A Numinous Hope

<u>Other books by Carl E Creasman Jr</u>

Songs on the Wind

An American Family

*Success for Life: Answers to the 77 Hardest Questions
College Students Ask*

Servant Leadership

Full Throttle: High Octane Insights on Achieving Your Dreams

Tracking the Storm: Uncovering the Pattern to Great Crisis

A Numinous Hope

A Compilation of Theological Writings on the
Nature and Purpose of Ecclesia:
the Church, the Body of Christ

Carl E. Creasman Jr.

Published by:
Carl E. Creasman, Jr.
P.O. Box 217
Winter Park, FL 32790

www.carlcreasman.com

Printed in the United States of America

ISBN #: 978-0-9814638-3-4

Cover Created by Christopher Kutcher

Christopher Kutcher Designs
www.christopherkutcherdesigns.com

Table of Contents

Preface

Numinous. It's an interesting word. I first stumbled into the word while reading C.S. Lewis back in 1997-98. It was in his wonderful, challenging book *The Problem of Pain.* Early in the book, Lewis begins unpacking his theology of dealing with pain by explaining the concept of "The Numinous." Here's how he says it:

> Those who have not met this term may be introduced to it by the following device. Suppose you were told there was a tiger in the next room: you would know that you were in danger and would probably feel fear. But if you were told 'There is a ghost in the next room', and believe it, you would feel, indeed, what is often called fear, but of a different kind. It would not be based on the knowledge of danger, for no one is primarily afraid of what a ghost may do to him, but of the mere fact that it is a ghost. It is 'uncanny' rather than dangerous, and the special kind of fear it excites may be called Dread. With the Uncanny, one has reached the fringes of the Numinous. Now suppose that you were told simply "There is a mighty spirit in the room', and believe it. Your feelings would then be even less like the mere fear of danger; but the substance would be profound. You would feel wonder and a certain shrinking – a sense of inadequacy to cope with such a visitant and of prostration before it – an emotion which might be expressed in Shakespeare's words "Under it my genius is rebuked." This feeling may be described as awe, and the object which excites it as the Numinous.
>
> (*The Problem of Pain*, pp. 5-6)

For myself, the idea of a spiritual presence connected with my own vision of the lost world around me, particularly my generation called Generation X. It is our lot to be among what is known as the "Nomad" archetype of generations...not well-loved, not necessarily well-received, somewhat always a loose ends or unable to establish deep roots in a society that has somewhat rejected it. In 1998, when I felt God moving me into a "next step" for my personal journey with him, this word, this idea of a "spiritual presence," of a "mighty spirit" reflected well my own feelings about God.

Those feelings about God, about what I thought He wanted with me, wants for us all, became fleshed out in the organization that my wife and I started in August 1998. At the core of the vision lies a hope, a dream of actually being a united group of fellow nomads on a journey together, experiencing the life of a believers connected deeply to one another. The writings to follow are my attempt to define the concept, explain why and demonstrate how to do it. I have written these over the 14 years of Numinous, though many of the ideas or beliefs stretch back further to my earliest experiences as a Christian.

The first section, *Letters from the Front,* was first written in 2003. I worked to get this book published then, including in the work some chapters from my close friend Garry "Gaz" Kishere who lives in England. We came close to publication, especially with two different small publishing houses, but in the end, the publishers that we spoke to passed and ultimately, I let the work settle into my files, guiding my work but not really seeing the light of day. The point of the book was to explain my theological position and how my friends and I were attempting to live that theology out in real life, in what was becoming known as "Numinous the Church." For this compilation, I have removed Gaz's chapters to improve the flow and isolate what were my own thoughts, doing some final editing now in the year 2012.

Four years later after finishing *Letters*, in 2007, I took a 10-month period to write more about my "theology of community" for our newsletter sent out to my prayer & financial supporters. The idea of community, of the Christians' lives together, is core to my theology. Even today, I often get asked about our theology, what it is that we believe; in general, I find people are simply asking "why another church" or "why aren't you just with a typical church; you could be a Pastor there?" Having explained this many times, and previously having put it into the book form of *Letters*, I decided to take the newsletter format as a way to put the essence of our theology on community into these brief "chapters." I did it as a multi-part writing, and each "part" was sent out about a month apart. Thus, some of the chapters will have a few sentences making sure the audience was "up to speed" with where we were at that point in my explanation about theology.

The last section of this compilation comes from emails that I have written to the body of Numinous over the past decade. Over the years with this specific group of people, I have taken the opportunity to state and restate the theology. Ultimately, there have been 100s of emails where I explain some aspect of God's vision for His people, especially for those collected into a local body of believers.

I certainly am someone who has a specific view of who God is based on what He has revealed in the Bible. These words are all an attempt to explain that, hopefully helping others see God better. He is, as Lewis demonstrated, the real Numinous, that deep spiritual presence with whom we are wise to remember that He is beyond even our genius. That, again, is why the word Numinous was used to title my ministry effort in His name...there is that Spiritual presence that wants to draw near, yet He is also beyond us. Working to comprehend what He has shown us is an effort to at least be faithful to what is revealed.

If you still feel lost in understanding our name, hence even the point of these writings, then consider this idea from another Lewis work, *The Lion, The Witch and The Wardrobe*. In there, the central figure representing Jesus is the lion Aslan. One of the children who stumbles into the world is being told about Aslan by another set of characters.

"Is - is he a man?" asked Lucy.

"Aslan a man?" said Mr. Beaver sternly. "Certainly not. I tell you he is the King of the wood and the son of the great Emperor-beyond-the-sea. Don't you know who is the King of Beasts? Aslan is a lion - the Lion, the great Lion."

"Ooh!" said Susan, "I'd thought he was a man. Is he - quite safe? I shall feel rather nervous about meeting a lion."

"That you will, dearie, and make no mistake," said Mrs. Beaver; "if there's anyone who can appear before Aslan without their knees knocking, they're either braver than most or else just silly."

"Then he isn't safe?" asked Lucy.

"Safe?" said Mr. Beaver; "don't you hear what Mrs. Beaver tells you? Who said anything about safe? 'Course he isn't safe. But he's good. He's the King, I tell you."

God, the Eternal One, is like that - not safe but good ("the fear of the Lord is the beginning of wisdom"--Ps 111:10; Prov 9:10). To be in His presence is to experience The Numinous. I hope you enjoy finding out more about Him in the pages to follow.

Letters from the Front

a postmodern theological study of the church

by

Carl E Creasman Jr.

are you ready?

1

The Introduction

In the dark of the early morning, the captain rose up to start his day. It was similar to many days, yet the tension of the future hung in the air like the morning mists. Has he groggily wiped his hand across his tired eyes, he recalled the words of the general during the staff meeting. Tomorrow they would attack.

They had been dogging their enemy for almost 2 weeks, probing, testing, tempting, pushing and now they were going to attempt to force the issue. The outcome was not certain, though their enemy was weak. Yet, he was in prepared positions and usually, in war, a defender in prepared positions was a force to be reckoned with, no matter how weak he was.

In the early moments of the next day, the now of the immediate, the captain knew he had a few moments before the call to duty. He took that moment to take up his pen and began to write a letter to his loved ones. He had been away at war for over 2 years and though the end perhaps was in site, things were still uncertain. And regardless of how it was going from a national level, he knew that every day brought the possibility that today would be his last day.

So he wanted to write a letter from the front. He had written several letters like this as well as keeping a journal of his life. Several entries are nothing more than "we marched 11 miles; camped about midnight" or "fortified on the ridge; rested in camp."

His letters to his loved ones were filled with tales of what was going on, though not in too much detail so as to not worry them. He'd ask about the growth of the children and he'd profess his love. Then, mostly, clearly with thoughts about the prospect of this being the last day, he would offer advice.

There's something about being at the front that brings out a strong desire to educate those that you love. The hope that your actions there might be enough to keep others from ever having to come to the front. In those letters, filled with expressions of love, also comes advice and care about taking care of the family, the family farm, the children, finances and the like.

So, our captain of the United States Army took a brief moment to write a letter home. Perhaps, after he finished, he was able to get it to the general postmaster for the army or maybe he gave it to one of his commanding officers in the hopes that he would be able to mail it back for him.

Then, off he marched to the sounds of war. To an uncertain future but with the full knowledge that he had expressed the important details of life to those that he loved, he headed out of his tent.

It is this same desire to write with urgent news that has pressed me to write what you hold in your hands. The sounds of battle rage around me in the spiritual realm and over the past decade, have become evident in the life that is before us.

Immorality grows by leaps and bounds while nations rage against nation. Various religious groups have emerged and tell competing stories about multiple paths to God or gods. Much has indeed changed in the previous 70+ years.

In 1998, God led me to the next step on my journey. My wife and I started a ministry, a church, a "thing" called Numinous. I first read that word in C. S. Lewis's awesome book *The Problem of Pain*. The word "numinous" is of Latin origin and means, "filled with or characterized by a sense of a supernatural presence."

Our initial aim was to reach Generation X, our generation (depending on who you read and believe, those born between 1963 and 1985) with God. Today, we say that we are a community of post-modern soul searchers on the journey of life. Anyone. Everyone.

As we thought about our generation, though, we noticed the negative feelings toward them, toward us. Yet, we believed then and now that our generation is, in fact, filled with a supernatural, spiritual presence. That presence provokes feelings, as described by Lewis, as "less like mere fear [but] profound. You would feel wonder and a certain shrinking. . . . This feeling may be described as awe." (Lewis, *The Problem of Pain*, p. 15)

In 2001, the world for Americans changed internationally. We went from a sense of detached invulnerability to a nervous concern about the fragile nature of security. In 2008, the economic world for Americans also negatively transformed, and as I sit here in 2012 writing this, nothing has been the same sense. Some believe that we've seen the worst; I actually believe we are merely at the start of the crisis, but be whichever is correct, clearly we are into something new.

The church and the Christian in America live in what I believe to be an anti-Christian country. Perhaps we are currently only viewed with a sense of bemusement at our old values and concepts, but increasingly, if a Christian or church dares to defend values from the past that contradict the current culture norms, watch out. The attacks will come often and unrelenting; surprisingly, some of the attacks will comes from other Christians quickly seeking to distance themselves from whatever old value was being proclaimed.

It is, then, to the Christian world, that I present this book, these ideas. I believe in a radical departure from the norm of what passes for the "American Church" and I think we Christians, the "Church," are as much to blame for the current setting in America as any other group. In fact, one might hypothesize that we Christians are already the equivalent of the nation of Israel being marched as captives to Babylon. God did not come to their rescue because He had already proclaimed their punishment for failing to honor Him and uphold His commands. Rather than rescue, He said that they were to build their lives there, to prepare to stay and die there, far from the Promised Land.

In that world, then, we can no longer be concerned if our ideas confront or are controversial. We need that direct approach now. The idea of a battle, a spiritual struggle about the correct path to take as a society, a civilization, is not a new idea. Trying to describe the gospel to England, C. S. Lewis wrote, "Christianity agrees. . . that this universe is at war. . . It thinks it is a civil war, a rebellion. . .Christianity is the story of how the rightful king has landed, you might say in disguise, and is calling us all to take part in a great campaign of sabotage." (Lewis, *Mere Christianity*, p. 45-46) Sadly, today it is clear that our side is losing, yet to engage in that struggle is a noble quest.

Research by experts like George Barna bears out what my own personal experience has seen. Most of the major denominations are in serious decline. Over 80% of active church members said in a survey from 1998 that they had not experienced the presence of God in their church. That stat has remained true in the following years. The church, and by extension, most Christians, are seen as non-credible by those we are trying desperately to reach. Or at least, by those we are supposed to be trying to reach. It is this fact, this situation, that the "thing" my wife and I started, Numinous Inc, attempts to participate in rectifying. We must engage in this struggle, to be "real" in our faith, constant in our calling, willing to go into the hard places, even to suffer if need be in order to faithfully fulfill the mission He has called us to. But it won't be easy.

Somehow, we've gone from knowing that our war was with a real enemy who once stood with God to believing that our war is with our culture, the very people our God came to save. In the process of the past 40 years, if not longer, the church has given her influence away. So, what is going on?

Have you noticed how the world seems to be spinning out of control, in a situation where no one seems to know what is going on? It seems to all be moving far too fast; I recently read a report saying the IT industry feels swamped as their certification programs cannot keep up with the swift pace of innovation and change.

Well, back in 2003, I was already feeling the quickening pace. I wrote then:

It feels that no one knows what is really going on, not just inside the church, but also across the country in many fields. In the September 2002 issue of Wired, eminent quantum physicist Isaac Chuang of MIT said, "Nobody in this field really understands what is going on. It defies intuition." Yet we are pressing on into this critical, amazing and provocative field that will impact computers, science, warfare and probably all of society.

In domestic and global politics, particularly since 2000, things are confusing and at times, scary. Many of the conventional rules from the past 50-70 years in diplomacy no longer work. I watched on TV (in 2003) as a national pundit acknowledged that neither party seems to know what direction to take right now.

The Internet seems to also defy understanding. The Internet is not going anywhere any time soon, but we simply do not know what to do with it. J. Bradford DeLong, professor at UC Berkeley and coeditor of The Journal of Economic Perspectives said this in the November 2002 issue of Wired. "Nobody knows anything. . . . The titans of the silicon age continue to calculate the pace and direction of technological change. . .but nobody knows what works."

Later in the article, he proclaims about the Internet "what we don't know. . .is how [new technology] will be used—how valuable those uses will turn out to be, and how rapidly they will diffuse." We simply do not know and those who try to tell you they do understand are wrong.

So, what does that mean for us? If we don't know what is going on in the community of faith (and we seemingly do not as evidenced by the current state of the church), where do we turn? The cry for answers grows louder every day. A week doesn't go by that I am not confronted with a "Christian" who either doesn't go to church at all or who goes yet feels completely empty from the experience. Where are the answers? Is it in better leaders, more programs, or more energy at worship? Or perhaps, are none of those the real answer because they point not to the real problem, but only to symptoms.

My hope is that these essays, these letters are written as words of promise to the people who are lost and desperate in a sea of religion with no Godly "permissioning" of any kind to be real and to ask questions. These people, of all ages, have long ago left the church or (if their own conscious won't allow them to leave out of a sense of duty to some past upbringing) remain increasingly frustrated with a very real sense of hypocrisy and lack of meaning inherent in their experience. We hope these letters reach their ears with a cry of "you are not alone" and "you are asking the right questions!" These are people who have something new to build, people who are perhaps alone in their thoughts, many of them leaders, but whom God has given similar sight.

At the same time, the essays are written as words of challenge to the religious community of our day. They are written to challenge long held assumptions about what "church" means and how it is important for today. With the same sense of fervor of Jan Hus and John Wycliffe, these essays demand, for the very sake of the church, that the church, its people and its leaders, wrestle with these questions. Perhaps, to many like this, these essays will sound harsh, perhaps shrill, but they are written as commanded.

So these essays, these musings, these letters from the front, are not theory of what I think might be up, but honest reflection born out of my experience. We must turn back to the messages and the person of God. The hope of the world is God, expressed through God's people in loving communities. In the coming pages, I will attempt to help us make some sense of our current setting. I hope you'll stick with me through the process.

Come with me through the following chapters as we look at the situation, confront how the American Church has largely become invisible, and then see how Numinous, Inc attempts to challenge the status quo.

2

We are the children of the ghetto.

We are the children of the ghetto.

We are the offspring of an idea turned into an organization twisted into an institution gone awry. Once there was a family of friends who had believed the same story of Truth about the Eternal One. But over many years, this family had been forgotten or had drifted away and in their place, a power hungry group of men emerged. Through these men, who probably had some idea of what the original family of friends had been about, the idea became an organization. And as with all organizations, the more it grew, the more it dangerously drifted toward institutionalism and all the inherent evils that come with institutions.

Then a man came decrying the institution that the organization had become. Many heard his words and looked hard at the Ancient Documents that the family of friends had left behind containing stories of the originals and the actual words of the One who was the idea, the One who provided the way to the Eternal One. But sadly, though a few people went looking for the family of friends or maybe they just became a new family of friends, others quickly took this man's words and made his name a new organization. And since one man's name could become an organization, why not many men's names. And thus, within years, similar powerful men, albeit with other names, came with their hunger for power and their names became organizations that became an institutions.

We are the children of the ghetto.

Now we sit in a strange world with tales almost mystical of a time when there was a family of friends who had believed the same story of Truth about the Eternal One. We look around at the institutions that supposedly contain some kernel of truth, some image of the family and see nothing. Or we see a picture not much better than the glassy black and white images of our own past, frayed at the edges with many details missing. Often, as we look at the picture, we can tell that some have tried to re-paint it, but the colors they used have highlighted many things that the One who came to provide the way never said or never implied or never even, probably, thought about.

Many devout followers of the One who came to provide a way have dreamed of a place where all will willingly follow His teaching. Of course, He told us about that place and that He was going ahead of us to prepare it, but these people, they don't seem too content with that. Or maybe they are content, but regardless, why not help Him out with things down here? So, in their efforts to provide this place, a place that really could not be built here, apart from the Eternal One and the place He resides, they have attempted to make society that place now. But since we know that not everyone will understand or even want to know the Eternal One, thus negating any desire to hear the teachings of the Ancient Documents or the words of the One who came to provide a way, everyone must be forced to act a certain way in order to have this society. Or, as some have tried, these people who believe must find a place where only the insiders can live. And control. And have power.

We are the children of the ghetto.

Of course, unless you inhabit an island, it's hard to keep outsiders out, especially if where you choose to live is, well, a nice place to live. So though many have tried this, in many places and times, each time the attempt has failed. But in the process, the attempt at this society, this attempt at heaven on earth has created a concept in the minds of many who think they are following in the footsteps of the family of friends. This idea is the ghetto.

Arguably, no one would call it such. To do so would be to cry out the truth about the Emperor's new clothes and, well, we are much too proper for that. What is the ghetto? It is two things, if it is anything and it certainly is something. First, it is the twisted offspring of this desire to have this place that the One who came to provide a way spoke of. And that is a good thing, of course, but He also was fairly clear that the place He was preparing was in no way this place, this planet, this celestial ball. So instead, this morphed thing has arisen that tries to keep the members of the institution insulated, separate, clean. In the ghetto, you learn a new language that only the members can understand. You learn to avoid many things that the outside world obviously can't see the danger of, like say, eating fast food, listening to the radio or shopping. Why, the ghetto has it all—its own TV stations (for the weaker members who have not seen the light that the little box is demonic), its own celebrities, its own rock stars, its own stores. Why, to quote one who has escaped the ghetto long ago, "you can only drink milk from a Christian cow!"

We are the children of the ghetto.

The other thing is fairly insidious and not the least less dangerous. In this realm, the ghetto is merely a safe way for a person to experience the spiritual, to try to keep the Eternal One happy while all the while living happily as if the Eternal One never existed. This desire to keep the spiritual and the secular separate is not so much to protect oneself, as with ghetto #1, but to keep the spiritual from "cramping my style." For this member, the ghetto exists so they can live like hell and still get heaven in the end. As long as they accomplish the simple requirements of the ghetto— attend the ghetto meetings, at least once a month or so, give money to keep the ghetto lords happy and, well, maybe there really aren't too many issues—then what they do the rest of the time is nobody's business.

These two. . .uh, things, these two ghettos or aspects of the ghetto are real. And in living in the ghetto, the whole concept of the original family of friends has long since disappeared. Ghetto members are either dismissed or laughed at for their obvious hypocrisy (Ghetto issue #2) or they are ignored as irrelevant (Ghetto issue #1). Yet whole generations have been reared in the ghetto. It did not used to be so bad, so noticeable, but little by little, the veneer has cracked, revealing the obvious issues to everyone but those on the inside. But some have escaped.

We are the children of the ghetto.

Yes, tales have emerged that there really is an escape. But man, does it take courage to attempt an escape for most of the time, the ghetto lords will hunt down and silence anyone who attempts to get out and speak truth. Over the years, most of those persecuted were ones who had escaped and tried to point out the issues, the flaws. Back to the man who decried the first institution, his salvation from this persecution was his betrayal, as he had to allow one of those men of power to protect him, or else his death would have been swift. Later, whether it was men of power from the old institution or men of power from the new ones, those who attempted to get out were not allowed to speak without reprisal.

Today, though death is not really a fear, words that wound like bullets fly quickly against the ones who would step outside the ghetto. Accusations fly, rumors spread, reputations are smeared or merely called into question. Finances dry up. Friendships and relationships are cut off. In the end, the one who seeks life outside of the ghetto finds that path a lonely journey. But you can get out. To do so takes a return to the Ancient Documents.

We are the children of the ghetto.

There in those texts, one can see clearly what the One who came to provide a way intended. He minces no words. He clearly lays out through example what life as one who follows him would be like. It's not the complicated, cheap maze of the ghetto but a simple costly life of living God filled. When one returns to those documents, one can see how the first family of friends lived and how they understood their task. There one can see the issue is first and foremost to live in unity and in love. And amazingly, through that, the Eternal One will illuminate himself for others. Individually, each member of the family of friends has a task, but not the tasks put forth by the ghetto. Many of the tasks of the ghetto, which border on inbreeding through self-perpetuation are not the same tasks as He laid out in the Ancient Documents. The task from the Eternal One is bigger than that, and simpler. Let Him live through you, changing you all the while, and as He does that, we represent Him wherever we are, wherever we live. In doing that, we are to be a seasoning, a flavoring to whatever is tasteless. And we are to illuminate whatever is dark, not through hateful words of judgment, but merely through His presence in us.

Of course, it's easy to see how impossible those tasks are if we are stuck in ghetto #1 (what could seasoning do to more seasoning but take up space in the bottle) or ghetto #2 (pretend seasoning does nothing but make the tasteless thing taste worse). So, all the while, ghetto members are busily working, feverishly striving to keep the outsiders at bay and inbreeding all the while, missing the direct commands of the One who came to provide a way. Amazing. So you can escape, but to do so is to turn your back on the majority of positions put forth by the many institutions that came from organizations that were once a man's name. Turn and walk away. Or perhaps, to paraphrase Tyler Durden (from *Fight Club*—definitely a non-ghetto movie), "brokenness might be the answer." And in allowing brokenness, in seeking to gain a handle on what things the Eternal One believes are the things that truly matter (and then caring for those things only), in walking away from the ghetto, you can find yourself in the company of the family of friends.

We are the children of the ghetto.

Why does this matter? Why blow the whistle and expose yourself to the words that wound from the ghetto lords? The reason for caring lies in the very thing that the ghetto seeks to contain or keep out—the Outsiders. For fear of contamination, they long ago shut the doors. Real followers of the way don't dance. So, those that do obviously are a threat. The walls went up and surprisingly, there were few, if any, doors. And in the process, those on the outside, those who can not hear the words of the One who came to provide a way, are lost. They walk away seeking to fill that spiritual gnawing in their soul in some place that does not seem to be as twisted as the ghetto. Even if they know of the Ancient Documents, they then speak similar words to Thomas Linacre, physician to Henry VII and VIII after reading the Ancient Documents for himself for the very first time (probably after the age of 40 or 50)—"Either these are not the Gospels or we are not Christians." For these outsiders see the ghetto for what it is, and somewhere, deep inside, they instinctively feel the error. Whether it comes in the many forms of rejection or lack of acceptance or the absence of any real fervor for the great Truth, the ghetto smacks as a cruel joke played on the whole of the earth.

So outsiders turn away to imposters. And any efforts to reach the outsiders usually contain language that only the ghetto dwellers can understand or such condescension that to even listen is an insult to who you are. Of course, the ghetto lords teach that reaching the outsiders is the main thing (even though the Ancient Documents state that the One who came to provide a way said loving each other and being unified were the laws of the land, the prime directive, the whole point). They mantra-fied one sentence into a guilt-laden obsession and at the same time, removed the elixir for accomplishing that sentence's intent. So mind-numb, but good-hearted ghetto dwellers crawl out against their will into the outside to accomplish something that they have no power to accomplish, come back feeling defeated and guilty and all the while, the outsiders are insulted or are laughing at the nerve of the hypocrite to try to sway them to something that person obviously does not really believe.

We are the children of the ghetto.

Get out. Start living life as He intended, in contact and context with your world, in your world. Start living life infused with His power. As one of His originals wrote, live a life worthy of the calling, proving He Himself has called you. Seek to be unified in the family of friends. Seek out first those that are like minded, also weary of the game of fame that the ghetto foists upon us. Then, believe it or not, seek out the very ones who will shoot first, ask questions later, the ghetto dwellers and try to be unified with them. See, as His followers, we know that no one of us can see from His perspective and though we are to be fruit judges, only the Eternal One can allow anyone in to His place. Or, again to paraphrase one of His originals, the seal upon one who follows the One who came to provide a way, is two fold: first, the Eternal One alone knows who is His, second, those who follow will give up wrong living. So, He alone knows who will live forever with Him. And living in the ghetto are many who will, even some of the ghetto lords.

And so while you are getting out and living in context and contact, focusing your energies on unity and love, season and illuminate the world around you. Doing this will also take much time and some risk as many on the outside know of the ghetto and they believe the ghetto is the only representation of the Eternal One. To really help them understand so that they can truly have a chance to decide if they want to hear the music of the Eternal One and dance as He intended, you'll need new words. And you'll have to allow Him to live through you in order to pursue righteousness. Without Him doing so, we are merely playing ghetto games. And they can see that. But by letting Him live through you, you authenticate the tales, the stories of the One who came to provide a way. You demonstrate the marks of the family of friends. You deprive power to the ghetto and point the way to the Truth.

We are the children of the ghetto.
But we don't have to raise any offspring there.

3

We've Lost Our Way

World War I, an event that many thought would be a quick conflict, much like the Franco-Prussian war of 1870, soon bogged down to become the archetype of futility. Hundreds of miles of trenches cut across Europe and for 4 years, the youth of nations was casually cast across the aptly named "no man's land."

The horror of the experience was expressed by many in their letters home. Home. What a glorious thought. For most, the great shock was as they attempted to remember why they were there. How had it come to this?

The sheer audacity of climbing "over the top" to advance upon an enemy, under withering fire was incredible. Many broke under the mental strain prior to even taking the leap. One such letter, written July 20, 1918 reflects the fear and frustration at being in such a situation. The British Sergeant wrote:

> *My own beloved wife,*
> *I do not know how to start this letter. The circumstances are different from any under which I ever wrote before. I am not to post it but will leave it in my pocket, if anything happens to me someone will perhaps post it. We are going over the top this afternoon and only God in Heaven knows who will come out of it alive.*

Like that soldier and most of the world's leaders back in the midst of that war, I'm not sure what has happened around here. When I was a young Christian in the 1970s, it seemed as if we had the enemy licked. Why, there was constant talk about ending the war by the year 2000, a seemingly easy task considering the resources at our disposal. And then, well alleluia amen, Jesus was coming back and it would all be over.

Back then it seemed that we were doing great. But who knows, I was just a kid, the son of a minister and 4th generation pastor and perhaps I have no idea how bad it was then. I've done a careful study of our history, but I've never seen a time like this when our credibility has been so challenged.

And credibility about what, you may ask? Well, about our job as the representatives of the rightful King. Now there are many other organizations that are saying that they instead represent Him. Never before has it been this way. Oh sure, some of these armies, these organizations, have been around for a long time. But now with our ever-increasing total connection worldwide, it seems that over the past 15 years at least, these armies have surpassed us in credibility worldwide.

Do you doubt this? Except for icons Billy Graham, Mother Teresa, and the Pope, no Christian leader commands the credibility of say, the Dalai Lama or Deepak Chopra. I would venture that the author of the wildly popular *Harry Potter* series probably commands more credibility in your community than any of your religious Christian leaders.

This is a major issue. For no longer are we merely able to speak to someone about Christ and know that they will at least respect our position enough to consider it. The church used to reside by the bridge between the temporal and the eternal, pointing the way. Now, we are far from that bridge partly because our audience is no longer considering our bridge as a possible path to the Eternal One and partly because, we've simply walked away from our task. And in some respects, the church and Christians are standing *between* the outsiders and the bridge. In our many efforts to redeem the culture, we have merely pointed a castigating finger (maybe the middle one?) and in the process, we have lost any ability at communicating about the one True God who loves that very person and community.

The one thing that we should be known for, the one thing that He told us to do as a group, as an organization--we aren't well known for that. And here's a surprise, it's not what you think. While I'll discuss this in a later letter, let me simply say now we should be known for our unity and our love for each other.

Instead, as mentioned above, we're more known for all the things we are against. As Leonard Sweet says, we've lost our ability to give a holy kiss to the culture. I'll add that we've lost that same ability to give the kiss of love to those on the inside, to those who claim to be Christians.

Maybe we're confused. Maybe we've just forgotten what we are here for. As I say to my church, "do you know who you are?" Or maybe, we've just stopped reading about our task in his book. Instead, we accept what we've been told and what we've seen as the way to do things. But if those things are right, then what is wrong?

One of these chapters was actually circulated around the Internet via email. It generated a variety of responses, mostly positive, but many responding sharply to what they perceived as an attack or critical way of approaching the topic of that letter. In one exchange with a dear friend over what I had written, I stopped his challenge with this question. "Is what I wrote true? Is it right?" His pause told me all that I needed to know and his response confirmed, that, well, "yes its true. You are right. I just did not like the way you said it."

We are no longer in a position of having the luxury of trying to worry about how we say what needs to be said. We've already lost most if not all of the credibility we ever had in this country and if we don't respond, well. . . . Barna said in 1999 at a seminar with his organization that "the church in America has less than 4 years to turn this around."

My point is simply this: it is not about "being right." It's about being Biblical. It's about being willing to lay down what I want my church to do (or what I perceive it as always having done) and take up the tasks that God has dictated for us. And if what I suggest does not fit well, just hear my question again "Is what I am writing true? Is it right?" You might want to scream "NO!! You are wrong." OK, great—prove it!

If my observations are wrong, then why are the statistics screaming otherwise. Why are so many churches dying? Why have so few churches seen any conversions besides those of their children? Why has the stat of the past 20 years that "85% of all conversions happen before the age of 18" become a self-fulfilling prophecy, admitting that we have no credibility as adults to impact our friends and neighbors?

I tell my church "welcome to the revolution." I'm not Luther or Calvin, but I am a spiritual leader, a man racing hard after God giving whatever breath is left in me to see our world at least give God a chance. And in the way of that, often, is the status of our organization. It's in our minds. It's our attitudes towards each other and the culture around us.

Let's dream for a minute. As hard as it is for many to accept this, God may indeed postpone Jesus' return for another 3000 years. We can't think that the problems of the church are merely an "end times" issue. Perhaps God will allow society to roll on for eons past your death. Your offspring will multiply; your descendants will still live here. Your children's children will live in North America. Yet what kind of society will they live in if the leavening agent of God, the church is bankrupt and has moved far from God. That society may look like something resembling the USA but do you want those who come after you to live here in a society that has totally dismissed the one True God?

For me, I will not go quietly. I will go down swinging, fighting to my last breath, to pass on a legacy of pursuing God. What about you? Will you go there with me? Will you challenge me to my socks, to my very being? Will you consider with me the Holy words that He has given us to guide us? Will you declare nothing sacred save the things He has clearly declared as such and in doing so, open your mind to the possibility that how we do what we do in church is confused, maybe even wrong?

Welcome to the revolution.

are you ready?

4

The surveys are depressing, but true

So what are we here for and why are we so passionate about the credibility of the church? George Barna of Barna Research Group, LTD. has recently finished yet another survey (actually a series of three surveys) that further underscores the current malaise within the church. While many pastors and leaders are singing the praises of the church and how their churches are just doing great, the research demands otherwise.

In these three surveys, the evidence rolls in that those who claim to be Christians (almost 80% of adult Americans claim to be Christians or at least claim a religious affiliation) have no idea of what exactly it means to be a Christian. In on survey on the morality of practical life issues, respondents over and over demonstrate either a lack of understanding to what their faith supports or they consciously go counter to their own faith's position.

Consider just these findings—45% of mainline denomination attendees (Methodists, Lutherans, Presbyterians and Episcopalians) and 26% of other Christian churches say that having an abortion is morally acceptable. On the issue of co-habitation, both groups were around 50% stating that such a living pattern is morally acceptable. Viewing pornography? 42% of mainline church attendees and 25% of other church attendees say that is morally acceptable. On the issue of drinking in excess and becoming drunk, 30% and 20% state this action is morally acceptable.

Of course, not everyone who says he is a part of a religion or even a Christian actually goes to church. But even of those people who attend regularly, the percentages were remarkably high to those same questions. Call me naïve, but it should be 0% state that those issues are morally acceptable. We're not talking about obscure issues that have no Biblical basis.

Yet, that is exactly the problem for the Christians of this country do not believe that the Bible is accurate. The surveys looked at 8 core beliefs of a theological nature. The results are not pretty, no matter which denominational group you are a part of. On the first issue, that of the accuracy of the Bible, the strongest denominational group on this question was Pentecostal/Four Square denomination, supporting accuracy at 81%. However, that means that 19% of people attending a Pentecostal or Four Square church do not think the Bible is completely accurate. The low end of this continuum was the Episcopal denomination where only 22% of its members believe the Bible to be completely accurate. Catholics—26%, Lutherans—34%, Church of Christ—57%, Baptist—66%.

Obviously, our faith relies on the Bible, on the written evidence that can be tested or that demonstrates the validity claimed. We are not Christians merely because of the stories that have been passed on over the centuries. If that were true, then our faith would be no stronger than any other group. Then, it would revert back to "my story is more convincing or compelling than your story." Instead of that, we state that our story is based on fact that is provable in a historical document.

And from that document, the adherents to the faith can find their moorings to determine their actions. If the Bible is not accurate, how can we expect a morally correct answer on say, getting drunk? Worse, how can anyone base his or her theological position? We obviously cannot find a firm foundation.

On the issue of a personal responsibility to share the faith, clearly communicated in II Corinthians 5:18-21, Matthew 5:13-16, Matthew 28:18-20 and others, the church miserably fails. Again, the Pentecostals led the way barely crossing the 70% mark. Even Baptists, supposedly known for their evangelism, barely crossed 50%.

The issue of the reality of Satan, that Satan is a real person rather than an idea, was widely disputed. The Bible clearly states that Satan was angel in heaven (Revelation 12:9) cast down to the earth (Isaiah 14:12-17, Ezekiel 28:12-19). Jesus, Peter and Paul speak him of, yet today within the Assembly of God denomination only 50% of the members believe Satan was real.

How about salvation as a gift of God, or to state it another way, whether salvation was something that could be earned? There was no denomination over 70% and most groups (all but three) were under 50%. Yet when you look in the Bible, there it is in black and white, most famously in Ephesians 2:8-9.

More shocking was the admission that many Christians do not think that Jesus lived a sinless life. According to II Corinthians 5:21 or Hebrews 7:26, the idea of Jesus' life with no sin is critical to our faith. So, by refuting this idea, these respondents undercut their own claim to be Christians. Sadly, more Mormons believe in this fact than do Christians.

Is it any wonder that non-Christians consider Christianity with a mixture of bemusement and disdain? The "church" has no idea about what it supposedly believes, or perhaps they know what it is supposed to believe and they simply refuse these core facts. This lack of under-girding is revealed in the practical outworking of Christian lives.

Another Barna survey considered basic actions that a person of the Christian faith should do, based on Biblical teaching. How can anyone ever convince a non-Christian to accept this faith when the church itself supports co-habitation or getting drunk? Not just in moral issues though, does this weakness rear its head, but in the lack of acceptance of these normal Christian activities. Here the illness of the church becomes even more apparent.

The simplest action that the early disciples and church performed immediately after Jesus left was meeting together. Today, most Christians say they attend "church" about 1/2 of the time. Jesus said the central issue for the church, for the believers, was unity of the body (John 17:20-23); if this were true it would seem obvious that attendance to the main gathering would be essential.

As I'll attempt to demonstrate later, "church attendance" is not the real issue—unity of the body is! But, for many of my generation and from many voices that I hear, the desire is to have God and claim rightness with Him and yet abandon any gathering point. How can we attempt to care for each other, to make sure no one has any needs if we don't really know each other? And how can we ever know each other if we are never together? This is not about "guilting" someone into attendance; it is about desiring to be with those that you are in community with.

Other core activities also are embarrassingly low.
- Those who read the Bible at other times during the week other than a church service: Baptists 55%, Episcopalians 30%, Methodists 43%.
- Serve in any volunteer capacity within the church body: Adventists 16%, Catholics 12%, Church of Christ 22%, Pentecostals 25%.
- Donate money: Baptists 22%, Lutherans 21%, Adventists 16%.

Those facts are simply amazing. In one sense, I knew it was bad, but my goodness, these statistics are horrific. If only these respondents had not claimed to be Christians, then perhaps it would not seem so bad.

Interestingly enough, there was one activity that gained universal support. Prayer. Every group was over 80%. Thus, we can state that in our country we note the idea that we should talk to God. After the events of September 11, 2001, those statistics rose higher, but fell back to normal levels. But why such a high percentage belief in prayer? Why would any of these people even think of speaking to God? His Word back to them is not accurate, his son was not sinless, there is no compulsion to share about His working in their own lives. Heck, they don't even feel like his commands or even suggestions about how to live better in this world apply. Did you know that even atheists admitted to praying? Amazing!

The Christian faith continues to slip into, as Barna states, "theological anarchy."   Sure, 80% and then some of all American adults claim to be Christians, but only 41% of those actually understand the idea of being born again. The researchers do not ask if a person is born again, but merely asks normal questions regarding their relationship with Jesus Christ and where they think they will spend eternity and why they should be allowed into heaven. Obviously, the church, Christianity in America, is sick.

I've been asked again and again why I am on this mission. "Why are you out here?" "Why don't you just pastor a normal church?" After this letter, does it really take a major explanation? We've been on this mission for at least 5 years as a group (that being Numinous, Inc.), but this has been my message and cry to the church for at least 16 years. We cannot merely stand around and assume all is well in the body. It's not!! This confusion about the faith causes us all difficulty in attempting to "make a difference."

If the vast majority of America imagines it is "Christian" and yet thinks like this, our task is not really evangelism but education. We must first demonstrate to individuals that actually they are not Christians. Wow!! What a difficult assignment. And that is made even more difficult by the fact that there is no discernable difference between the world's opinion on theological issues or moral choices and those who claim to be Christians.

The times are desperate. We are out here on the front lines and where there should be others who labor with us, there are none. America, perhaps the world, is in greater need of a spiritual reformation or revolution than any time in its history.

are you ready?

5

Are we asking the right questions?

If we are looking towards a revolution, we had better have some idea as to what we are revolting against. It's easy to stand on the corner and loudly complain, but those complaints need elements of truth, of seeing real problems and then at least make some attempt to provide a response.

I was riding in my truck with an older Christian, the father of one of our elders and he asked the crucial, critical question. We were talking about the book of Acts, that wonderful history of the early years of the church.

The question was raised, "what I read in that book and what I have experienced most of my adult life are not congruent. What I see those early Christians experiencing is not what most, if any, Christians experience today." So, was the book of Acts written merely to provide history about the early church? Or is the book of Acts there for Christians in the future to know what the collection of believers should be like, look like, and be doing?

It is a critical question that must be addressed. I agree with my older friend, that for most of my adult life I have not experienced what I read in the book of Acts. Note that I am not really talking about the miracles, though perhaps I should be. No, I'm merely talking about the sense of community, of togetherness that the early church seemed to have.

In fact, as I have looked around at various churches, engaged many of my Christian friends in discussion, read as much as possible, I find that most if not all Christians would express the decision that the do not experience the community inherent in Acts either. Sadly, it is this revelation that those outside the body of Christ can not get past to see the Father.

Sure, many of them would not call it that, but in their questioning the church in its lack of love towards those with AIDS or the racial separation seen in most churches or the lack of compassion toward the lost or the almost outward hatred toward a minister (or deacon or leader) who "sins," the lost world is not casting stones. They are, instead, asking the church "exactly what do you believe?"

It's not an easy question to deal with as it strikes to the core of the issue. Is the collection of believers supposed to be a community of friends, of lovers of God, or is it an institution to do good things for people?

When we started Numinous, it was an idea with several implications. One of those ideas was that as people heard the call of God, they would need a "church home" that understood the core teachings of the Bible. While we knew that perhaps, these people touched by our ministry at Numinous, Inc, would turn toward us to provide them that community of faith, we really never set out to start or form a church. God had other ideas though since He eventually birthed a community of faith. But what would it really be?

For years, I had been studying and praying and watching and discussing (with myself, with others, with God) what the church should really be. As we started on this journey we call Numinous, we knew that we wanted to put our ideas into place. Once God brought a true nucleus of a community to light, we saw that our ideas had to become reality or we needed to stop spouting off.

Foremost among those ideas was the notion that community is the key thing that the church should be noted for. Of course, in doing this, we knew that we would risk running afoul of many inside the church who, while agreeing that community was important, would nonetheless push that other aspects of the church are more important.

Actually, what most people would propose is that their church also believes community is critical. But as my older

Christian friend noted, their church budgets and calendars don't support that contention. We wanted this claim towards community to be the core of what and who we are as a gathering of Christians. Why?

Well, to explain that, will take an entirely new letter, which we will get to. My point now is if we are so "on target" with what the Bible teaches, then why the loss of credibility in the world? If it were because we had all of a sudden started saying our God was not the one True God, but just one of many Gods, then it would be easy to see why the world might start to question us. Sure, some of them might add, "it's about time you got of the exclusivity kick." At the same time, though, I think they would question our hearts if we so quickly left such a core teaching. So, what gives?

In my view, the problem for the Christian today lies at the heart of what the nature of the church should be, or is commanded to be in the Scripture. By confusing that issue, churches FUNCTIONALLY have gotten off the mark. What is the mission of the church really supposed to be? That is indeed the question as I see it. We can create new programs, try innovative services, play cutting edge music, dress more "like the word," dress less "like the world" and a host of other ideas. None of that will be effective if we have missed the point of the mission.

What I am trying to say is we have a problem. Just look around at the world and you can see it. People calling themselves Christians do not live out their faith and indeed don't even seem to know what the faith should be. Churches, while still teaching the basic core theology, seem incapable of preparing the people and in fact, churches seem to be the problem, not the solution. The reason why is that the Church has forgotten what the mission is.

What is that mission, you ask? Well, let's just say this: if the local bar in your town is the only place where everyone knows your name, then I would offer that the churches in your town have forgotten their real mission.

are you ready?

6

You can only drink milk from a Christian Cow

Recently, I was driving along I-4 through Orlando and I see it. Up ahead in bold letters was a billboard promoting another college/university in the Orlando area. Like many other industries, the higher education industry apparently has determined that having a satellite school in Orlando is a good thing for business. I know this because there are approximately 25 different schools in the Orlando area. Well, this billboard is representing yet another one, but it has a twist.

"Your Christian Alternative" is the title for the school (which I won't name so as to not embarrass it). So I start thinking, "now what is this about?" Are they saying that they are the alternative to normal Christian education? They have a relatively hip looking college age student posted on the board too, so maybe they are saying, "we are the cool, hip Christian place where you can even use a modern translation of the Bible, instead of that stodgy old King James Version." Or maybe, it's the somewhat normal idea of "we are your education alternative, and hey, we're Christians too." That's better said with a snappy smile.

Are we out of the ghetto yet? So many times I get asked exactly what do I mean by all this ghetto talk. Are you just trying to be abrasive? Are you always that sarcastic? The answers there would be no and yes, but back to the question, what do I mean by the ghetto?

Well, that billboard sums it up no matter what they were thinking. In either case, you see in that billboard a perfect example of ghetto thinking. "The education system is screwed up and we sure don't want the world influencing us—so, hey let's create an alternative." And just like Steve Taylor's infamous song states, you end up in a setting where you "only drink milk from a Christian cow."

Why not take the audacious stand of saying "we are your education alternative," leave the "Christian" part out of it, and mean that you will be producing the very best in education in the area. Why not take that approach to the level that people begin to understand that the strongest, brightest and sharpest educators are at your school. That the top professors in their field teach there. Sure, let them be Christians. In fact, encourage that—I would, but you don't have to flaunt it, especially in a culture like ours that then agrees with you, that you belong in a separate camp, away from all of the normal people.

You can see this best in the arena of the arts. Try finding a review in Rolling Stone of an album from an artist who is better known in the Christian world. You won't find it. Try calling your secular radio station in your town and requesting a current song by a Christian artist that would fit their format. Odds are you won't get rejected due to the nature of the song, but rather on the grounds that they have never heard of that artist and they don't have the song in their play-list.

See, by starting all Christian labels within the ghetto, we have further cemented the idea that Christians are supposed to be kept apart from everyone else. "Hey, if that's not what they think, then why do they have their own TV and radio stations?" It won't surprise me in the future to hear of an ownership group who are all Christians trying to bring a professional sports team to their town so the Christians can have their own professional sports team. Or more likely, they'd try to create their own sports league that would air on TBN or some other Christian-only station so all the Christians in the ghetto would have something to watch.

Think that sound ridiculous? Well, you're right, but how else do you explain the proliferation of ghetto-like things such as "Christian radio?" We won't debate the merits or lack thereof of Christian music. That has been done before by other writers than I in magazines. Go read those articles, but understand that the music is not the problem. We should have people writing songs like "Awesome God" and "Shout to the Lord" or "Watch the Lamb." Groups like Point of Grace or artists like Twila Paris or Larnelle Harris should have the right to create the beautiful music that they create. But what Christian radio and the industry at large has done is create a system whereby "Christian music" has become a genre much like "rock" or "country" or "pop." Yet, that is logically not the case because the type of music being played is rock or pop or country or adult contemporary. And it is on those very stations that artists should live or die.

In magazines like Rolling Stone, those same artists should compete as well as the many bands and singers who are out there trying to be heard. And the good ones will make it and the not so good ones will continue to play wherever they can get a gig. That's the way the music industry works. If it did not work that way, it would be like a professional sports team holding a couple of spots open for the best Christian they could find. It would not matter if he/she was good enough to make it on their own, just that their Christian walk was up to snuff. And of course, that would be ridiculous.

I think that many artists that I read about actually wish for that opportunity, to compete on a level playing field, but because of the genre created by the existence of the ghetto, they never get that chance. Many of the old Christian labels are actually owned by the mega-labels that control most of what you hear on the radio. Yet, instead of that opening doors, what has happened is that the industry knows when it has a cash cow and so, it keeps producing "Christian artists" for their "Christian label" that they own. Instead of someone saying "hey, this band is good—let's sign them" what happens is more like "this band is good—they're Christians—let's put them into the ghetto group so they'll have more instant success and besides, isn't that what they want, to be separate from us anyway?"

Is that what we want, to be separate from "those people" anyway? Is that what "your Christian alternative" means? Are we so afraid of young adults being unable to discover for themselves the truth about the beginning of time? Many scientists today admit that evolution as a theory of the origin of life has many holes. Are we afraid of letting our young adults search out this question? Are we afraid that the previous 18 years of training at (assumedly) a Christian home and church are not enough to keep them on track to believe God's word?

Remember, according to recent surveys, not even the members of the church itself actually believe that the Bible is completely accurate. So I guess the conclusion is that, "no, we don't think that training is enough" and "yes, we are afraid." So, lets hole them up for four more years and hopefully, they'll marry another ghetto dweller and they'll all live happily ever after.

The only problem with that is, uh, you know, there's a world going to hell out here and they are not going to drop into the ghetto anytime soon. Even with the recent events of September 2001, people are trying to find God but they're having nothing to do with the church.

While working in the construction field from 1998-2002, I remember talking with one of the sub-contractors on one of our job sites. This was two weeks after the bombings of 9/11 and I turned the conversation to God. He talked about Allah, I responded, telling what I believe about Islam and then we headed over to Christianity. He's response was priceless and tragic, yet one that must be heard by the church. "Well, how do you know what you people even believe. If there are seven churches on the road, side by side, you walk into each one of them and you get a different story."

Wow!!! What a telling revelation that should shake everyone who thinks he/she is a Christian. We're supposed to be telling one story about one faith in one savior who is also one God and we're supposed to be doing it in unity in the midst of the unsaved world. Instead, according to this man (and others that I personally have talked to and you too, if you actually talk to unbelievers), we are telling several stories, competing stories about this savior and there, all the facts are not consistent and there is

absolutely no unity and usually, this message comes in the form of info being lobbed over the walls of the ghetto.
He asked me "What religion is your group?"

I responded "Well, we're just Christians."

"Right, I knew that, but what type? You know they're not alike. They even have different Bibles."

Besides wanting to cry at that moment, I quickly explained how there is only one Bible and in that Bible, God says that there are only Christians, nothing more, nothing less. I left him with some challenging questions and ideas and I pray that we get to pick up where we left of sometime soon.

Am I being critical? Perhaps, but we must wake up and smell the coffee about our little world we have created. I'm sure that the educators at this Christian college are good ones who want to serve their God by using their education for Him. And perhaps at other schools, they might feel confined. Perhaps they want to open each class with prayer and feel as if that might not be okay at non-Christian school. I understand all of that, but the problem is, we weren't told that our job was to be salt and light inside the salt shaker and in a lit room. It's a dark and tasteless world out there that He commands us to be a part of.

Come on church—we've got to go out and be a part of this world before it's too late. The world is wondering about God. They are even asking for His blessing over our land, though they really have little idea as to what that means except "keep us safe" and "let us win all the conflicts." How can you be a voice to explain Him if you can't have a conversation with them? And you can't have a conversation with them if you never venture out and live in the community in which you live.

are you ready?

7

A splinter in your mind

So you're ready to move on, leave the ghetto, make a change. That attitude often prevails in war situations. I feel the same way right now and that is why I'm out here anyway. I sometimes I wish I could be somewhere else, but I feel a very clear command to this post. That concept of sticking it out for the end of the war comes clear from men in all issues of war.

General U. S. Grant, speaking after the Battle of Shiloh in 1862 wrote "Up to the battle of Shiloh I. . .believed that the rebellion. . .would collapse suddenly and soon if a decisive victory could be gained. . .[afterward] I gave up all idea of saving the Union except by complete conquest."

A soldier writing from the American 35th Division in World War I expressed the idea of the need to give it all to accomplish the end result of victory.

I have not seen a whole lot. It rather seems at times as if I were not in the big game at all when I see what some of the fellows have done and are going through. Well, if the Germans like war, the Yanks are giving them plenty of it. For the life of me I can't see how anyone can be so devilish, brutal, fiendish (many other words that will better express it), as to say that war is necessary for the natural growth of nations. I have seen wounded men, my own soldiers in arms, coming back to the hospitals and, well, it just gets you, that's all. I am willing and ready to go to the limit (and you know what that is here) to bring this business to a decisive end.

So you're ready to move on, and like Neo in *The Matrix*, you are looking for a way out. But to what, more aloneness? To a separateness that leaves you safe from backstabbers, but walking trails in a fog? That can't be right. The answer we all are looking for is right before us, unbelievably so, in the image of the church.

I think that there are a lot of people like Neo. The story of *The Matrix* is a powerful spiritual metaphor. In the story, the world has moved into a dark future where computers control humans. In fact, humans are captive and they don't even know they are captive. They are, in essence, blinded to reality by a clever deception by the computers.

There are some humans, however, who have gained freedom, led by a prophet-warrior named Morpheus. His team is looking for a special human who might be able to defeat the computers. When they find him, they have to first free him to see what is really real. To do this, Morpheus has to communicate clearly to Neo, yet he can't tell him everything, mostly because Neo would not believe him. Neo has to trust Morpheus enough to take the plunge; he has to believe Morpheus to do something drastic that will enable him to see the real world, blinders removed.

Once he does so, all that Neo believed to be true comes crashing down and reality comes blinding in. But first Morpheus must convince Neo that he, Neo knows inside that there really is a problem in the world. Things are not what they seem. Here is how Morpheus put it:

> "Feeling a bit like Alice, tumbling down the rabbit hole? You know something. What you know you can't explain, but you feel it. . .that there is something wrong with the world. You don't know what it is, but it's there, **like a splinter in your mind, driving you mad.**"

While it is true that many do not want to think about it, would just rather be left alone to themselves, there are others who hunger for the truth. They want some answers, someone to

45

remove this splinter from their mind. They know something is wrong with the world, but they can't really put their finger on it. Worse, when the Church tries to explain the answer, these outsiders often reject their testimony out of hand. Neither the messenger nor the message has any credibility, at least not in their minds.

For the person who already thinks they are a Christian, or who grew up in the church, they, like I, want their experience as a Christian to match what they read in the Bible. Or they want someone to put them out of their misery and prove that there is no God. Of course, they, like me, are clinging tightly to their faith and believing that the problem is not somehow with God, but with the expression of God in the world...."the Church."

As Morpheus continued in his conversation with Neo, he asked a question that I ask you now: "Do you know what I'm talking about? Do you want to know what [the thing that caused the problem] is?" While the rest of that wonderful exchange can be a lead-in into an evangelistic encounter, I challenge you to think of that question as someone who is already a Christian, and yet still has this nagging feeling that something is wrong.

Don't hear this as some attack on the church, as if I might suggest the church isn't Biblical or not worth the effort. This is no such attack. In fact, over the past 15 years, God has been working in me to become a defender of the idea of church. However, what the "official" church has become, a massive institution much like a "Christian mall" is NOT what the Bible even describes. This problem is where we must begin our investigation into what has gone wrong.

We aren't post-Congregationalist. We don't want to dismiss what the Bible says. We just want to get it right, and to get there, we must make sure we are letting God define the terms.

are you ready?

8

Ill-defined Words

For too long we have misunderstood what the word church even really means and in that, we have lost our way. The concept behind the word, truly a Biblical concept, has changed to something else.

The Bible describes those who receive Jesus as being part of a group, all together. The Bible actually uses several metaphors for this group. You will read of the body, an army, family, citizens of a city, a holy priesthood and others terms. The word however that is used more than others is *ecclesia*, which is best translated into a phrase—"the called out ones" or "those who are called out." This is this word that is translated "church" in English.

How that came to be is still up for debate among experts; the word "church" has a contentious history from an etymology point of view, and that history is instructive for our discussion here. Keep in mind first that English was not widely used until the 6th century or so. And the Bible was not translated into English until the 14th century. Through the first 300 years or so after Jesus, there was no single word to somehow describe the place that people met.

How we got from *ecclesia* to "church" is the part that most do not know about. There is some agreement among scholars that the Greek word *kyriakon* forms the historical background for the word "church." This Greek word means "of the Lord" and thus, was used to imply "house of the Lord" as a name of the Christian house of worship. Some of the earliest cited instances are around 300 AD, such as in the Apostolic Constitutions or cited by Eusebius. From then, it appears to have been in fairly common use in the East: e.g., Emperor Constantine named several churches built by him *kyriaka*.

As we have said, the ordinary name for the gathered or the believers, in Greek was *ecclesia* and this was the name that passed into Latin and all the Romanic languages including all the Celtic languages. Yet the Germanic tribes did not adopt this name for the house of worship, using instead the derivative *"kirika"* or *"kirikja."* *Ecclesia* was actually adopted as the sense of the Christian society or assembly, which would be theologically correct.

Thus the point being made is that our early English word "church" actually means the building and *ecclesia* means the assembly of the saints. Tyndale, in his wonderful translation in 1534, tried to fix the problem by using the word congregation in the several places that typically now use the word "church." But, the publishing of the King James Bible in 1611 cemented the Germanic image of "church" to mean the actual gathering together. In doing so, we have created the confusion that now exists with the church. Today, you might hear pastors and leaders saying something like "the church is the people, not the building" when the opposite is true. "Church" does mean the building and not the people. The people of God are the *ecclesia*.

Beyond that confusion over the word "church," we know that the Bible uses several different metaphors for the collected Christians as we have already stated. We would probably be better off if we could eliminate the word "church" altogether as it relates to *ecclesia*. We are trying to help people see that they are to connect to God through his Son Jesus. We are not trying to say that they need to join an institution. We should demonstrate that after accepting God' gracious call to himself, each Christian belongs to a family, to the gathering, to the "called out ones. We are not trying to tell them that they belong, post conversion, to the church. As we say at Numinous, "you don't join the church when you become a believer, you just ARE the church—church is a state of being." You ARE a "called out one."

I just got off the phone with a brother in the Lord discussing this issue, asking similar questions. In his mind, the idea of church is wrong. I would say rather the problem lies in the fact that the *ecclesia* has been morphed into something else. Now we must reclaimed its true definition by returning again to how the Bible describes things.

Yes, it is the idea of the church, that idea which morphed sadly into a ghetto, a spiritual vs. secular enclave, where we can see a faint image of what we should move toward. It's not that we decide to destroy the idea of church, of a "together" that is beyond just me. It's that we return to the Ancient Documents to see what is there about how we are to live, together.

And there is information there. God did not "leave us hanging" with how we go about this. Sadly, just as in Luther's day, most have no idea what is in the Bible and we have accepted the status quo. But as we have seen, in accepting it, we have given birth to a status that prohibits, rather than encourages, outsiders from seeing Jesus, and from seeing He is the reason for us gathered.

In the end, the church is about community—that idea of a gathering of people who have chosen to reside together, to connect intimately, invasively into one another's lives. Today, in America and Europe, we have lost all sense of what that means and have accepted a cheap substitute in its place.

It's an "us" thing; community, the great mystery of our days. Of course it's also one of those things that no one really thinks or worries about, except for weirdoes like me. Of course we talk about our communities, especially the places that we live. But that kind of community exists only in our minds.

Seriously, do you know even 4 neighbors who live around you? And in a metro area like Orlando, real towns like Maitland and Casselberry are just swallowed up by the metropolis. Some might say that is where they are from, but in general, most will say they are from Orlando, the larger more vague city, or even more broadly say "Central Florida."

We know nothing of community. Over the past 6 decades, America has lost that sense that comes with community, the idea that you live and surround yourself, usually willingly, with others.

They know you. You know them. Parents raise each other's children. PTA and YMCA are places for neighbors to see each other and share life.

Today, in most American cities, we individually live within the four walls of our house. We stay uneasily in our jobs, prepared for the coming move when we either find greener pastures or the boss has seen our faces enough. Our participation at city things like the YMCA is merely another gathering of strangers. Casual, friendly chatter ensues, but with a safety net of the knowledge that I will not see this person ever again.

Each morning, we let the drawbridge down over our moat and venture out in our steel encased armor, a horse with four wheels and move isolated toward our rendezvous with our work. There, we have "work friends" who don't really know us and would think us strange if we ever really asked questions to discover who they are. Each night we travel the same dusty roads home, raise the drawbridge behind us, and disappear for the night. Safe behind our castle walls.

We could spend pages discussing why this is the picture of most of America, but what's the use of that. We have crossed the bridge into this new land and burned the bridge. So what do we do? How about looking beyond the "what used to be of 1930-50 America" toward the "what could be" of an Acts-copied community. It is the secret to life. There we can find the wholeness and health to life that many of us are missing. And surprisingly enough, it's in the life of the Christian to demonstrate this to the world.

are you ready?

9

Last words of a dying man

The strangest aspect of the current church context is that most Christians understand the idea that they are part of the movement to help others. For more evangelical churches, most often "helping others" translates to evangelism. For other groups, "helping others" means more socially active forays.

But at the same time, few of us actually do those things. We basically act as if it's the job of the leaders or it's just a part of the fabric of the church. "Personally my responsibility? No way." I think most feel it's just far too dangerous and at the same time there pervades a feeling that none of us live a life good enough to go out and supposedly represent God.

Much of this conundrum (that we know to do evangelism, but we don't do it) occurs due to one idea in the Bible. The Great Commission, as Matthew 28:18-20 is often called contains one report of Jesus' last words. Clearly, there, He tells everyone assembled they have a job to do and more evangelical churches paint that verse as the key.

Thus, from this one report, the notion that the church has a mission emerged. And, from one point of view, I totally agree with that. There is a clear presentation, Biblically speaking, that spreading this news that is good is a critical task.

But is it the "mission" of the church? Of the collective? Does Matthew 28:18-20 de facto become the last word on the role of the church? Does that question shake you? Anger you? If we are considering the ills of the church, contemplating how we got stuck in the ghetto, dreaming about any move that might help save us for the future, then we must take to task what exactly is the mission of the church.

If we cannot firmly establish a mission, then how can we know that we are being successful or not? And complimentary to that, if the current direction is discovered not to be the actual Biblical mission, then pursuing that aim would be unwise. If there is a mission for the church, let's find it and do that first and foremost.

Certainly, I could be out to lunch here, but the facts lead me to at least consider what exactly is the mission of the church. If we can see our current product and see that it is horribly flawed, weak or something--it is producing a terrible end product—then we must ask the hard question about the mission. Whatever it is, currently we are failing miserably. Let's just be honest about that. And, perhaps we are failing for the same reasons I've heard for many years—that people are lazy, not interested in evangelism and the like. Perhaps. Or maybe, the problem is that we've been pursuing the wrong mission for the church.

In 1863, General Robert E. Lee decided that his best effort to win The Civil War was to re-invade the north. He mustered his best troops, broke off contact with the Union army and headed for Pennsylvania. To accomplish this, his army was more or less broken into parts working its way north. However, before his cavalry units made it across the Potomac, they were surprised by a Union cavalry unit. The resulting battle was basically a draw, but to the prideful leader of the CSA Calvary, J.E.B. Stuart, it was an embarrassment.

To prove his worth and to save face, Stuart took off with his unit into a ravaging ride through Maryland and Pennsylvania. This event would, in and of itself not be such a big deal except that he never bothered to communicate with General Lee his plans. Stuart assumed that his mission was clear and that this tactic would be fine. He had done much the same thing other times, perhaps most famously in 1862 when he road completely around the Union army as it lay encamped outside of Richmond. His ride then struck terror in then commanding General McDowell.

This time, though, his mission was not to ravage the northern countryside. Though he was very successful in his effort in a numbers kind of way, he was not actually accomplishing the true and intended mission. And, as it worked out, he was not where Lee needed him to be on July 1, 1863 when advance elements of the CSA army stumbled into scouts of the Union army. It would not be till late July 2, 1863 before Stuart would ride up and by then it was too late. Lee was blind without his cavalry and it showed in his worst performance of the war. A group that is making strides in its effort is not really doing that well if the effort is not in keeping with the true mission.

I spent a year or more looking and studying the Bible to see what, if any, commands or directives were given to the church. Of course, accepting the idea that the church exists as every individual Christian, then one can state that the entire Bible contains the mission of the church. Granted. However, what I mean by "given to the church" is asking if there are any direct statements to the collective, to the group. Who knows—maybe there is nothing there?

I looked. You should too. If you study the Bible for this topic, one can see some fascinating facts. What I saw there was astounding to me. We know that the Bible has wonderful teaching for how a specific Christian should live, irrespective of what other Christians do. Yet, as one looks in the Bible, a companion teaching is there for the collective group of Christians living in a certain city, instructions for how they should live.

Among the various statements to the church collective, there is direct mission given to the collective body by Jesus. It appears in a very logical place, in his last time of intensive communication with the disciples prior to his going to the cross. In John 13-17, we are given an in-depth report of this last meeting that Jesus had with his followers. These last words of one who was about to die (He knew it even as no one else did—He also knew He would come back in three days--Praise the Lord) are very important. All that Jesus teaches there is very important, but two aspects jumped out at me that I had never seen before, at least not in this light. There in chapters 13 and 17 lay what I consider to be the prime directive for the church.

First, in John 13:34-35, Jesus states the following:

> A new command I give you: Love one another. As I have loved you, so you must love one another. By this all men will know that you are my disciples, if you love one another.

Notice the hook here—this is tremendous. It is not just "love one another." No, while that would be fine of course, but instead, Jesus says this is a brand new command. It has never been uttered before. Thus, He adds something to the old love as you want to be loved command. It is a corollary that impacts or defines evangelism. "Love one another as I have loved you" and hey, as a bonus, everyone will then know you are my disciples.

Part of our problem today is that Christians are hard to discern. What makes a person a Christian? Church membership? Just a personal declaration that you are one? Baptism? People have no idea exactly what Christians are supposed to believe. Christians don't know what Christians should believe. Many people run around claiming to be Christians. How can anyone tell? Jesus, here, says clearly that one can tell a Christian simply by how they love other Christians. He is not talking about loving everyone in the world this way. Nope—this is to the disciples, those who would stake their claim with Jesus. Inside, where relationships are hard to maintain, in that place, Jesus says you must love as I have loved you and by that fact, the world will know you are my disciples. Amazing.

Loving the world and loving those who are not in agreement with you was covered already back in the Sermon on the Mount (Matthew 5-7). There, Jesus said to love your enemies, to love those who attack you, to love as you want to be loved. In John 13, though, he is clearly speaking to his followers, to the embryonic church. For them, on the inside, the level is jacked up a notch. Now, it's not just love as you wish others to love you, but love as

Jesus loved. Leonard Sweet called this the Platinum Rule, a higher, deeper call to love than the Golden Rule.

What Jesus is talking about is a credibility issue. We face problems in proving that credibility, don't we? In my discussions with people, the one issue that comes up over and over again is the credibility issue. One young mother told me that she was a Christian, but just could not deal with going to church because no one there had any credibility. Our credibility is a personal issue; it comes down to us. Yet here, Jesus is telling us that He has a plan for guaranteeing our credibility.

Of course we all know why loving each other will prove out credibility. We've been in enough different groups to understand that if you put 15 strangers into a room to become a group, some normal things occur. Natural affinities step in and people click with different people. Also, natural friction occurs between other people. People just don't naturally "love" each other—not over time. They can fake it for a while but after a while, the little idiosyncrasies begin to really irritate and before long, annoyances form walls between people. That is what naturally happens. Jesus is saying that by breaking that cycle, we demonstrate that something beyond natural is at work here and that "thing" can only be a spiritual God thing and that should point to Jesus.

He did not stop there, though. Jesus reiterates his point during his prayer of Chapter 17. In that prayer, he first prays about himself, then he prays for his disciples and finally, Jesus turns his prayer to the future believers. He utters a cry to God asking God to give the believers a unity that was equal to the unity that He (Jesus) had with God.

Again, this in and of itself would be a great prayer. We need unity if for no other reason than it is good practice for heaven. Yet again, Jesus shows how much he actually cares about evangelism, about getting the word out about himself and his mission. He says this in John 17:20-21:

> My prayer is not for them [the disciples] alone. I pray also
> for those who will believe in me through their message, that

all of them may be one, Father, just as you are in me and I am in you. May they also be in us so that the world may believe that you have sent me.

What he is saying is that through our unity, the world would know that God had sent his Son. In other words, the entire aspect of evangelism—the good news that Jesus came from God and provides us a way to have relationship with God now and forever—only becomes discerned by the world through our unity within the body.

Again, what is really at stake here? While individual credibility is a crucial issue, the credibility of the message is also important. That credibility gets attacked in a variety of ways, but the gist of it usually involves an implication that Jesus was not who he says he is.

And it's not just non-Christians who attack the credibility of the message. As we saw earlier, people who call themselves Christians also doubt the validity of the Bible, of the fact that Jesus was perfect, that Jesus even knew what he was doing and on and on. In our journey, we have attempted to lay a very strong foundation in our theology as we teach it and live it out. One young man that I was teaching, after the session, came to me in full amazement. "I never knew any of that," he said in reflection of my full defense of the Bible. "I always thought that the Bible and Jesus was just a bunch of good stories."

We are fortunate to have many apologists who attempt to provide support for the credibility of the message. They are important, but at the same time, with Jesus words and the call to unity, He is providing His own evidence for credibility. The unity proves that he came from God. If our love for one another provides the personal credibility, then our unity provides evidence that the message is also credible.

Do you see this? The church for more than a few decades has taken the focus off of our true mission—being in love with each other and in being unified—and placed the focus on "doing" Christianity. The result has been disastrous, as we have seen. Guilt racks many Christians who feel inadequate to pull off this task. Churches misallocate funds that should be used for the mission (love and unity) into evangelism, service, poverty issues, environmental issues, etc.... The church becomes an institution trying to accomplish a task rather than a loving state of being. Church should not be something you join; it should be an existence in continual devotion, closer and closer together as community, with an end result of reaching others who are not Christians.

Don't lose sight of what I am trying to demonstrate here. Jesus wants evangelism to happen! He wants the poor ministered to. He cares about babies and orphans. He cares about the earth and her inhabitants, human and otherwise. It matters tremendously to him! However, he has his own plan for how these things are to happen and it does involve the church, but not in the way that we've been taught or heard. The church really is to be constantly moving closer and closer in love and unity with one another. And as that happens? Tah-dah—the world knows that Jesus came from God and they see that we are his disciples. The credibility is established! The lost person "gets it" and they come to believe in God and His Son Jesus.

Amazingly, the very thing that many pastors want and often try to drive their people towards, is accomplished by NOT doing activities, but by being something as a collective. These two commands CANNOT be accomplished individually, but are given to the group, the collective as a whole. These are not merely good ideas for a Christian, but are the core foundation of what the church is to be—a community.

are you ready?

10

The Acts Gamble

So the basic idea is that we are to love one another and be unified, huh? One could demand some proof of this idea because if you look around at the Christian church today, you can clearly see that we are failing on both accounts. If you just look at any large American city, you'll find "church row" where, side by side, sit a variety of Christian churches.

Supposedly, all of these churches are of one faith, yet in practice, these difference churches represent to their city different pictures of faith. While not true everywhere, in many cities, these neighboring churches barley admit each other's existence. What is that about? Remember the story about my construction colleague? His entire issue was which version of Christianity I stood for. It took some time to convince him that in reality, there was only one version, but in his mind and his personal experience, there were multiple versions of Christianity with multiple versions of the Bible.

Is it any wonder that non-Christians disregard the faith and members of these churches? And when they consider that most of those same members are not even sure of the core tenants of the faith, it is even worse. It's not supposed to be this way. When I was growing up in East Tennessee in the 1970s, church was our life. My father served in many ministerial settings within the Southern Baptist Church and God was an active part of my family. Yet, church was really nothing more than lots of activities and it sure seemed as if many people had no real connection beyond the Sunday experience.

Even more troubling to me was that most of my friends who were not Christians saw little need for all the activities that my youth group and church offered. They were very happy with their own friends and settings. Of course, from a theological point of view, I can demonstrate how they were still in need of God, but in practice, they could argue back that they did not have any need for the thing being offered them. Without knowing, what they wanted (then and now) was community, love and unity, to be known deeply by others and find relationships there that mattered. What they were being told they needed was Jesus and lots of activities--a place to join.

That was never Jesus intent or purpose. But can I prove this? Well, let's keep looking at the Bible for our answer. I will clearly accept the charge that Jesus words won't really work (which is part of the point—we've never really seen this kind of love and unity in action apart from God, so the doubt factor is really high here). We need to see evidence in practice, not just theory.

In Acts 2, we see that Jesus/God has moved from the theory of John 13 & 17 to the practice of Acts 2 community. It would be one thing to have the verses of John and no picture biblically of it ever working. Perhaps it would still be right, but we could honestly complain that such an idea has never worked down here, especially the part about evangelism just being a by-product of unity and love. Nope, we could honestly state that all we've ever seen done is evangelism as a duty or an act of the church.

But right there in the Bible, in Acts 2, 4, 5, and 7 we are given snapshots of the early church and what they were doing. In each picture the underlying image is of a group of individuals who come together around the cross and form community.

And it's not just there—throughout the remainder of the New Testament, unity and love for one another within the body is mentioned again and again. In fact, there is an entire set of commands that further provide support for our contention about the mission of the church.

We call these the "one another" commands, so titled by my friend Dr. Paul Cornwell. In these commands (see the Appendix for full list) we are told many things such as "be devoted to one another" or "exhort one another." The most oft repeated is, not surprisingly, "love one another." Throughout, writers like James, Paul, Peter, and John all extol the virtue of the community of faith operating together. It is as if they understood that full success only came as the group interacted properly with one another.

Of course that is not surprising since they were all there when Jesus gave his final commands, as recorded by John. They heard his promises that came with these commands. They were also there at the very beginning as recorded by Luke in Acts—they saw the result of the promise of Jesus.

Certainly there are many things that a "good Christian" should do and many of them can be done individually. Meaning, I don't need you to accomplish a command like "turn the other cheek." But these "one another" commands cannot be accomplished in isolation. To fulfill what God has asked of me, I must have others, the others of the body of Christ.

It is in this community that we see care for one another. We see the disregard for self and a larger concern for one another. Here we see the proof of God's promise in John. How do we know that? Well, we are told that people, outsiders, joined the group on a regular basis.

So there it is. While today's evangelical church strives to "do" evangelism as a task and win converts, God desperately wants to do the whole enterprise a different way. Rather than a lot of work, money and effort on random "outreach" efforts (things that usually come up far short of what should be expected based on the time and money spent), God asks us to do something else.

Love and Unity—if you asked most churches, they'd exclaim that of course they are about those two things. But if you investigate, you'd find most of their effort and money not spent on love and unity, on community. Rather, it is on buildings, salaries, and "outreach."

Sadly the one thing God tells us WILL bring the ultimate goal is an often overlooked or dismissed. Community, it is assumed, is a given and is easy to do. It is not as I'll discuss later, but consider if we could move our effort towards maintaining our love and unity, perhaps God would be faithful to his Word.

Of course, a lot of this all rides on your interpretation of Acts. Is it merely a history or does it also contain a didactic element demonstrating how we are to proceed as the body gathered? I believe that Acts is indeed didactic and not merely just history. So, I decided to accept the challenge of Acts. I call this the Acts Gamble.

"Gamble," you ask? It is a gamble in this way, particularly for leaders, but not them alone. What if this idea doesn't work? Meaning, what if they can't get enough people at their church without doing a lot of Christian ghetto programs that everyone seems to expect? What if they only have "real serious" Christians come? Meaning what? Well, meaning, "we won't be able to pay all our bills financially." And that is the rub. Is paying the bills really the point of the church? I think we have demonstrated that the answer there is a resounding "NO!" So, choosing to base the core mission of the church exactly like Jesus laid it out is a gamble, especially in the US.

Currently, there are many books and philosophies teaching how to accomplish church growth. I've always wondered about that phrase "church growth" anyway. What is that supposed to mean? You hear it from some church leaders—"I'm just trying to grow the church." I thought that Jesus had already done that or, at least, that it is his job to build whatever the body gathered together should look like. Well, these books and efforts are tried and true in the attempt to get people into the church building. I'll even admit that some of them do bring in new people. Most of the time, the majority (the vast majority?) are Christians who are just on the move or new in town, but sometimes, a non-connected person will attend based on some "church growth" effort. But then what do you have—a crowd? Are they community? Are they disciples? I suppose that if we were commanded to draw a crowd, perhaps the fact of people coming into the building would be good. Is that our task?

So in the end, what you end up with is this Hamster wheel theology of many churches. That philosophy of church growth demands more people (for good Bible reasons surely) and at the same time, believes that you need more money to pay for the events/programs to bring in those people. Then you need more money to pay for more staff (really?) to minister to these new people and then of course you need a bigger building to house the more people, so that also demands more money, which in turn demands more people. And all these people need "resources" that the church is supposed to provide, programs to satisfy our consumer appetite, so that takes money too. And of course, while this is happening, you end up back at the point where there is 10% of the community doing 90% of the work (and the paid staff pulling a huge load—"hey, they get paid to do that, so why should I do it?"). But they can't handle too many people, so you expect within these new people are some leaders and/or hope that some are mature enough to come on and become like the other weary, worn workers. Can you see the wheel spinning round? Can you see and feel the exhaustion?

I am not saying that programs are intrinsically bad or wrong. I am also not saying that having more people is wrong. But if the underlying philosophy is wrong, then what is built on top cannot be right. And when the underlying philosophy is NOT community, then the workers end up feeling used and exhausted from all the things to have to do, guilt gets thrown around, others start to wonder why all they hear about is money, etc...

So the Gamble relates to aspects that are financial and philosophical. We are spending major money on trying to draw a crowd, but not focusing on the actual stated task of the church. So, the gamble is that through God's promise based on our love and unity, God will do what he said, that the result would be the same as in Acts. That is not to say that any certain number of people is promised. I don't think you can look at Acts and demand 5000 converts every time you open the doors. Our belief here at Numinous is that we must focus on community (love and unity) and let him worry about people coming to us. And that is a gamble. If He lets us down, then there is no money for any staff (we'll talk about that later), there's little money to pay for a rent to be in a building (is that really a problem?), there's a question about God (that is the scary part).

In reality, the Gamble leads us to seriously entertain the question of what is success in the first place. I'll write more about that in a later letter, but suffice it to say now that I am growing further and further convinced that numbers are NOT the way that we should evaluate.

I know by now many of you are screaming to me that there is more to church than that. You are thinking of verses that indicate something about a responsibility to reach others. Verses that talk about how we live our lives. Or, you are confident that the church is really to be a service organization. I know, I know—we're getting there, but we cannot race past this. Trust me, the individual Christian's call is part and parcel to this entire process. Yet the danger is that we skip this foundation and only make demands for individuals to "do their jobs" and thus, revert back to the old system whereby everyone plays a game that takes us back where we started: that the church institution (and the paid staff's job) is to do the church stuff.

Hear me well—no one is supposed to do this evangelism stuff in the way you think. Yes, we are to be about evangelism. That word is in the New Testament. It's there, explicit as well as implied. But the issue I am raising is how it happens. Jesus is clearly stating in John and demonstrating in Acts that He will do this for us as we work towards a deeper community.

How's it going for us? So far, we've seen God to be true to his Word. Not as quick as I would like perhaps, not in mass numbers, but steadily we've seen people come to believe that we are his disciples and that Jesus came from God based on our community and love for one another. Do I think the gamble is worth continuing? Yes. Do I wonder about it? I wish it would happen quicker. Am I scared as someone who has laid his life on the line about this? Yes. If I wasn't, then it wouldn't probably be a gamble. Yet my trust is in the same God who says that He will let me be with him in heaven. I still have to work outside of the church to pay my bills, but I like that and I am totally confident that even if we had a very large budget, I would still only receive part of my salary from Numinous. So it is a gamble I will continue to gladly take.

Look at it this way—for the past decades, much hand wringing has occurred about the state of the church. Much has been done to increase evangelism and the profile of the church.. As of today, things are worse rather than better. The under 40 crowd has clearly walked away from any concept of a Biblical position about life and the churched crowd (the majority of American adults, particularly 40 and over) reflects a deep loss of what it actually means to be a Christian. Do you honestly think that all of these people are really Christians? That God will admit that He knows them? As the old adage states, you can't expect new results from the same old methods.

To me, if someone has a better idea, I'm open to it, but here's the rub. We have not tried the simple two things He told us to do, not since the early centuries and in scattered pockets here and there throughout history. Love each other and be unified— that's all He told us in his last words to us. And they come with a promise! Sure there's more about the church, about the gathered believers (see appendix 1for my study of that), but those other passages about the church describe its attributes or facts or leadership—not its mission. For that, this is it! It is clearly tied to the thing in God's heart, to wit, that everyone would know Him and be in relationship with Him. Numinous is about trying to fulfill those commands and in doing so, put the challenge back to God as we go forward.

What about you? Ready for the revolution yet?

are you ready?

64

11

Invasive Community

The small talk of the evening was winding down quickly as she came to the main point of why she wanted to have dinner.

"So, anyway, let me tell you what I really need to say," she said.

Not wanting to interrupt her train of thought, I stayed silent and continued to eat my sandwich.

"I'm going to start attending another church. Whew! Man, that was hard to say, but I had to just blurt it out."

The words started coming quickly at that point. Stuff about not wanting to hurt me, about how it had nothing to do with me (well, not really), about how we'd really helped her get on her feet, yet now as she viewed the church landscape, just couldn't see a reason to stay.

She stopped talking and looked at me. I had been silent through the entire exchange. The restaurant was basically empty.

"Well, do you have anything to say?"

I looked up. Paused. Got up and walked to refill my drink. I looked very calm but inside I was a bundle of confused thoughts and images. What was I really being told? What had happened? Just two weeks before, this person had announced that, as part of a committee, she was very committed to the coming church event.

Long sigh.

"I suppose I'm supposed to talk you into staying around, but that is just not my style," I finally announced. And with that, I launched into a nice explanation about what I really heard her saying, my observation of it, the pluses and the minuses. And, how, in the end, I couldn't make her do anything nor would I try if I could.

The evening did not end too well and was rather bittersweet. What you are reading here, a true story with some details changed, is an example of the real struggle of love and unity. In the end, what this person was breaking free from was the invasive nature of community.

What this person said they were leaving for was not exactly what was really happening, as later events proved out. What she did not really know how to say, as she was leaving for the bigger church that held more "bells and whistles," was that she did not like the intimacy of community.

Therein lies the rub of what Jesus asks us to do in this mission of the church. There is a sense in which most Americans that I know really chafe against the concepts inherent in communal connection. Oh we know internally that we want to know and be known by others. We do want that. However, when it comes time to live it out, we run from the intimacy.

I think that partly is a cultural thing specific to the United States and partly I think it a result of the last 50 years of American history. We have moved far from the culture of community, at least in much of the US, where people grow up in the same setting as their grandparents, in that place where everyone knows everyone else.

In those places (and some do still remain), everyone did know everyone's business. A handshake was as good as a signature in business. The community raised the child. When a person was in need, the community knew it and rallied to meet that need.

Today, in most places, we have casual relationships much like people now have casual sex. "I'm glad to know you and am interested in sharing something, some parts of me, but only on the surface and I certainly don't expect you to get to know the "real" me." We go to work, having casual friendships there. In our neighborhoods, we barely get to know our neighbors' names, usually rushing home to lower the drawbridge of the garage door, shutting down the outside world. Events like youth sports or group activities occur on a much larger community level with people that live in disparate sections of town, so we know that we'll only see them for these 3-5 months.

Thus, all of our communal settings maintain a transitory nature, rather than a permanent one. We all know the pain of loss when a co-worker leaves or is fired. We know what it is like to experience a good neighbor moving away. For many postmodern young adults, we know what it is like to have our own parents move out. So, we think, "why waste the effort getting too close to these people."

In the end, we are alone. We hate being alone, yet we fear being too close. That reality is the underlying foundation in so many stories like the one that I relayed at the beginning of this letter.

For that person, in the end, what they experienced at the big church was what they had experienced before—they were invisible and no one really knew them. Before long, this person told me that they had quit going to that church. Today? Today they are basically alone, not going to church at all, having no real intimacy with anyone of faith and maintaining casual relationships within some activities and work.

That story is a tragedy that we need to understand if we are indeed to move beyond just talking about real community. If we really are excited about God's glory and seeing Him connected to our lost friends, then we had better get excited about community. God certainly is.

Yet, we have to also comprehend the fact that most of us struggle with invasive community. We WANT to be left alone.

There is some pull to privacy, especially in the USA with our independent streak, well seen in our history.

The reality of community is that it is invasive. You can't "love one another as I [Jesus] have loved you" and not become intimate. So, as many of us struggle with that aspect, the aftereffects can be seen in many different places and people. I've seen it in big cities. I've seen it in small towns. In large churches and small churches. It is unavoidable and unmistakable.

Is there anything we can do to change it? No, I don't think so. In our current culture, most of us cringe when people start getting too close. We have trouble being very close to our own immediate families.

How can we help people prepare for those feelings? Well, besides teaching about the truth of it, not much else has worked in my experience. What we have done at Numinous is illuminate the facts. That way, when each person starts feeling the effects, they can resist better, or, at appropriate times, take a vacation to be alone and catch their breath. When we know the enemy that we are facing, we can prepare better.

Knowing what I am feeling is half the battle in my opinion. Understanding that it is coming and that I've been sensitized to this by my culture allows me to fight back. So, if start to feel like I want to withdraw, I instead force myself to get closer. When I feel like staying home from the gatherings, I will intentionally must decide to go.

Seeing the invasive nature of community helps me understand when people ask about me, they really are caring for me. It helps me take the time daily to call someone in the group to just check in and try to get closer. Here in Numinous, I created something known as the "Five Minute Phone Call." Knowing that we instinctively rebel against community and its invasive nature, I challenged our group to take five minutes each day to call one person in the community.

Five minutes is not a big deal as we all know and it basically allows for a simple conversation that everyone can handle. It allows you to say hello and ask how you can pray for that person.

Or, if you've called them before, it allows you to simply check up on them, telling them that you've been praying for them. That is a very simple plan that works to defeat the feelings we've discussed.

At the heart of what I am trying to say is that the invasiveness of community is not a bad thing. The word "invasion" sounds bad, war-like, but really what I mean is that intimacy is coming. Community as Jesus lays it out demands intimacy, not casualness. To love as he loved and to pursue unity at all times is hard, requiring a closeness not experienced by most people. How in the world are we to expect that others will sell their possessions to provide financially for one another when they are not close? It won't happen.

So either Jesus is wrong or He knew that what He was calling for required a move toward one another rather than a move into isolation. And such a move is costly. It means that someone will call wanting to have your time. It means sharing the meal table with many people. It means finding others in your house at all times. It means late night phone calls in crisis.

All of those things and more are the real meaning of community and that is invasive. Rather than running from it, Jesus wants us to embrace it. Accept the intimacy as He sees it—not something to be endured but something to rejoice in. For those that fight through the initial feeling of invasion, the sweetness of community is very rich.

Let me close with another story, another sad one. We've had a couple that has been on again, off again with us, with the wife coming deeper than the husband. They've actually been "active" at two other churches at one level or another all the while being around us. One of those churches is what most would call their "home church" (serving in some ministries there).

Recently, they've gone through a crisis in their marriage. The husband called last week asking for help. While discussing the nature of their need, he volunteered that he was turning to us since we were the only one's who ever were really there for his family.

That is not the tragic part, though it could be. If we were the only ones "there for them," you would be correct to wonder why in the world they had not given themselves more deeply to our community and group than they actually had. Why would you subject yourself to some institutional experience that was less that fulfilling when you could find real community in another place? The answer is simply that the other church could provide a normal sense of church programming that they thought they needed for themselves and their kids. But that is not the tragic part.

He went on to add that he did not want to call the others because they always made him feel uncomfortable. That is also not the tragic part, though it could be. Here clearly is another case of church as institution, though both churches he is involved with would protest that they indeed are community churches. Yet, here is just one more testimony that I have personally listened to about a person feeling quite lost or unimportant or a bother to the institution. But that is not the tragic part.

No, the tragic part was that he could not see that he had so isolated himself from community (ours in particular) that no one knows him and most have no real reason to want to help him. In a moment of need, he began to realize that he was alone and that not only would some of the churches not easily want to help him due to their own issues, but that even a community centered group like ours was reluctant. He could not see that he had run away from the invasive nature of community and in the process isolated himself.

If we hope to move the church in the direction that God wants, we'd better start illuminating the invasive nature of community well. And, as individuals, we must recognize that community is challenging and that we have to press on and into.

He never said it would be easy, but the reward on the other end of invasive community is sweet. To be known deeply by others and to know others deeply is a rich, comforting experience. I would not have it any other way and I have certainly had to fight against and through invasive community. How about you? Ready to move deeper?

are you ready?

12

Welcome to the Revolution

I was on the phone today with a dear brother in the Lord, but one that I did not think understood all that I have been saying. Put another way, I did not think that he had come to join the revolution that I believe God is trying to spark. But I kept hoping and as I hung up the phone, I was encouraged. As I ended the phone call, based on what he shared, I told him "welcome to the revolution." He finally gets it.

He and some friends had started a church 8 months ago. I spoke there once. It was fine, but typical. Now he tells me that issues are emerging, and part of that stems from the things I said when I spoke there and the very ideas that I have written about here.

As we talked, he began to verbalize what I've said here, but coming at it from a different direction. To honor him, let me just let his words speak here:

Well here is what I've been thinking about. Tell me what you think about it. As an individual believer, I've been given some tasks to accomplish. I think there are at least 5, maybe more. In no certain order they are these:

- Fathers are to teach the children
- Husbands are to instruct the wife and bathe her in the Word
- Maintain my own private worship and prayer with God
- Become intimate within the body

- Be a light that shines to my neighbors.

Obviously, the first two are for me as a man and would be similar for a woman [Mothers are to teach their children; Wives are to help their husbands become a godly man]. Anyway, what I am thinking is that, as I look at the church, all I see is that we've allowed or forced the church to take all these roles for me. So, that is why I think the church is wrong or confused or something.

As I listened to my friend, I was struck by how God is communicating this message to many. I thought of my friend Garry Kishere in England who has said much the same thing. And I thought of another brother in ministry, Tre Cates, in Boulder, CO who is living out these same concerns. And there are others who I don't know yet.

My friend on the phone was right, you know. Stated another way, the individual Christian has given up his/her God-given mission and in their place, the collective has taken up the burden. And of course, in taking up that mission, the collective has dropped it's own mission. I don't really think that there was some insidious plan somewhere for this to happen. Just, over time, as more and more Christians have been allowed to think that being a Christian is some easy club you join, where there is a difference between believers and disciples, where you can choose not to obey God and yet think that you have a free pass to heaven, believers have stopped trying to do what they were commanded to do.

As this happened, Christian leaders felt compelled to step in. Sometimes, probably, it was over a hunger for a larger church, for an ego to be satisfied, for a personal kingdom to be built, but mostly it was just the desire to do more for God. Kind of a "if the people are not going to fulfill their mission of representing God, well, we'll set up a program here in the church to do that." But instead of jump-starting individual Christians, such actions further deadened them to their real tasks.

As more churches moved toward a professional staff setting and they were paid in cash rather than with a pound of corn or a chicken, there became more of a demand for the paid guys to do more. As more churches set up these "helpful" programs, more people began to accept the church doing by proxy what they individually had been told to do.

In the process, great verses like Matthew 28:18-20 got moved from a personal command for each believer into some grandiose purpose statement for the collective. And as the years ran along, the split between what Jesus asked each of us to do grew. Ministers applied more guilt to get action and dreamed up even more creative programs designed to try and get some action out of people. Yet, the more stringent leaders found their words falling on deaf ears and churches that were sensitive and speakers that told happy stories found greater success.

Church growth experts come along saying "create church growth this way," or market yourself that way, speak with these types of stories and on and on. People, deadened to the real mission of either the church or individuals, became more consumer oriented and less disciple oriented. Ministers like myself who aren't really concerned with leading a consumer church find themselves challenged, accused like I was, of pushing for some "commando Christianity."

All I want is for real believers to act like it—not perfect, but with a willing, desiring heart to be like Jesus. All we tell people is that church should be less demanding of complicated schemes and be more simple with the message for the collective—love and unity.

Put another way, the current status of the church ends up usurping the very things that we are supposed to do as individual Christians. The roles get confused and eventually, we have no idea if we are coming or going.

Think I'm crazy? Well, take a look at my generation. Generation X. The New Lost Generation. The Busters. Whatever title you want to give them. Throw in the young boomers while you are at it and keep watching the next generation—the Millennials.

But look hardest at my group. We are the product of the church in its new lost pattern.

Talk to someone aged 18 - 39 if you want a taste of how people feel about it. Most hate the church but will claim some connection with God. They can't see that the two statements are in conflict. They were forced to go to church at some point, most of them, yet hated their parents for it. They saw nothing in their parents or most adults that demonstrated any conviction or integrity. Those adults were beginning to live out the confusion, the lack of mission and the beginning of the end of community in the church. Church was beginning to really be this strip mall experience where the best ones provided all that a person needed in the spiritual realm. And hey, there were little requirements. Just toss a little cash in the plate, give a little time when you can and all is well.

Think I'm kidding—let me relay stories for you, from fellow journeyers—not drug addicts, not crazy people, but honest-to-goodness Christians who hunger for God.

(The following stories are true, but the names have been changed to protect the innocent and the guilty. They are offered in first person or the way the speaker related them to me.)

Story #1—I was brought up in church. I went to church all the time, but the older I got, the more lies I saw. I never saw love; I never saw acceptance. To fit in, I had to be what they wanted me to be and not who I was. I had to dress their way, speak their way and think their way and usually those things had nothing to do with God. Finally, I walked away. I thought I'll just love Jesus and God and hang with my close Christian friends and my family and be done with it. I did that for 3 years till Julie brought me here, to Numinous. Here, for the first time I was accepted as who I was. I, of course, did not believe it. I kept my walls up, but over and over again, I found myself being drawn to this community. They really did love me for who I was. I found myself staring at a picture of what God said the church was supposed to be, for the first time in my life. Know I am home and I want to try and get as many of my friends here as possible.

Story #2—I used to go to a really big, corporate, "seeker-sensitive church." I thought I had found a home; I really enjoyed my group of closest friends and we really started building community together. Then, we ran afoul of the institutional leadership. We were in trouble for not asking them for permission to hang out, to minister, to love each other. All of a sudden, since they could not change our leadership from within, they just shut our group down at a corporate level. They "re-organized" and I watched as our leaders were told they could not lead. I was made to feel unwanted. I got hurt. I determined then that I was never going to go to an organized church again, that I could love Jesus on my own. I know I am wrong about that last part, but it was how I felt. I just thought "I'll never find a church like the Bible talks about." Then my friend Mark asked me to come here, to Numinous, for fluid [the worship service]. I went, reluctantly and was transfixed. The speaker, Carl [that's me] said things I had never heard a Christian minister say. So, I started to come back, regularly, but I withheld myself. I just could not believe it was true. I kept waiting for "the other shoe to drop." I'm still waiting and I am so happy.

Story #3—I cannot believe the deep honest humility I find here in Numinous. I am blown away. People worship like they want, no pressure, no rules—people are genuinely touching God, the Eternal One, each time we worship. And the community is so real, every day of the week. I used to go to church—I've been in just about every church there is. And you know, I just got tired of playing all the religious games they ask you to play. Everyone is fake; everyone is judgmental. I just wanted someone to be honest and real, with the ups and the downs.

Story #4—I spent years growing up in church. But let me define that for you: it starts like this: getting up early, putting on stupid clothes, getting into unholy fights with family on what is supposed to be a most holy day. [They] preach God's love and his word, but whatever you do, don't believe it or worse yet live it. Church is about love, it's about people it's about reaching out, but from where I sat they are all just full of shit. It's sad and shameful that I really feel this way. And likewise that I felt so condemned by such a loving God. And then came along a "good church" for my family and me. Or so it started out. I had never seen my father excited to go to church till then. God started to show us what church was, not dead hypocrisy. It was good. And for that I'm thankful. But, a few years down the road and people forgot! The concern changed from people to numbers. From life to religion. Quality worship that's honest to production and putting on a show. Welcome to church a division of corporate America. I'll pass thank you. I found that by trying to be honest, real and open, you know the way it was supposed to be, I was in many ways frowned upon, turned away and ignored. I CRAVE WORSHIP, UNADULTERATED, FERVENT, ARDENT, HONEST, TRUE, WORSHIP.

Story #5—I'm tired of playing the religious game. Church is just a big game. Everyone talks their best and dresses their best on Sunday but the rest of the time, they live like hell. All I want is just someone to be honest about it.

Story #6— I remember asking Jesus to come into my life last summer, and soon thereafter Steve brought you [Carl] to me. I feel a new chapter is starting. Before, I was wandering, looking for direction, wondering if God was real. What I had seen in church was fake, plastic. You are the first person I've ever known who really lived this out. Now I believe God is speaking to me.

I could give you more, but I think you see my point. When I speak with my generation, except for those fortunate souls to have been brought up in a setting where their spiritual experience was true to the Word, they inevitably are dismissive to the church and yet hungry for Truth.

In the end, these passionate cries are directed at the church. Note, these cries are not only aimed at the traditional, "old" church, but at today's "contemporary" church. The lament is against those church leaders who felt as if they were offering a better product (the contemporary church) than what the traditional church. However, in the process, I believe these leaders lost their way, and my generation grew up wondering what in the world they were talking about. It all seemed so plastic, so fake and it was in competition for my entertainment dollars and you know, it, the church, was coming in way short. So, why go through all the hassle?

My generation is the most aborted, unwanted and unloved generation in history. Why, the very people who were talking about love and should have been demonstrating unity could not even stay married. Remember the statistics from chapter 4? They increasingly show a church membership that simply does not act on the things they claim to believe. All along my generation was and IS begging for God. A God that is real, that is bigger than me.

Douglas Coupland said it best in his book *Life After God*:

My secret is that I need God—that I am sick and can no longer make it alone. I need God to help me give, because I no longer seem to be capable of giving; to help me be kind, as I no longer seem capable of kindness; to help me love, as I seem beyond being able to love.

Don't forget that Coupland makes no pretense that he is a Christian, yet he is communicating what most of my generation feels at one level or another.

We need the body of Christ, the community to be real. I need it to be real. I cannot play this game anymore. In fact, part of my constant conflict with "church people" is that I have always had that splinter in my mind and I've kept screaming about it. It's not supposed to be this way.

The community of the Bible is rich, warm, for one another. Sure they had conflicts. I can read Corinthians. I can read the first chapters of Revelation. Things weren't perfect, yet the concept was there.

We cannot simple accept failure as an option. Regardless of what went before, we must accept the error of our current situation and make adjustments. I play war-games. I have for years. Sometimes, as you move your forces, you discover that you are going off course, that your aim is now wrong. Occasionally you can fix it from where you are or make do, but usually you have to admit your plan is wrong and adjust. You have to move things around. You cannot keep going the way you were, getting the same wrong results and somehow expect it all to just work out. Life is not that way.

Now, at this time and place, we've got to get this right. We are losing too many battles and the body of Christ withdraws further and further into the ghetto. Closing their eyes tight, pulling the covers over their head hoping it all goes away. Begging Jesus to come back so they can get out of here. Worse still, from an American perspective, the inability of the church to get this right has obviously and greatly impacted the culture. From schools to politics, business to youth sports there is a very evident loss of moral groundings. Much of that blame can be laid at the feet of the church institution.

And maybe, just maybe, God is withholding the return of Jesus, in mercy, in hopes that we'll get back to basics and back to the things he called us too. Maybe, he can't return until we finish the task assigned and for the past several years at least, we've gotten way far from that.

We've looked to the church to complete those tasks of the individual and all the while the mission of the church languishes. We are lost in a confusing wood and very few are actually trying to make their way out. It is frustrating. It is sad. It must change.

Are you ready for the revolution?

are you ready?

13

The Secret Mission

Remember the cool intro music or the trailing line of burning fuse? Remember Tom Cruise hanging very calmly from the side of a mountain? *Mission Impossible*. The images of them going undercover for a secret mission are irresistible. Watching them rip off their fake face to show their true identity is one of the coolest parts of the show and the movie.

Being a Christian, to some degree, is just like that. Often as I explain my position regarding the church, I get a strong reaction. "What do you mean the Great Commission is not the mission of the church?" Usually, the underlying implication is that what I am proposing is totally non-Biblical and probably heretical.

They miss the fact that I do believe that each individual has a responsibility as a Christian. This individual mission provides the other half of the picture we are painting. The collective mission is the other half—as a group, our entire focus is to love each other and be unified, displaying the actions portrayed in Acts 2 and following: teaching of the apostles, fellowship, worship, prayer, community, sharing resources. Yet, the individual has a job to do also, it's just that (as we've attempted to show) the church collective institution has usurped that mission and in doing so, lost its own mission.

Recently on our website we had a very lively discussion about this very topic—the nature of the church and the role of the individual Christian. One member of our forums said this:

> I don't feel like "The Church" is doing the job that we should be doing in the church. With all the debates going on in

every denomination regarding the "Unerring word of God" and pastors and preachers saying that they're not sure whether Jesus is the only way to God and all of the other political stuff going on I just can't see where our worship of God in the physical buildings is going.

At my request, I asked the forum members to check out Biblically what they could find about the mission of the church. In this search, the same member came back with this:

> OK, so all these things that I have considered to be jobs of the church (jobs that we do in the buildings) are really jobs of the body, individually. It's MY job to seek the lost, not my churches. If my fellow believers know more about the Bible and what we're supposed to be doing than I do then it's YOUR job to teach me. We all just have to keep pulling each other up to the next level.

And there you go. In that simple statement is the answer. So, let me unpack this idea of mission impossible. If the mission of the church is community, love and unity, then what is our individual mission? Do we have a clear message from God about this?

The answer is a simple "yes." He has laid it out, but our failure to do this mission too has created the great loss of credibility mentioned in earlier chapters. You know what I'm talking about. God, over and over, from Adam and Eve of Genesis has been on a journey working to bring all of us into relationship with him.

Representing God is the mission or main task of each individual Christian. We all get that, right? Well, no, we don't as evidenced in the last Barna surveys. It's also fairly clear as seen by what happens in churches today. While most churches, particularly evangelical churches, demand that their leadership is very involved in doing and planning activities for evangelism, most individuals don't participate. They just want to have it done for them by proxy. The same can be said for the idea of serving in the community;

while many are happy to toss some dollars at poverty, don't ask them to actually serve physically. And if it's not being done in the church, then they'll join the unhappy chorus of voices demanding a new staff or at least a change somehow.

Part of the problem here is that we don't honestly believe that any of this is our job. We've heard about calling, we see verses implying perhaps that it takes a special ability to do this; we are given the implicit impression that only a leader gets to do this. None of that is true, but we want it to be true because, honestly, we really don't have time to be bothered with all that.

That reason also is the impetus behind the desire for large mass evangelism efforts. Year after year, tons of money is put into area wide evangelism efforts, great crusades to win the world (or at least "our" town) to Christ. Well, as often as we do those around the US, you'd think that all our problems would be solved, wouldn't you? I'm not saying that those efforts are somehow bad, but in the end, for many people, such events come at the expense of individually getting involved. The underlying position is as if we are saying "let's get everyone saved, then leave me alone—let me live my life my way and stop hassling me."

Well, are we allowed to see representing God as a duty of the church or church leaders? Is there some kind of special call that only certain people get in this area that somehow protects me from having to do evangelism? No!! In fact, it's the other way around.

So often I run into people who are frustrated about their life, usually young people, and they are seeking to know "God's will for their life." That is a noble quest of course, but in the end, it often becomes very debilitating. We become convinced that our task in this world has to be clearly spoken by God through a burning bush or by hand writing on the wall (don't pray for that, it did not work out very well for that guy). And all along, we miss the fact that God has already given us our task.

"He has," you ask? Yes indeedy, he has. Let's look at it. Individually, God has long ago laid out what our purpose or path was to be. II Corinthians 5: 17-21 says this:

What this means is that those who become Christians become new persons. They are not the same anymore, for the old life is gone. A new life has begun! All this newness of life is from God, who brought us back to himself through what Christ did. And **God has given us the task** of reconciling people to him. For God was in Christ, reconciling the world to himself, no longer counting people's sins against them. This is the wonderful message he has given us to tell others. **We are Christ's ambassadors,** and God is using us to speak to you. We urge you, as though Christ himself were here pleading with you, "Be reconciled to God!" For God made Christ, who never sinned, to be the offering for our sin, so that we could be made right with God through Christ. [emphasis added]

There, as clearly as possible, we are told that we have a task, a mission, as individual Christians. It is a great mission to represent a King, a power greater than yourself. Certainly, here (as in Matthew 28:18-20) plural pronouns are used to express that this applies to all individuals in the group. And also just as certainly, there is nothing wrong with a group of Christians actively doing something for the purpose of sharing about Jesus or doing some service project together. But the thrust here is toward each individual.

It is as if Paul is saying here, "We, each of us, are Christ's ambassadors. Even if your Christian buddy does not do this, does not go out, you are Christ's ambassador." Even if other Christians around me fail at this, God expects me to do my part. If, to use the language of Matthew 28, if other Christians do not go or do not make disciples, I am still expected to go. I can accomplish this alone and alone will stand before God giving an account.

You should quickly tell the difference between this and the "one another" nature of the church command and mission. I cannot accomplish "love one another" without "an other" Christian. I cannot be in unity with others when I am in isolation. So, while of course there is nothing wrong with a corporate concern for representing God, for corporate evangelism, for corporate service to others, the focus here (and in other places) is to the individual.

Amazingly, for some reason, God has refrained himself from personally entering this fray (since Jesus ascended) and instead has chosen to work through us, his creation. Of course, He has not left us alone, having given each Christian His Spirit, so in essence, He resides with us. Yet, He will never override our own free will, so he is in that way constrained. If we, knowing we have a mission and a purpose, refuse to go through with our task, then God is bereft of hands and feet to accomplish His great redemptive work.

The Apostle Paul is not the only one to share this news. As we have mentioned elsewhere, Jesus himself told us this in his own wonderful style. The most obvious place is of course Matthew 28:18-20 and Acts 1:8, but let's look at an earlier message from Jesus.

In Matthew 5, the gospel writer begins to share with his readers the great message Jesus shared sitting on a hill in Galilee. After starting with the long list of blessings to those who follow him, He then shifts gears to get to the heart of the message—our mission or job. His first word to the crowd is a command to those who wish to follow Him, a teaching about our task. He tells his listeners that they are like salt or light for the world.

To those Jewish listeners it should not have been a surprise. From the time of Abraham, the promise of God was that the entire world would be blessed and in communion with Him through His chosen people. So, here, Jesus is in one sense reminding them of their task.

Looking through Gentile, Christian eyes, we can see that the same command lies upon us. And that command? Much as what Paul wrote, that we are the salt of the earth and the light of the world. Into this dark and tasteless world, we are sent with the message of hope. Individually, that is our task. If we think about it, that is obvious to see.

Think of your own life—it's possible that where you work, where you go to school, where you live, you are the only Christian there. Well, as we have seen, you might not be the only person who calls themselves a Christian, but you might easily be the only one there with the knowledge of the Word about the task. You might be the only one not living in the ghetto. So, in your world, who else could be salt and light? Who else could be the representative of the King?

Recently, I made a new friend. A new girl started coming to our worship and began to feel at home. In an email to the entire group, she expressed some of what I'm saying here. The email is lengthy and she begins with a complaint, a similar one to those that I've heard and mentioned here—the church as an institution has gotten lost along the way, especially the American church over the past 60 years. She then zeroes in to express the hunger of what every Christian should be when she says this:

> I know that there are good churches out there, I'm part of one, the best one, the true meaning of church and community, where it's not about corporate America and its stupid backwards principles.
>
> How can I help?
> How can I show you that it's not what people tell you it is?
> How can I tell you the truth?
> Do you really know who Jesus is?
> This journey is long and we all weep and grow tired. May the God of peace grant us strength and wisdom. Please encourage me God.

Those ideas stand hand in hand with the great final commanding statements of Jesus. "Go into the world"—in essence, go and live among the people. "Be my witnesses"—you are the salt, the light, the representative. "Teach them the truth about me"—if no one else goes and shares, you are still under the force of this command, this mission.

For too long, we have looked at those verses as the command to the church and in doing so we have stripped them of their power over us individually. Instead, we think that we are obeying the command by proxy, but that is not what was said or taught to us. Often we think only that a gifted person is to do this, or only a missionary into a foreign land. While certainly there are those who God moves to foreign lands to share, and yes there are those who are specially gifted in sharing the faith, ALL CHRISTIANS are under this command.

Perhaps my focus on this lies in the fact that I was raised in that Southern Baptist church and so, with a strong evangelical tradition, I was exposed to this over and over again. I know that for others, especially from more mainline denominations, that perhaps has not been their experience. My wife was raised an Episcopalian; her church experience was not one burdened with any overt pressure on evangelism. In the end, regardless of what our traditions taught, we each have an individual responsibility. There, the focus can be on doing service, "good works" for others; again, the individual responsibility is to go into the world as His representative, not merely sit back waiting on the church or on someone specially called.

Part of the problem is that we refuse to believe what God has told us--that this world, the physical world is really not the real world. He tells us that there is a real world, a spiritual world that is eternal that currently exists around us and that only those with His spirit can see it. The story of *The Matrix* again provides a great illustration. We think we are awake in a real world when all along, we are sleepwalking through a dream world. We think the job we do is somehow our real job. I'm a painter, a teacher, a lawyer, etc... and in that, we then come to conflict when we think about ministry. "How can I do ministry [in our minds, that is somehow a church profession] and do my job at the same time?"

As Morpheus says to Neo in the movie *The Matrix*, "What is real? How do you define real? If you are talking about what you can feel, what you can smell, taste or see, then real is merely electrical signals interpreted by your brain." We know from Paul's writings to the Corinthian church, we actually are living in a setting where we've had "the wool pulled over our eyes." We do begin to believe that this is the real world when all along God is telling us that this is merely a starting place. As theologian said it, we are not fleshly humans who die and then have a spiritual transformation; we are instead spiritual beings having a fleshly human moment.

So, all along, God is crying to us that we have a real job and the thing we do (for a salary) is merely our cover. Hear the words again of II Corinthians 5 and realize that they are our prime directive:

> And *God has given us the task* of reconciling people to him. For God was in Christ, reconciling the world to himself, no longer counting people's sins against them. This is the wonderful message he has given us to tell others. *We are Christ's ambassadors*, and God is using us to speak to you.

It's as if we are part of a grand large undercover operation to over throw the current ruler of the earth. He (our enemy) thinks he is immune to attack, but he does not know that we know he is merely an interloper and that the real King of the world has already invaded and is currently raising up troops. So, this real King sends us in to all manner of places and environments to begin to spread his message of love, grace and hope. For most of us, we do this undercover—to the world and the false king, we are merely construction workers, bus drivers, doctors, secretaries. To the King though, we are his ambassadors of love. So, we are undercover, in secret and we constantly are looking for any new information from the King, in case He wants us to move to a new position or a new city. Generally, like He has for most of eternity, for most of us, He just wants us to be happy and do the thing in front of us, all the while completing the task as He laid it out.

Simple, isn't it?

It really is quite simple when you think about it and it should give you real gladness to know that you current job, no matter how little you get paid or if you feel appreciated or not, really does not matter. It's just your cover, your way into part of the world, your place to work your real job of being his representative.

I was speaking in North Carolina at a Youth Conference in 2001. Of course there were the requisite adult volunteers there to chaperone. Usually in those settings, the adults come to the event with an "I'm only here for the kids—nothing this guy says will apply to me" kind of attitude. This event was no different. Yet, at the end of, after teaching what I am writing to you now, an older gentleman came up to me. In fact, he basically ran out in front of my rental car to stop me. He had been crying and began to tear up again as he spoke to me. He said, "I've been church a long time and I've never heard anyone say what you just said. All these years I have hated my job and my life and wondered why God did not let me do something better. I felt as if my life was a waste. Now, for the first time, I understand that He has given me a task, a mission and I'm undercover like you said. Thank you. I really doubted that I could learn anything from a young buck like you, but I was wrong."

YES!

That attitude is exactly what God is intending. He wants us to take the red pill just as Neo did in *The Matrix* to see the real world for what it is. He wants us to understand that we have an individual mission that is critical and that the church is NOT supposed to worry with. He wants us to understand the value that each of us has in our place of service.

Of course, if we are stuck in the ghetto, then we won't really want to talk to those outsiders for fear of contamination. Or, we won't talk for fear of being discovered as a fraud, that they know you are not living a credible life as a Christian. So, again, what we really want is our "church" to do it, so we don't have to and we can keep playing our little game.

Instead, wake up to the real world and understand that you have chosen this mission when you accepted his invitation to be His child. You may not have been told this (and I am truly sorry that you were not told), but it's the truth. You are in and now is the time for you to realize that, while in the world, you wear a clever disguise as a doctor, a lawyer, a housewife, a clerk, a salesman in order to help you blend in. Can you see it? Just like in *Mission Impossible* you are there undercover. You've been inserted by the

Mission Commander; you may be the only one there who is part of the Master's team.

Remember you are not of this world and deep inside you is a longing to return home. You watch the eastern sky hoping for his return, but seeing it not, you return with hope to your task, to your cover. And all the while, you look always for the chance to perform the real task. In disguise, you work hard, as unto the Lord and you perform the best you can in an attempt to gain more credibility with those around you. As you do, you gain the confidence of those around you, "your world" and you merely act as salt and light. They will notice.

They will hear of your love for others, those like you and those who are different, and they will be amazed. They will begin to see that you must be a disciple of One Great. They will see the unity of the community of faith that you belong to and long deeply in their hearts for that kind of relationship. They will silently understand that this Great One you follow must have come from God. They will notice that when you are around, the atmosphere seems to taste different. They will begin to see how the darkness recedes from you when you pass by. They will finally begin to ask questions or begin to share their life with you, perhaps not asking directly, but hoping inwardly that you notice their longing. They are waiting for you to fulfill your task and then begin to teach them about that same task.

That's when you'll remove the mask, just like the actors in *Mission Impossible.* You'll show them why you REALY are there...to help them find the Answer for life, Jesus Christ.

are you ready?

14

The President called this morning

I hope you don't find these writings too disparate. The press for community and the responsibility of individually representing God are not two separate points, but reflect different points of the life of a Christian.

The place to start is with God, not us. God is after one thing when it's all boiled down. He wants every tongue, every person to give him glory. From Genesis to Revelation, we are reading one long story about God and God's pursuit of gaining glory.

That is not an arrogant or misplaced aim of God's; on the contrary it is what we should expect to find in a true God. If there were a God (and we say there is), one would expect it/he/she to be perfect, holy, and glorious. We would expect it/he/she to attempt to honor the most wonderful thing in the universe. Well, if it/he/she is God, then that most wonderful thing in the universe IS God. That God, the Christian Father of all, the Creator and Redeemer, stands alone as the most glorious thing in all creation is right; that He then calls us to revel, to worship, to give Him that glory is equally right.

So, God's real aim (and we see a great picture of the end result in Revelation 19:1) is for the entire world to worship him and give him glory. It was for this end that we were created. Theologian and Pastor John Piper has excellently communicated more of these truths in his powerful work *Desiring God.*

If God desiring his own glory is the deal, then humans were indeed created for that purpose. As Piper says, "Man is given the exalted status of image-bearer not so he would become arrogant and autonomous. . .but so he would reflect the glory of his Maker whose image he bears."(*Desiring God,* p. 256)

The foundation then of life as a human is giving God glory. Want to know your purpose in life? To give God glory. So often I hear young adult wondering about what to do, what job to take, etc.... They are begging for direction as if it has not yet been given. The need for a foundation becomes huge in them, but the foundation has already been made clear.

Thus, God's wants glory, and giving it to Him is the foundation of a human's life, but the problem, as you already know is that humans are at war with God. They don't want to give Him glory. So, He is engaged in this great struggle to communicate to his creation that He indeed loves them and wants to be in relationship with them. Some of us have heard that word and believed. Since we have believed, we then are in a position to know the mission of our lives. If giving God glory is the foundation of life, then communicating about God's love and desire for relationship is the mission of life.

Here is the place where the individual mission begins. As Jesus put it, since you know Him, you are to be salt to a tasteless world. You, as a believer, are to be light in a dark world. God, for whatever reason, has basically limited himself to just using the same humans that used to be at war with him. Of course He can and does communicate via creation and His written word, but by and large, the strategy is to have those who believe "go back in" to rescue the others.

Morpheus in *The Matrix* again provides an example for us. In the movie, his mission is to prowl the "fake world" attempting to communicate to those willing to listen, to those ready to hear, that what they see is not the real world. That there is a way out, a salvation, but they must take a leap of faith to get there. They must swallow the red pill.

As a rule, I don't think most Christians really believe that they have been so called. I've taught this truth around the nation and am constantly caught off-guard by the responses of people that can be summarized thusly. "I've never heard that before and I've been in church for _____ years."

For those that know about it, I wonder if they actually believe it. Think of it this way. Imagine that the President of the United States summoned you to the White House. There, standing with several other people, you are told about a somewhat secret mission that you have been chosen for. The experts have told the President that you are the perfect choice to be his representative back in your hometown.

There, if you are willing to accept the mission, you are to communicate to your town about a new strategy that the President has embarked upon. You'll need to talk to anyone and everyone, people you like and people you don't like. The good news is that you won't be alone. Most cities are far too big for just one person, so you discover that there are several other people who have also accepted this call.

You will meet with them on a regular basis, both for encouragement's sake and to hear new information from the Commander-in-Chief. You'll get written communication from the President and his advisors and you'll need to read and study them. You won't quit your job—this isn't a paying gig. But you'll have to be ready to sacrifice some time and energy. Never forget that the mission is vital to the success of the USA.

Now, let's assume that you accept the task. Were that story true, would you actually blow off the mission? Would you refuse to read the letters? Would you refuse to attend the meetings? I suppose some of us would, but you can imagine what would happen. If nothing else, you'd get taken off the mission.

For the vast majority of us, though, I think that you would endeavor to accomplish the mission to the best of your ability. You would take it seriously. You would work your hardest. You would never doubt the validity of the calling.

Can you see the problem here? I have already shown you that supposed Christians everywhere DO NOT do the things communicated by the Commander-in-Chief. While we would have no problem doing basically the same thing for the President, we blow off the assignment from God. Same deal, same type of mission—"represent Me to the people."

Well, for those who get it, we finally understand our mission in life—it is as God's representative. I certainly understand that you may think that such an answer will not pay your bills or help you find a mate. Showing the deep connection between those functional, temporal issues and the deeper mission of our life is beyond the scope of this book. Let say simply that the normal questions of life such as those are not silly or wrong. Yet, we get things out of order when we replace our true mission with some other mission.

If you will keep your foundation of life sure (giving God glory) and understand that you DO KNOW what you are to do with your life (be God's representative), then it is easier to relax about those other questions. In the midst of those, you can use your foundation and mission as a filter through which to answer those other questions.

We know, then, that we are on mission and we have a solid foundation. We are out there with the others (out of the ghetto), telling everyone we know about our God and his love. Again, this is the core of the individual Christian's mission. It is summed up in the Great Commission verses—a perfect explanation of the mission of the individual. As you are going through life, tell others, disciple them, teach them, and help them get close to God. Where do you do this? Acts 1:8—wherever in the world God has you. Your world.

So off we go, but instantly we run into a different issue. People are skeptical, particularly in these days. As we say at Numinous, "credibility precedes being heard." The crowd wants to see that we are solid witnesses and that we have something worthwhile to say.

Are you ahead of me yet? You see it? Of course, that leads us right to the community. The church is THE ANSWER for the world. It is God's plan for the world. Yet, it is not the answer because it contains the evangelistic stuff, but because the community provides the support for the very thing people are looking for.

As we have already demonstrated, God's mission for the church is love and unity. End of story. Everything else rests on those two things. Why? To provide the two things the unbelieving world is looking to see: credible witnesses and a credible story.

When they see the gathered loving each other as Jesus loved, total acceptance, sharing resources, the weird, outcast and unlovely embraced by the supposedly normal—well then the world is stunned. They are left to know that these people must be from God. They must be Jesus-followers, Christians. Credibility.

Then they see the body united. Not divided by creed or personality, the outsiders are stunned to sense the similar unity that they know instinctively must exist between Jesus and God. In that truth, in that expression, they can see that indeed only God could pull off unity among such a disparate group. And, if God is doing that, then the thing they are talking about, a relationship with Jesus, must be true. Jesus must indeed have come from God.

Do you get it? Do you see how connected that is? That cycle is core to all of life. While we waste time with programs and events that do nothing but make busy schedules, the world is subconsciously (and often consciously), looking to see love and unity. They demand credibility, both in you as the messenger and in your message.

What happens next is up to God. Not everyone will take the red pill. As Paul said to the Corinthians, the leader of this world has blinded the eyes of people and many will never believe. While we can and should pray for them to see, salvation is a power that lies with God. And there is should stay.

But for those that get it? Well, guess what they start doing? Giving God glory! Praise his name! They finally understand their own foundation of life, realizing why all these years life has not felt perfect or was weird. As they draw into close community, they finally taste something they have longed for—to be known.

Intimacy and relationship, created first in us to have with God and secondly lived out here on earth with one another, is experienced.

What do they do with that? They go tell another and the cycle starts again. Beautiful.

Simple.

God.

are you ready?

15

Permission granted to close the book now

So far what we been talking about is theory, theology, and philosophy. The teaching about the real mission of the church under-girds the teaching about my individual mission as God's representative. But I can hear you wondering—"How does this actually happen?"

Functional theology is what I call this and out here on the front lines, theory must connect to reality and practice. I believe that for much of functional theology [how things actually get done in your church], you have a lot of room to create what you want. Sure the Bible does lay down some functional commands, but overall, it leaves a lot not discussed. You can choose to rely on tradition if you wish or you can choose much of your functional theology based on what the Church growth experts think.

Or, you can try something else.

At Numinous, Inc., we've been attempting something else. Instead of continuing to do the same things in the same way that we've seen done for years, we have stripped church down the essence of community, of the gathering, and we are going from there. We still face the same questions that others do regarding leadership, money, advertising, children, music, and on and on. We've just taken an approach that says that "let's do the things that we know for certain are commanded in the Bible and we'll cover the other stuff as it comes up."

That may not be too comforting if you are looking for me to provide you a quick "how-to manual." Part of my reticence in that regard is the fact that I do believe that the Bible allows us to be aware of our times, our culture and those that we are ministering to. Thus, what "works" for us in this urban setting in Florida may have no basis for success where you are.

I initially planned on ending these letters at this point. We've clearly lain out that there is a problem within the institutional church. Christians cannot even agree on who is or who is not a Christian or if there is even a problem. There is no denying the issue regardless of how great you think your particular church is. The facts are clear that the vast majority of people inside the church have little understanding of what they have supposedly agreed to once they became a Christian.

J R Vassar, speaker and leader of iWitness, calls that ATM Christianity. Most Americans have approached the ATM of God, punched up their access code "sinner's prayer" and out has popped a "Get out of Hell" card. Off they go assuming all is well and that nothing more is required of them. They do not live lives that are anticipating and hoping for change. They consider a verse like Luke 9:23--"If any of you wants to be my follower, you must put aside your selfish ambition, shoulder your cross daily, and follow me."— as merely some statement about "serious Christianity," and as such has nothing to do with them. After all, they merely wanted to get out of hell, so, if that means they have to admit something about Jesus, well, okay, just as long as they avoid hell.

Christianity has little to do with that. Yes, we do get an eternity with God rather than without God, but the point of the call of Christ is to a relationship with God. Lives that call themselves Christian but never desire or move toward allowing Him to change you are pointless...and not Christian.

As such, they have no witness. Or better stated, the witness they provide is in conflict with the message of God. What we are directly commanded to do in II Corinthians 5 is hampered, thus, for the people who stand outside of a relationship with God. They see no clear message. When the invitation to them comes about God, they look at this person who is supposedly a Christian and think "She lives a life no different than I do." Thus, why go through the hassle of change. They see no point.

96

On the other hand, a person's life that has a relationship with God does provide clear evidence of change in that person. In a community where there are several people who are showing that change, the community will change. You cannot look at America and see changed communities, so either God is failing at his job or we have a problem on our end.

This failure is hampered by the corporate group, the church as an organization, failing to focus on its real role. We can teach all we want about individual change, but if the organization that I choose to connect with is failing at its mission, then I as the individual have little chance to succeed.

So, we know there is change needed. We must wake up to the fact that we have drifted from the mission and we must return to the mission. That is the answer, not what style of worship music you choose. Not whether you use liturgy or not. Not in whether you allow women in ministry or not. The issue comes initially by knowing what the one thing is that must be done and doing that.

People are actually hungry for this change. As I have spoken about our theology, I get plenty of questions. They want to know more about the theology. They also want to know about the core concepts of our functional theology that we use. So, while these ideas may not actually work for your group due to a variety of factors such as the culture in which you live, I did want to share how we do this.

In particular, I get asked, "are there any core concepts that I have found that are important?" Yes, I do think that there are, particularly in the area of leadership. Leadership is a very hot topic in America for the past 10 years if not longer. And truly leadership is where the costs of what I am talking about must be paid. Remember the Acts Gamble? In all reality, most of that gamble is taken by a leader; if the church or ministry fails, then it's usually them left holding the bag financially.

At the same time, core leaders invest a lot of their lives in a dream like starting a church. If these ideas fail, they are often destroyed or hurt emotionally, even if they don't have a financial setting at stake. A leader who is not ready to embark on this path will thwart any changes that the corporate group desires. When you consider the Acts Gamble or the mission of the individual, the leaders must embrace what is clearly in Scripture.

Worship is another topic that I get asked about often, so I've written a chapter about that as well. But probably where we need to start is in the minefield of Biblical Interpretation. I call it a minefield—it may be better known as a killing ground for it is here that many Christians have been laid low by others.

I probably should have written about my view of Biblical interpretation earlier and I did touch on it briefly, but I must go into some detail or you'll never understand the things that I am trying to tell you about worship, leadership or other issues.

Just know that, if you want, you can close the book now and quit reading and start living it out. You know what you need to know. I think I've been clear enough. My letters have hit their target. We know we've walked away from the direct mission of God, so let's return. Let's get out of the ghetto and start living with our community. We can avoid the fate of the Dodo and once again become a vibrant influence on our surroundings. We can stop trying to create a "Christian" this or a "Christian" that and just start being the leaven in the dough of our world.

You can do this. You can change the world. Release yourself to God and allow him to change you. If you want help here or suggestions beyond what I've written, then go read the words of wiser people than me—go pick up a book by Brennan Manning, C.S. Lewis, Dietrich Bonhoeffer, John Piper, Beth Moore or John Fischer. They can help.

Then, while you are digging in deeper into God, releasing yourself more to him, allowing him to mold and shape you (you know he's waiting on your permission—he won't break your free will), you can also begin pushing your community, your church, to re-examine its priorities. Where is the money spent? How about the time? Leadership? Membership? Push these issues with your group. Insist that the group return to the Scripture and put first the things God has told us. Request that you do those things and just those things. Beg your church to stop pretending that it is focused on community—love and unity. Ask them to start actually living community through the budget and the calendar.

I was counseling a young pastor about his church. As we talked about the various issues facing his church, I was able to zero in on the major area of struggle. So I asked him "do your people like being together, enjoy hanging out?" He responded immediately—"No!" I told him that was the problem. As long as the community of God does not enjoy being together, they will always see church as this thing you join, something apart from their real life. The worship experience will only fall into this requirement of God that they must endure. They will not desire to be together like we are commanded to be. My prayer and advice to that young pastor and to anyone else was to go back and demand (in a loving but clear way) that they decide to pursue community.

You can start living the life that Jesus asked for and that Paul wrote about. You can. Just start doing it. You may get criticized. Some may call you a radical or a freak. Others may ask you to stop talking about that stuff. They may tell you that they are completely fine with church the way it is, that they see no evidence of these things that I've talked about. Ignore them! Keep living. Oh sure, watch the attitude and run from arrogance. And always at least acknowledge your critics—God may be speaking through them about something that demands your response. But unless there is a major change in the Bible, you have God's word on your side.

So go for it. You can close the book now, if you want. However, I am going to take the time to write at least 3 or 4 more letters about some of the issues that I've been asked most often. If you want to read them, well come on and let's go. Time's a wasting.

are you ready?

16

"You allow tattoos in your church?"

In the 1988 USA Presidential election, Presidential candidate Bill Clinton was greatly aided in his campaign by one simple phrase. "It's the economy, stupid." By that, he and his campaign was able to stay focused on the one aspect they thought paramount. As a Christian theologian, I have determined to live my life with another simple phrase: "It's not about being right, it's about being Biblical."

We, as a group, Christians, have far too often fought over things that divide us and these things are usually not a Biblical issue at all. For Numinous, we run quickly to change our stance in order to agree with God. So, when I travel and speak or while in Orlando, I am quick to let people know that I welcome their opinion. I want people to ask me hard questions about what I am saying. If I begin to take a stance that implies I know all, then I have stepped into God's place and that is not only dangerous, but evil. To keep myself in check, I want listeners to challenge me.

If I cannot defend the various positions that I take based on Scripture, then I have no basis for sharing about it. For example, I believe that all Christians should embrace the concept of "Simple Living," meaning that they should have their budgets agree with their theology. Far too many Christians talk about their desire to walk with God, but their lifestyles do not match up. Usually they have a conflict between their possessions or budget and their theology. OK, so that's a nice idea, but if I cannot demonstrate to you in the Bible that we should live that way, then it's not better than be telling you that we should all move to Mars in order to avoid global warming. It would be just one man's opinion.

So, I choose to make myself vulnerable to attack or contradiction from others because I want to always find myself siding with God and that is seen through his revelation to us through his word.

I suppose I might have to defend that statement, but others like C.S. Lewis, Josh McDowell and most recently Lee Strobel have done that so well. If you have any question to the validity of the idea that the Bible is the bedrock of the Christian faith, I urge you to read the works of those apologists. Stated simply, as a trained historian, I believe that the Bible is the most accurate, trustworthy and credible book from antiquity. Without it, we have no faith. At best, our idea of God is merely one of many ideas, just one story to compare to many stories.

So, we start there, that the Bible is our basis. But here is where it gets tricky. For about 1800 years, since Christian leaders put the books of the New Testament together, people have argued about various parts of what was written there. Friendships have ended over these theological tussles and new denominations have arisen. The attempt to comprehend and work out what is written in the Bible and then apply what is there is a very difficult task.

Thus, I am now clearly walking into a minefield. Really, no matter what I say at this moment, some of you will vehemently disagree with me. Perhaps you will write the publisher demanding a retraction and if you ever see me in public, you will be quick to let me know how much you disagree.

This fact was recently brought home to me. I was presenting at a conference for college students and after my first day, I had at least 4 different people challenge me and finally tell me they did not agree with me. I felt fairly bad about that for the very reasons I have mentioned above. I want to be in step with God and to be able to explain myself within the context of the Bible, thus I want to have everyone agree with me. Well, at this same conference were John Piper, one of America's foremost theologians, and Gregg Matte, one of America's most dynamic college speakers. Four days after my confrontations, I was with 3 other leaders in a casual setting. There, the various conference speakers came up and to my complete surprise, all of these leaders found a variety of points to which they disagreed with Piper and Matte. One summed it up this way: "I like most of what he says, but the rest of it I just disagree with." I thought to myself, if they are going to argue with Gregg Matte or John Piper about something relating to the Bible and the application of it, then I will not be able to get 100% agreement either.

So here we go. In the theological landscape, there are at least a few different viewpoints to interpretation, as I see it. The first is the very liberal approach that starts from the position that the Bible is NOT the direct word of God and that it can be dismissed as irrelevant whenever it suits you.

This opinion comes out of decades of liberal scholarship that has attempted (and failed in my opinion) to discredit the Bible's accuracy. So, in this view, since the Bible is not accurate to begin with, then one can merely refuse to consider it at all.

Opposed to this is the fundamentalist claim, which at its heart, is a cry for the entire Bible to be lived out to the letter. For the Fundamentalists, their teaching (if not their practice) is to demand that every rule and word of the Bible be obeyed regardless of any context. Much of the fundamentalists approach actually is born out of a response to liberalism, thus, it is easy to see how they have gone far in their attempts to withstand the liberal position.

For me, neither position is correct. So, my position has come down somewhere in the middle and I suppose that will make me susceptible to attack from both sides.

I call this a dynamic approach to Scripture. For me, the Bible is alive and dynamic and as such is able to be viewed in the context of my times. We have the ability to interpret and apply the teaching of the Word in a way that fits our culture. Yet, at the same time, we do not have the freedom to dismiss or ignore what God says MERELY because our culture does not like it.

Now, as soon as I state that position, I know that most conservatives will gear up for the attack. They will claim that we have no wiggle room in relationship to the Bible and we must do exactly what it demands and implies, regardless of our culture or setting.

However, what they say and what they do are not congruent. Actually, I can respect a fundamentalist more easily than I can a liberal. That is, I can support a fundamentalist to his/her position as long as they hold to it completely. One can't tell me that he disagrees with my position as not holding to Scripture unless he also holds to that full measure.

Case in point, the Bible clearly teaches that a woman cannot come to worship within a week of having her period. Yes, that teaching is in Leviticus. Quickly you shout, well, that Scripture has been covered in the New Testament, so I ask you to show me. Of course you cannot. It is not there, but nowhere in America do you have a church pushing women out of church (at least not that I know of). Yet, in that same book is a prohibition or warning against tattoos. I don't personally have a tattoo, but I support people who do and I hear about Leviticus 19:28 all the time. These same people who would never keep a woman out of worship who is on her period easily find the voice to attack the young man with a tattoo, something they find scary or distasteful.

Here's another example—very few churches command their women to wear head coverings to worship, yet the Apostle Paul clearly laid this out in a command in I Corinthians. This is obviously in the New Testament yet churches all across America allow women into their worship service with no head coverings. However, in that same book is a prohibition to women in ministry. I support women in ministry (as you will see in a coming letter) and I hear about the I Corinthians verses about women all the time.

My point is this—you cannot claim to be a conservative fundamentalist unless you embrace the full scope of the Bible. You cannot claim that position and then abandon it when the words do not fit your need. We could easily start in Genesis and make our way through the book and find many commands and verses that clearly appear to have a cultural basis, but if you are a fundamentalist, then you must embrace those verses. There is no way around that.

I have tried to make that point strong enough in order for you to understand my position as we head into the other letters. I believe that I am a conservative and I fully embrace the validity and accuracy of the Bible.

Let me give you another example to attempt to help you see what I am trying to say. We all believe that discipleship, that action of a younger believer spending time with an older believer in order to learn more about the faith, is a critical action. We base that belief on a variety of verses and we see it best demonstrated for us by Jesus. So, we can easily state that, if we are a conservative fundamentalists, to accomplish this Biblical command or directive, we should just copy Jesus.

But how did he do it? Well, he allowed people to hang out with him for starters. But further, he had at least 12 people who were with him 24/7 for over 2 years. They walked around, traveled together, and ate together with apparently only a few brief moments apart.

Now I don't know where you live, but here, if you tried that, not only would you be labeled as a cultish group, you would be hard pressed to have anyone accept your offer. For starters, they would not be able to afford it. And you probably would find it hard to support them yourself. And no one walks around, so where would you find and afford a vehicle that could transport 12-20 people? Yet rarely do you hear that someone is attacking a ministry because its leaders are not doing discipleship just like Jesus. And to be accurate, everyone would have to be in the role of Jesus as well as in the role of the disciple. How would that work?

So, what we do instead is morph discipleship into something that will work in our society and culture. And we can't make our new strategy for discipleship a kind of new rule for other cultures might find that it would not work there.

What we are doing is dynamically interpreting the Bible and applying it to our culture regardless of what the Bible actually says. And we do this all the time, yet it is a hard thing to deal with. But, why is this a hard thing to accept?

Well, we generally do not like it when the theology in question is contrary to our own view. And often, without too much trouble, we can and do find a verse that supports us. But when we don't think it's a big deal, we let it slide and do not concern ourselves with the Bible at all.

Honestly, I'll admit that this position scares me. And I wonder if I will not find myself before God and hear him saying, "You were wrong on that." And what He'll mean is that I SHOULD have demanded that no woman enter the church on her period. Nor should I have allowed tattoos. But at the same time, I see in Scripture that even within the New Testament, God reveals himself as a dynamic God that re-establishes norms based on current settings. Thus, as I look at my world, I do not think that I am wrong if I teach that discipleship can occur differently than Jesus modeled. Or, I am okay if I allow women to come to my worship service with no head coverings.

Within that setting, I am willing to deal with the opening of Pandora's Box in this arena. And it has its dangers, no doubt! But the alternative seems to me to be short of full integrity. Again I might be wrong about the head coverings thing, for instance, but it's a chance I am willing to take.

So how do we do that? Well, for me it is really quite simple. The thing to check for is whether or not the law or rule or idea that is being overturned is a cultural thing or is it seemingly in God's mind as being for all time. So, for instance, though our culture would cry out for a change in the area of sex, God has a characteristic reason for maintaining his want of purity. His claims about purity and holiness, expressed in the sexual arena, are consistent throughout the writing of the Bible. So, though culture seems to demand it, I am going to maintain that God's law of no sex out of wedlock is one for all people in all times.

Yet, when I look at a thing like head coverings or tattoos, I see a cultural aspect. When I read about women on their period's not coming to worship, being unclean, I see a cultural law that does not really reflect something from God that He demands be kept for all times. As we know, Jesus Himself led the step into changes, and those changes are further elaborated on by his followers Peter and Paul. I know it still sounds somewhat less than clear. I agree that the clearest thing would be to hold to either the liberal position (nothing really counts anymore) or the conservative fundamentalist view (every word must be maintained). But both seem to be holding a certain lack of integrity.

In any case, we look to see how this impacts us as we deal with functional theology. We see that though we are told in Acts precisely what they did for church, we can take the principle of the teaching and apply it. Thus, we don't try to meet for worship every day nor specifically in or on a porch. Instead, we see that the principle of community is that we should be involved in one another's lives and that comes from spending time together. We know that though we are told that Jesus did discipleship through a hands-on 24/7 experience, we can take the principle of "intentional hanging out" that will happen and apply it to our times. We won't demand a person in discipleship to live with whoever is discipling them, but we will and do ask for an intentional gathering to happen between them as often as possible.

All of that may not make you feel any better, but it is our approach. We think it's done with integrity and with a heart to honor God, not just get our own way. Fair enough? Alrighty then, let's move on.

are you ready?

17

Leadership Questions

Leadership gets a lot of press these days and obviously there are gifted writers flooding the book market with tons of books on the subject. So, what I want to talk to you about is not really how to do leadership or how to be a better leader, but more a continuation of our story about how we chose leaders.

The entire concept of how we do leadership is in keeping with the rest of how we do this thing others call church. We do it in opposition to how it is currently done. And to do that strikes at the core of what passes as leadership.

Leadership in the Christian realm is a funny thing for while the world demands the sorts of leaders seen in the corporate world, Jesus asks for a different style of leadership. So we are caught between a rock and a hard place. If we hope to lead an organization toward some victorious future (victorious as defined by the world—large numbers, power, money, fame, etc...), we should utilize the leadership style of the world. However, if we hope to stay true to what the Bible teaches about leadership, we cannot utilize much of what the world demands of leadership.

Probably the place to start is in the Bible where God says, "My ways are not your ways." Follow that with Paul reminding us that God uses the opposite of what the world claims is best: wise, powerful, rich. If you were to go to any Fortune 500 with two candidates for their top leadership and told them that one person was very wise, powerful and rich. They would be very interested. If you told them, however, that the other person was weak, foolish and poor, they probably would tell you to let that person out the back door.

Yet over and over again, that style is precisely God's way in all aspects. It is hard to understand, yet He knows what he is doing. Today, we are as badly confused as Samuel when he went looking for Saul's replacement. Remember that story? He so thought David's brothers were perfect choices to be new king for they looked and acted the part. Meanwhile, God had another plan. He used the scrawny kid, the runt, the smallest. And he used him not merely because he was not yet a great leader, but because God knew David was weak in certain areas.

My point is not to debate about leadership in general, but to state one of our values that I put forward from the beginning. It is this: we will not allow any kind of "cult of personality" setting to emerge surrounding me. I have had leaders and other ministers directly tell me that if I ever hope to make Numinous successful, that I had to bank on me. That it was I that people would come to be around to hear, to follow.

I have watched the American church for over two decades and if I have seen anything that turns my stomach more is the hero status that we elevate one person, usually a man. I determined that even if it meant that Numinous would fail, I would not allow a setting to emerge around me.

There are several ways we work to protect ourselves in that area. Left to myself, I would gravitate toward any stroking of my ego. I would probably stride atop of any pedestal given me and I would eventually start to believe that people actually came to hear me rather than God.

Here are some of the protective devices that we've used. First, I am not the only person who speaks at our worship service, fluid. I know that sounds simple, but it strikes hard at the root of the pride. Usually, a church leaders needs to speak on Sundays for good reasons. Some of those reasons are that the members think, "well, we are paying you to do it." Also there is an implied concept that no one else really can do it as well as the main leader. Finally, there is the idea that this one large meeting is the leader's one shot to push his agenda, for him to shape the group.

Each of these reasons is badly flawed. The gathering for worship is not some kind of public business meeting. It is a time for God, not for the organization or the leader. At the same time, Scripture clearly implies that all are gifted and there must be, in every group of more than a few, strong communicators, prophets and teachers. To think that only one person is gifted enough to lead or teach runs counter to what the Bible actually teaches. Thus, we live that out here in Numinous. We have determined who our gifted speakers and teachers are and we have unleashed them.

Another protective device for me has to do with exactly who is established as a leader. We believe that Scripture teaches that leadership happens in a group setting. While we also believe that vision is given to one person, thus there is one visionary who starts the group or communicates to the group from an overall perspective, protection from our own ego and pride comes in that same visionary leader submitting as an equal to the group.

Equality at the cross is a mantra that keeps every person from gaining a prideful stance. I only have to remember that I come from a small town with no stoplights and a few stop signs to keep myself from imagining that I am important. I am no more important to God than my buddy from grade school who is a loving husband and daddy and who works hard every day at his job. He does not fly around the country speaking and singing, but he is not less important than me.

I imagine that many leaders believe that same truth, but how many actually do something about it? I said earlier that the full force of what I am proposing in this book of letters would only reach its full impact if the leaders embrace it. We can believe all we want about equality at the cross and that the mission of the church is in loving each other, but if the leaders continue to demand the stage and spotlight and force a different agenda to keep their corporation going, there will be no change.

So in our case, we established a group of leaders. And we then empower those leaders to actually lead. What does that mean? Well, we do exactly what the Bible teaches about leadership for the community, that the elders (as the Bible calls them) are to shepherd (protect, guide and feed) the flock. That is a simple rendition obviously, but it gets at it. And my job as one of those elders is to allow them to do exactly that.

My job is perhaps the most challenging here because the natural tendency is to overstep my boundaries and do it for them. Or, make sure the others know that they really need to clear things with me. Or that the members really need to talk to me for counsel as if the other leaders are not equipped enough.

Do you see the subtle ways we undermine our team leadership plans in order to gain some kind of power to ourselves? If God really did place others in leadership, then that leadership must be embraced and allowed to soar.

Oh my mind is swimming with all the many things I want to say here, but I fear that you'll miss the main point. Leaders—lay down your leadership and embrace the fact that God has gifted so many others to lead as well. Let them and like Moses, find that you are able to concentrate on the more important things.

Our leaders are continuing to grow in this and it is so exciting to watch them. They have to fight the normal church training that says that leadership is merely a title for the paid staff does everything. They will often ask me about some idea they have for an activity to which I will almost always reply "Just do it." It has taken a while, but now they are finally over the shock. What they are used to is a strong centralized control deal where the paid staff is fearful of allowing the people to actually do for themselves. Their fear is that they will lose control.

To that I say—forget worrying about losing control, give it away instead. You don't have control anyway. And you don't want robots around you either. You want vibrant excited people using their gifts as God moves them.

But what about your leadership, I hear you thinking. I have found that the more I have given about power, the more respect I find sent my way. The more I empower my leaders, the more the others clearly see that I am the "God sent" visionary. To say it another way, they see me as I am, the leader of the leaders. I am one of them and fully submit to the elders as the situation demands. One of them came to me in shock and amazement after a certain event was over. He said, "I cannot believe that you really did submit to all that I did in leadership. Even when I asked you what to do, you kept telling me to decide. You gave me options as you saw them, but then you never added your weight to whatever you thought was best." That leader now stands in our group as one of our stronger leaders, eager to go wherever God sends him.

We call our leaders "elders." For us, the title "elder" does not carry baggage or mythical undertones but rather is merely a word that was in vogue when the Bible was written. I think we are on good grounds to state that you could call your leaders whatever you wanted to. We chose elder as a nod to our ancient nature of our faith. We knew that doing so might cause some controversy among some groups, but we felt that the name also helped the leaders stand apart from the crowd a bit. However, you could chose any other name you wanted---there is nothing in the Bible demanding any certain name for your leaders. But wait, why not call yourself or the leaders "pastors?"

Pastor. Did you know it's a word that is not even in the Bible? It's an okay word and its etymology works well enough to still be a title. And since it is so readily understood as a church leader, I use it begrudgingly. It's just easier. But it is not in the Bible.

What I mean is that poor linguistics are at play here. Around the late 16th century, something happened that contributed to the desire to use a new word for a common Greek word. Paul wrote in Ephesians 4 a list of 5 titles of ministry leaders or positions. For the 4th title, he wrote *poimenas*, the same word used 18 times in the New Testament. In each location, the word is translated "shepherd." Yet, in most English Bibles today, the word is now written "pastor."

Amazingly, the word "pastor" is not even known until the 13th century. In William Tyndale's translation in 1534, he rightly follows the Greek and translates it as "shepherd." Yet, by the time of King James in 1611, the word pastor was substituted for shepherd. Why?

Apparently no one seems to know. I have an educated historical hypothesis, however. Through the 1500s, the Reformation was in full-fledged war, literally, and "good" Protestants wanted nothing to do with anything that smacked of Catholicism. Thus, using titles like bishop or priest was out of the question. So, they adopted this new, fancier word, for shepherd—pastour "one who tends the pasture." It quickly became adopted by the common practice and before long, the leaders of the churches were being called this word as a title. Then, the leaders of the English church, inserted the word into the Book of Common Prayer in 1549 in two places:

> The Catechism – "To submitte my selfe to all my gouernours, teachers, spirituall pastours, and maisters."

> The Order. Priests – "To be the messengers, the watchemen, the Pastours, and the stewardes of the Lorde, to teache, to premonisshe, to feede, and prouyde for the Lordes famylye."

In the Geneva New Testament written in 1557, "pastour" is substituted for shepherd in Ephesians 4:11, compared to the Tyndale translation. The Authorized Version leaned on the Geneva Bible through their translation process and followed suit. Thus the King James Bible in 1611 also did not use the more common word "shepherd." By the time that Jamestown in established in 1607 and the Puritans arrive in Massachusetts in 1630 in the New World, the idea that the leader of the church was called pastor had been firmly established.

This is admittedly speculation, but it is educated on the facts as we know them. Regardless, it is our word and I am not trying to overturn that (I would if I could to get rid of the baggage that comes with the word), but I want to remove the idea that comes of one person (the "pastor") being elevated over all the rest (the "laity" or the "members").

112

I know churches where the leader seemingly no longer even has a first name—he's just called Pastor as if that name was what his parents called him at birth. I understand that for many that is merely a sign of respect, like calling a doctor by that title. I get that, but the problem is that God's established system for the community is that all should get respect, that all are equal no matter what their gift or calling, that only God deserves titles.

When we resort to that kind of setting, invariably the teaching creeps in that there is some kind of special difference between clergy and laity. There is none!!! So, we decided that we would use the word "elder," which is the more direct translation in the Bible for the church leaders.

We have women elders. Yep, I know that's shocking to many of you and probably make you want to stop reading. Please don't and allow me to attempt to Biblically explain this position.

To do so, you must remember what I said in the previous letter about Biblical interpretation. To start with, we must look at the writings of Paul to Timothy and to the Corinthian church. In both cases, those letters (I Timothy and I Corinthians) reflect a clear cultural setting. As I stated above, that does not mean that we blow off the words, but we must take them into context.

Again, feel free to blow off cultural relevance and demand a full allegiance to the letter of the word. Just promise me that if you are going to that, that you also force head coverings and that your worship service look exactly as Paul dictated. The commands to those two things are just as clear as his teaching on women in the writing to the people in Corinth. And, remember that you need to get on the phone to Beth Moore, Kay Arthur and other women and demand that they stop teaching, ever, to men. What Paul writes in I Timothy is clear. In no way does it somehow imply that he only meant a Sunday morning service. Nor did he mean or ever imply there that it's okay as long as some man is listed on a board of directors somewhere, covering a woman teacher. He is crystal clear and if you are going to follow the letter of the law, then follow it clearly and no sidestepping.

For me, I love hearing Beth speak and would gladly sit at her feet. How can that be? Either God is confused or the Bible is wrong or, better, *the Bible is dynamic and God moves in time knowing cultures and allows the Bible to work in culture.* I cannot accept either of the first two possible answers and I am not a fundamentalists (I don't plan on demanding the women of my church stay away when they are on their period—and the Bible demands that.) Paul's letters then, must be connected in some way to the culture needed at those specific moments in time.

But, couldn't that same claim be made for any other law or command in the Bible? Well, actually, yes. Thus, as I wrote in the earlier chapter, we have to work with the entire Bible. So, what does God teach about women in leadership in the rest, the fullness of the Bible? As I look across the breadth of Scripture, I see that God himself uses women in leadership. Deborah the judge is a clear example of that. If God was against all women for all time every being leaders, then what is up with that? There is no logical way to get around her existence as the leader of Israel at that time without accepting God's dynamic ability. Esther is another example of God using a woman in leadership, though Esther never had an official position or office like Deborah.

The New Testament provides even more information. Paul himself acknowledges and supports women in chief leadership. You can argue all you want that Priscilla was "under" Aquilla, but the text to the Romans never says that. Paul speaks to them as equals and lists them as the main leaders. Today, people would call them both pastors.

In the Romans 16 chapter, Paul lists other women who are clearly leaders and teachers. Now how can this be? Did someone other than Paul write to Corinth and Timothy? Did someone not named Paul write to Rome? It seems clear that Paul understood that the culture in these various regions demanded different instructions on this point.

Finally, we must address the fact that in his lists of Spiritual gifts, Paul gives no room for gender-based gifts. He merely lists the gifts and says that God gives them to all of his children.

114

Amazingly, one of the lists is in Corinthians. If he really did think that no woman could lead or teach, why would he not simply state that here? He could easily have said something about how leadership, prophecy and teaching were gifts only for men. But he did not. The obvious answer is that the spiritual gifts have no limit based on gender.

So, here we have a situation where God himself has chosen women leaders in the history of his chosen people, the apostle Paul (who supposedly is against women leading and teaching for all times and in all places) supporting and acknowledging the leadership of women in places that he knows, and the Holy Spirit giving gifts to all people, including gifts of teaching and leadership. How can I stand here today and somehow demand that no woman can be in leadership?

And one more thing—to say so would rob the mission field of a tremendous number of leaders for the international mission field is full of godly ladies who are wonderful teachers and leaders. I know why and so do you—as long as no one calls them pastor, everyone acts like that is okay. Sadly, all that does is make the church look hypocritical and silly to the world, in particular to strong women leaders.

Well, I suppose I've rambled on around in this. My heart is not to say that there are no leaders. There most certainly are and the leaders need to do their job, just like those called to teach need to teach, those called to give should give, those to serve to serve. However, those who are called to give are not the only ones who give or are not more important because they financially provide more than others; we must also teach all leaders, particularly those called to the front of the front, that they are not more special.

We need to see more service, not more hiding in the ivory tower. We need to see more teamwork and submission from the leaders, demonstrating their own confidence in their own leadership and calling, thus strengthening the ability of all the others to follow those steps.

As I've said elsewhere, either the leaders embrace that or hope for the church may really lost. The people will follow authentic leadership, leadership that allows for their truth about themselves to be seen. They want to be led properly, in a way that validates their own ability to fulfill their mission.

I'll end with a sad story. I had a young lady move away to college from our group here where she had been taught that she could minister, she could embrace all that God had called her to. She went to college and got involved with a fairly sympathetic church, agreeing with much of what I have written here. But she soon ran afoul of leadership in this church. Her crime was merely trying to minister to the lost as well as the body. After attempting to hold parties in her dorm or getting people from her home group to go skating or the movies, she received a phone call from the leader. She was told in no uncertain terms that she could not do that. "What," she exclaimed? "I can't hold a party?" He replied, "Well, you can hold a party but you can't ask people from our church to it without asking my permission. Then it looks like it's a church function and I approve and set all of those."

That is a tragedy. It happens all over America, someone like you, living in towns like yours, involved in churches like yours. Such is the American church. Leaders, if this is your idea of leadership, then you are not reading the same Bible I'm reading.

are you ready?

18

Keep it simple

I have more than a few mantras that I use to stay sane out here on the front lines. "Let it be what it becomes." "Church is not a thing you join, it's a thing you are." "are you ready?" One of the most instructive to me is "the church of Jesus is simple, not complicated."

The idea of simple vs. complicated is something that I use often to keep myself on the right path. I suppose at the end, it may sound as if I am attacking programs. I'm really not. I promise. Most programs have at their heart a desire to accomplish the community commands of John and Acts.

However, for most churches, the programs end up becoming a very complicated system that involves way more effort and work than really is needed. How did it get like that? Why less than 40-50 years ago, church was not so burdened with so many programs? It's through these various programs that we have drifted further and further into our little ghettos in the first place. "Why go to the YMCA and actively participate in my community when I can have my church program an aerobics class. Then I can be sure that they'll use only Christian music and I'll be surrounded by Christians."

Along the way though, as we layer event upon event, program for whatever on top of program for whatever, we lose sight of what we should be about. There is no reasonable way for me to actively be engaged in my society, being salt and light when I am needed at a church function 3-5 times a week. And those functions are on top of the worship services. There are many churches where their building is running 24 hours a day.

Perhaps they can pull it off and again, I am not saying that certain programs are somehow bad or satanic. What I am getting at though is that Jesus asked us to be involved in our society. We cannot do that when we are snuggled up safe in our little church ghetto.

To that end, we have focused on having just two ongoing functional activities. I suppose that could all change in an instant, but for us we must keep it simple. Recently we debated a proposed change to our schedule because of issues with the location where we meet for worship. As the discussion went back and forth, we kept reminding ourselves that a key point was to keep it simple.

Modern church structure/life is very complicated, yet it also presents itself and theology in simplistic ways. While there are several various meetings that I'm suppose to be at, I really don't have to go to any of it and no one will call me on it. In a simplistic way, I can live like I want. The "one another" commands are rarely used or embraced.

On the other hand, the church life/structure described by Jesus, that community experience he taught, is really simple, yet the theology is complex, deep. As I wrote already describing "invasive community," this complexity presents a challenge; people typically don't like complex.

So how do we put this into action? In our efforts to keep it simple, we chose not to ask for a lot of organized time together. The complex nature of that idea is that community is a 24/7 expression--something to live and breathe.

As we look at the Bible, we see that there are a few things that the organized group should do in a specific format: spend time together in fun, food, sadness, joy, pain, success and all that life brings; gather more depth as a believer by hearing more of God's teaching to us via the apostles; worship the Eternal One individually and corporately, and finally, seek God's face in prayer together. You can put those ideas into the categories of community and worship (you don't have to, but it brings it down to a foundational level). We don't mean to imply that this is an exhaustive list, but it is a clear list given at the outset of the existence of the church (Acts

2:42-47). Rather than complicating things by adding other meetings or things "we have to do," our aim is to do those foundational things well.

To that end, we have two gatherings in which we engage to help us accomplish the corporate tasks laid out for us. Neither one is somehow better than the other. Each accomplishes a specific task. Bliss is what we call our community focused meeting, and we hold it on Monday nights (though any weeknight could be used). *fluid* is our worship service, and we hold it on Sunday nights. If forced, I would tell you that coming to Bliss would probably precede coming to *fluid*. In fact, in our history, we started Bliss long before *fluid*.

Bliss is what we consider our horizontal meeting. It is our community time. While we need God there and expect him to bless our gathering, it only happens if all come. Bliss is a gathering of fellow searchers, a time of fellowship and community. We started it in September 1999 and have been walking together on the journey of life ever since. Our focus is a time for real life to occur in community.

We meet in each other's homes. We don't do this because "cell groups" are the hip new thing of the modern church. Rather it is to mimic the early church where almost 2000 years ago, members met in each other's homes to strengthen and encourage one another. That is being the church as we see it—the called out ones of God gathered together. Maybe if we really understood community, we would not need this crutch, but we find that it helps us on the journey by knowing that for sure, one day a week, we will be together for fellowship and to study the teaching of the apostles.

We do that in an atmosphere that is light and relaxed with the emphasis on sharing our lives together. We ask questions and tell stories based on the "one another" community commands of the Bible. If you want to participate in the "us" stuff of spiritual life, then Bliss is the place. There one can find the bridge as it were, for a soul searcher to move into relationship with the Eternal. It is also a place for Believers to connect with others who seek after something larger than themselves.

fluid was started almost two years after Bliss (and yes, the word is always lower case and italicized). It came in a time when our core group was moving deeper into being and seeing that we were an organized gathering. As such a group, we knew that the collection of believers was called to worship the Eternal One. For us worship is life. We wanted *fluid* to be like that.

We also knew what we did not want *fluid* to be—boring, stale, regular, routine. Thus, in our materials, we say that fluid is "innovativespareexuberantrealneeded." There are a few aspects of *fluid* that are probably noticeable from the start. We want the focus to be on God rather than the bells and whistles. That comes from our desire for simplicity. So, we sit on the floor, often use candles, and avoid the stage.

Another critical aspect of *fluid* comes in our expectations. We announce often that we expect to meet with God. We have come not for a religious program or ritual, but rather with the belief that we will meet with the Eternal One and that He wants to meet with us. We are told that God inhabits the praises of his people and that he longs to speak to us. Taking time each week to mentally and spiritually prepare is a deep part of *fluid.*

fluid is the vertical meeting. Some people question that or wonder about that aspect—can it really be vertical? We say yes. What we do there is not unique in the actual parts—we sing, we pray, we hear teaching, we read the Bible—the somewhat normal stuff required in the Acts 2 list of activities. Over the years, we've heard from person after person who, after attending, remarks about the intense level of worship. Even those who don't like it usually don't like it because it is so intense, so intimate, so vertical. I am driven by that statistic that I heard George Barna mention from 1998-99, that over 85% of church attendees during that time said they had NEVER experienced the presence of God in worship.

While we want everyone to come and expect to get a lot out of worshipping in community, *fluid* only happens if God shows up. Thus, it does have an intense personal direct tie between the worshipper and God. At *fluid* the focus is God and individually growing deeper in faith with him and as such, is a very open worship service for any and all, even if they call some other communal group their spiritual home.

For us, *fluid* is a time and place to worship the Eternal One, the God that has existed before time and space, the great "I AM." It is a time for the "called out ones" to gather together. *fluid* is for anyone who is hungry for an authentic time of worship, without the trappings or feel of an institution. *fluid* reflects the contemporary expressions of worship while at the same time practicing historical expressions of worship like Communion, silence, and reading from the Bible.

I love to worship God. I love the moment when all stills before him and I feel him breathing. It is that awesome numinous moment when I know that I am in the presence of something far greater than myself. It's that kind of feeling in which I am afraid to move in fear that the presence will leave or the moment will change. Let me tell you a story of what worship is supposed to be like to illustrate my point.

January 1999, my friend and disciple Chris Kutcher and I had the pleasure of attending Passion'99. The entire weekend was stellar, but I will never forget the last night there. After most of the day had past, they had planned for us to return into the arena for a late night worship event. As we came in, we were told to be silent. We topped the stairs up into the arena and were greeted with a darkened room and thousands of candles.

They had left the powered lights off and had put candles all over the stage and through the arena. The appearance was incredible. Then we started to worship. Nothing loud and boisterous, just a steady outpouring of words of praise to our God. I'm not really sure how long it lasted, but soon, the "official" praise band stepped off and we were alone, with 15,000 other people.

It was during this time that I no longer could stand easily. So I sat and cried and relished the presence of God. At one point, I looked up from my seat and noticed something over the floor of the arena. The place we were was a typical convention hall styled room, and the organizers had placed several hundred chairs on the floor. All along the sides, there were stadium seating and that was where we were sitting.

We were probably 30 feet above the floor of the arena, so, looking directly out from my seat, I could see above the arena all the way over to the other side. As I looked up, I noticed that at about eye level, there hung a great cloud over the entire arena. My mind instantly jolted to when Solomon was praising God and blessing the new temple. II Chronicles 5:13-14 records it this way:

> "they raised their voices and praised the Lord with these words, "He is so good! His faithful love endures forever!" At that moment a cloud filled the Temple of the Lord. The priests could not continue their work because of the glorious presence of the Lord filled the Temple of God."

As I sat there and looked out, I felt that same way, that I could not move, sing, pray or anything else. I am not one given to emotional rapture or excess, but that was how I felt. My rational mind quickly explained to myself that it was merely the smoke from the candles, but as I watched it hover over the room, I felt that numinous feeling of "beyond awe" at the presence of something so beyond myself.

Eventually, we were told to dismiss. Chris looked at me and wondered if I was ready. I told him "I can't move. Regardless of if I want to go, I literally can't move." He smiled a knowing smile and commenced to pray and praise more. I'm not sure how long I sat there, but finally, I leaned over to him and said, "I'm ready. I can go now." We silently got up and left the building.

That, my friends, is worship. I get asked so many questions about worship and usually, they are asking about style or parameters. My heart aches for them to really know that what God wants is so far beyond that stuff.

No, each week I don't see the presence of God in the smoke above our heads, nor is His presence so overwhelming that I cannot move. But I will tell you that each week we worship at fluid, the presence of God is very real for me and for others.

How does *fluid* process in real life? Quite well, I think, but we are still an experiment in motion. Here is one danger. Too many people, even in our setting, try to make the main meetings the only expression of community. I think I've clearly explained that community is an existence thing, but it is very hard to do. One reason is that we are all too lazy to make it happen, so we find in that one Sunday meeting (or whenever your group meets) a feeling of having accomplished what is required for community.

I recently had an email conversation with one of our elders on this very issue. He was admitting distaste for the large group and so I replied. His reply to me illuminated further his position, not of wanting to end the large group but to not get stuck there as I just described. Here is what I wrote first:

> Let me reply to the large group thing. We are so weak at community we must have the crutch [of the meeting]. Now Gaz would add that we should not linger too long on the crutch and that is well said too. But I look at [some of our group] and I think we must have this simple little time when I KNOW for sure I will see you. It cannot and will not be the only place for relationship and it can NEVER be the deep place. That's really what you are reacting too--people trying to make it the deep place, trying to run and thinking hobbling on a crutch is the same as running. But I think we [who at least think we can run, maybe we stumble some] who can run must still come and hobble along beside those on crutches, encouraging them to go deeper and further.

His reply:

> Let me expound on the 'large group' thing a moment. Tonight I spent about an hour and a half with Nick and Chris. Sweet time, exceedingly so. Monday night I

spent about an hour and a half with EVERYBODY. Not nearly the rewarding experience as tonight was... why? The answer I think lies in the depth of possible relationship. In an hour and a half I can dive deep into relationship with one person or play in the shallows with 20. I've come to understand that my soul longs for the deep. So, while I'm not opposed to large group gatherings, they no longer excite me. Having 500 people coming every week would hardly light my fire. On the surface I suppose we'd be successful but unless those 500 people were the rest of the week breaking up into groups of 5 or smaller and chasing what God is doing with the hunger of a starving man, I think Numinous would be a colossal failure. So, I've decided to pursue people in small group settings. . . I long deep in my soul for more [than large group]. It's time for a Song of Songs experience in community. My frustration is that not everyone else is here on the same page or as hungry for it. Like you pointed out they're trying to make the shallows experience on Sunday or Monday the 'deep' thing. Or they aren't ready for it at all.

If we ever hope to move the world toward what God called us to, real community where we love like Jesus and a place where I can gain the tools to live an authentic life so that I can succeed in the task of my individual mission, we have to learn how to move past the large gatherings. Our community must become a delicate dance between my spiritual hunger and my life.

To do that, we think keeping it simple helps us do that. We've lost religious people because we don't have all the correct programs. Maybe one day we'll add some of those programs, but remember our focus. What passes as Christian corporate living is broken. It must be or there is no other explanation as to why so many live apart from God.

Thus, we are experimenting in an attempt to find what we have lost. In that process, we have returned to the Bible to try and do merely what it says there and nothing else. Our heart is to focus

124

on doing that well and then, maybe, try to add other things. In other words, never allow any program to climb onto a pedestal to be worshiped.

Why not try this—for six months, drop everything in your church that is a program, that you cannot find solid Biblical backing for (like a verse that commands it). Then, for that same six months, teach, focus on and push community. Drive your people to love your remaining large group meetings but demand them push into one another's lives, deeper into community. Urge them to use the fresh time they have both for inner community and their own lives. Watch and see if they don't become more rested, less stressful. Watch and see deeper relationships form. Watch them, just like Jesus, take the light of God into places like PTA or the YMCA or the city council and do that without burning out because of all the church meetings and programs that also demand their time.

Risky huh? I think it is the way of the Word. Six months later, you'll probably find a program or two that someone is passionate for. They should be allowed to pursue that passion with gusto, but keep it from being a program. Just let them do it and let them take whatever support they get from others. Maybe it's a "Mom's Day out" program and several mothers will be excited to share it. Great let them.

Maybe it'll be a service thing and several members will, out of their own expression of community, do a service project. Great! Let them. Just don't rush in to add it under the banner of a program for your church. Just let it be their passion.

What you will find is a group of more relaxed members who love each other and are moving deeper into community. You can do this. Don't just copy us in our naming convention or days when we do stuff. Do it your way that reaches your generation and culture. But do it. Try my experiment. I think you'll find yourself and your church community more relaxed and happy.

Am I being too idealistic? Is this too simple or too costly to do this? Jim Collins in his wonderful book *Good to Great* says that for most organizations, the key question is not what is on the "to-do" list but what is on the "stop doing" list. This is not the only way to regain simple community. Yet, for many groups it is going to take this kind of bold leadership--bold leadership to merely focus on being community and freeing the people to really love on each other.

You can choose not to do this, but in the church, we know the result we are already getting and mere innovative programs are not the answer. Do you really want a Biblically sound church? A healthy church focused on God's mission? If my idea is too simplistic for you, then get to work coming up with something else to get you there, but please do something. Now!

are you ready?

19

Do your people like being together?

Back in 2002, one of our group was in New York and was invited to "a church thing like that thing you are doing in Orlando." Curious, she went. In she walked, actually with a church member. She sat down quietly, received little greeting. The service started with fairly tame worship for an X'er crowd. As she sat there, she tried not to evaluate, but just soak it in and enjoy the moment. However, as she put it to me later, "it seemed as if they were trying too hard, but they certainly didn't get it. It was just the same old religious thing with a somewhat different package."

In America somewhere near you, another new church has cranked it up with a young leader. They say all the right things and their PR looks hip enough. Yet, do they get it? Time will tell, but already enough questions are raised by the way things are done that one could start to edge to the conclusion that, sadly, they don't get it.

The entire reason I've spent the time to write this book is to try and scream to others that we must get it. And getting it will be costly. And it will demand radical change about the philosophy of ministry and the functionality of ministry.

While in New Mexico, I was counseling a young pastor about his flock. Finally, after listening for a while, I asked the critical question that I think easily underscores the difference between getting it or not. "Do your people like being together?" The question took him aback (I think he was expecting some really spiritual question). He thought for a moment and then sadly admitted that, "well, no they don't."

Tragic. The entire point of the called out ones is to exist together. That cannot happen if we don't like being together. Jesus mission to the church lies fully exposed as driving us to be together and enjoy one another. How can I be expected to share my resources with someone that I detest or at least have no emotion for? How can I share a meal together with someone that I don't like?

At its more simple level, "church" is a group of people who have all heard the same message, realized they have the same need of grace, accepted the same offer from God and now are in the same boat together. Of course, Jesus knew that as humans we are not all going to like being around everyone—that is why the command is so heaven sent and can only be accomplished by someone who has a spiritual power that is from without and above. Meaning, none of us can accomplish Jesus' command in own power. We are all too judgmental, too harsh, too picky and too selfish.

When it really happens, when the world sees an accepting, loving, likable group that really enjoys being together, sharing the ups and downs—that is attractive. Right now there is a young lady who wants to travel with us more than she actually does it. She is so attracted to our community, but she holds back because of "the church" where she goes has hooks on her. Of course I counsel her to continue to stay connected to her church, but her lament is that while that church provides good programming for her, there is absolutely no community, at least not that touches her. In other words, it fails at that same critical question—do you like being together?

Churches across America could do an easy self-check-up to see where they are by simply asking that question. Do people come here for worship and sharing because they like each other or because we have provided a spiritual mall ghetto experience? Again, while there is nothing wrong with a community decided to offer some program that comes from a passion of its people, why offer a basketball program when there are several in your community already? Why not participate, coach, play and share your faith there? Anyway, when those programs become the reason a person joins the club and they never develop or understand the true mission of the church that is not good.

Stated another way—if a church gathers a rather large crowd for its religious show, but fails at the God-given mission of love and unity, is it successful just because it has large numbers?

So, do you get it? Are you willing to pay any price to accomplish God's mission? As I've tried to demonstrate logically and Biblically, the church of America (at least) as lost the understanding of the true mission of the church. Actually, through my study of history, I would argue that the church lost that mission way back in time, maybe as early as the 250-400 AD period.

Let's assume for a minute that I'm right. Can you sense what kind of change is needed? Will you go there? If Gabriel himself reappeared to you and told you "that stuff Creasman wrote is 100% correct," would you take the steps needed to pull it off? Are you willing to discontinue a "good" church structure to accomplish the best, the specific thing God tells us to do?

I hope so or I think the church's slide into an irrelevant place is truly complete. Oh we'll keep having religion around here, but true church? Well, I suppose it cannot get much worse than it currently is, but in this loss, much of what has been of value in the United States will be lost as well.

I have been reading about the current and past persecution that the church has gone through over the years. How can you imagine that the church in America could survive real persecution, protecting each other, meeting clandestinely for worship when we don't even like being together?

So, what do we do? How can we return to what Jesus asked of us? Well, the change will have to start at the top. We have discussed leadership at length, but we cannot fail to see that if the leader does not get it, then it will be very hard for the "regular" churchman to affect proper change.

Leaders, are you ready to pay the price? We must quickly humble ourselves and step off of our pedestal. We are no better than any other Christian and it is about time we admit that. Sunday would indeed be a great day for the church if pastors around America knelt down in front of their body and begged forgiveness if they have this lack of humility.

Also, as others like Leonard Sweet have already said many times, we need to end this non-Biblical setting of clergy and laity. Perhaps I should beg that we go back and try to appropriate what the Bible actually says. Again, we've already spoken about Biblical interpretation and perhaps no one is reading at this point. I know I've opened Pandora's box in one sense and you may feel like throwing that up in my face with something like tattoos. Fine, but while you are majoring on the minors, let's at least see that the major issues are clear. God DID give some the gift of leadership, clearly. And they are to lead, clearly. But that in no way demands a paid clergy staff that somehow rules over the rest of us.

If your church cannot operate without a single paid staff person, then you probably don't have a church. You have an organization, a bureaucracy. The church can exist without any paid staff if need be. Let me say that again—*ecclesia* does NOT demand a paid leader! Yes, obviously in the Bible, we can see that some feel their calling in such a way that they no longer hold down traditional jobs in one location. But for the vast majority of churches in the first and second centuries, there were no paid staff at churches. That idea comes clearly from the church structure of the 4th-7th centuries as well as the Old Testament structure of priests and Levites. Yet, those early churches had leaders who led, all the while continuing to impact their communities through their jobs.

Yes, it is okay for a leader, locating in one area, to receive some financial support from the body. In the area of godly resource management, the Bible does teach that part of the giving of the body is for the leader, particularly the leaders who teach. But the church of today would do well to tell all of it's paid staff to go get a job. Sounds harsh? Well, I think there are some very compelling reasons why.

First, based on my experience and discussion with others, many clergy are disconnected from their people. For many clergy, coming straight from college to seminary to the pastorate, what church members go through on a daily basis, having to deal with non-Christians in the work force, is a foreign concept. Second, no "paid professional" staff forces the people to pick up their own tasks of ministry—no longer will it be just the leaders who get the "at all hours" phone calls in desperation, but the body would have to minister to one another.

Third, there are financial reasons. While the resources of most gatherings (i.e., churches) are actually quite extensive, at most churches, you'll find up to 50-70% of resources end-up specifically for paid staff. In many churches, then, the people constantly hear about how much money they don't have for "ministry" and how everyone needs to give more.

While I agree that most Christians experience a vast chasm between what they say they believe and how they organize their resources, one can hardly blame them for trying to hold on to more of their money. When they give to the church, what exactly is done with it except build bigger buildings and pay church staff salaries? To many, that seems quite offensive and perhaps wasteful. Again, you can prove that providing for the leaders (the priests) is part of why we give, but the idea of a "full time" or "professional" clergy is not a given in the New Testament for the majority of churches.

So the leaders have to take the first step. In relationship to my role as the spiritual leader of Numinous, I decided from day one that I would not receive a full salary from the church. I am attempting to receive a significant portion of my annual needs from my personal ministry as a speaker, singer and author. That income would be augmented by some percentage of our giving as a body. But I have also worked part-time from day one of Numinous. Thus, to be quite transparent, I receive about a small source of my total annual income from Numinous the church, another source comes from other ministry endeavors under the Numinous, Inc banner and about half of my income from my part-time job.

Finally, and perhaps most critical, if most church leaders went out to get a real job, that would put our supposedly most mature, most knowledgeable Christians out of the ivory spiritual tower and down among the people of the world. In my part time job I have had so many opportunities to share my faith, counsel, and pray for and over those people in my path. People I would NEVER meet if I were still working in a church office. Jesus was almost always out among the regular people and that is where we should be also.

This idea is not hard to comprehend. For most pastors, finding a church member who owns their own business or who manages some kind of store would not be too hard. Professional church leaders, go to work like the rest of the world. Even if you raise your support like with many para-church organizations—just think what you could do within your ministry if 45% of that amount was earmarked by you for other things besides your personal support.

I can already hear many complaining about how they barely have time now as it is. That is so merely because for most churches, they have ceased to be the fulfillment of the mission of Jesus and have become large corporations providing a consumer-driven program that they must manage. Having served in a traditional church and having watched my father and uncles and other friends in ministry, it is my opinion that most of what a pastor has to do, from a weekly preparation point of view, can easily be done in about 15-25 hours a week. That leaves plenty of time for them to hold a normal job and give them the chance to work like everyone else in the world.

What about ministry of visiting the sick or new members and the like? Well, how do you expect a normal church member to do that? Or, do you really think they don't do that and should not do that? In reality, again, each of us has the same general responsibilities as everyone else. Do you provide a paid time each week for your various Sunday School teachers to prepare their lessons? Is what they teach somehow less important that what the preacher has to say on Sunday? Isn't it all the same "teachings of the apostles?

See, in that we come back full circle—there is no difference in value between the leader and the other members of the body.

And we must act that way. Now this is not to say that somehow leaders are of no importance. Nor is it to say that God has ceased to call out leaders in the 5-fold ministry system of Ephesians. But as we say here, it is level ground at the cross and most leaders would do well to start acting like it.

I have a vision of heaven that speaks to this. In my vision, I see the multitude standing before God at one of the judgments, probably that which consists only of the saved. He speaks, calling forward all the leaders, particularly those like me who get to stand on a stage somewhere. We'll all move forward towards him. Then he'll have us turn and face the crowd. At that point, He will begin to call out the unknown saints who labored in service, prayer, giving, caring and other things, things that were never known by most or by any. And at his command, us of the more visible, will begin to cheer and clap and honor these very important but previously invisible parts of the body. They will get the honor due to them for their excellent service to God. Then, those like me, the famous, the known, will just be quietly ushered off to the back of the crowd again. For many leaders, a vision like that bothers them.

Well, if our leaders need to operate with change, so too does our structure. If our aim is loving each other and unity, then whatever it is we do should aim that way. One place to examine that is the church budget. Take a long hard look at your budget and ask this question: "how much of what we spend helps us as a body in loving each other and unity?"

As I have indicated before, for most churches and leaders, that love and unity thing is, at best, an "understood." However, for the average member, it's not really comprehended and it is rarely programmed in their church. So, in the end, most go away from Sunday not really caring whether they see the others during the week or not. Again, we should so love each other, there should be a longing inherent in us that almost hurts when we go more than a few days without hearing from one another.

We cannot let our budgets stand idly by and give short shrift to what Jesus says is the mission of the church. What would an appropriate budget look like? Body ministry and benevolence (meaning giving back to the body) would be a high percentage. We give, first and foremost, to ensure that no one is in need. Missions, which in reality is giving to a member of the body so that they can go somewhere else to serve, would also have a high percentage. In large churches, they could give money away to smaller church bodies if they needed supplies or their rent paid. Of course there could be programs that have financial support, programs that foster the sense of community that each body should be known for. However, those programs should not usurp the opportunity to actually do the same thing within the community that you live.

I will not sit here and try to formulate how you spend every penny at your church, but the fact is that our budgets speak to what we really value. So do our time commitments. In this postmodern world, time is really the chief currency. Is your church's schedule full of groups of the body being together or is it full of "ministry" activities that has people working (and feeling guilty if they can't be there) at something in order to accomplish some ministry goal? Most churches would do well to cut 75% of what is on their schedule and then tell their people to either spend time together or spend it with people they are trying to influence. Better still, do both at the same time. As we have said before, what the Bible implies is that as the non-connected see our love and unity, they will want to know more, they will believe you are his disciple and they will believe the facts you share about Jesus.

In the end, for us to really get it, we have to do it. We can't teach about a Biblical method or view of church life, and then not do it in actual practice. Those who are doing it must teach others about it. Both teaching and doing have to happen if we are ever going to get anywhere.

I know that what I am proposing is a massive undertaking. I also believe that there are actually many churches out there now that already have this plan, but no one has ever told them it's okay. Usually, their pastors go to big gatherings where they hear the latest plans to grow the church and they get both excited and depressed. They think to their group of 75 or 150 or 200 and think "all those people like to do is be together." What I want to say to that leader and that church is YES!! WAY TO GO!! That is it. Keep doing that. But these leaders usually complain and apply some level of guilt to remind the people that the church is not about each other but about some organization to save the lost—"so we need to get busy and implement some new program." That is the exact opposite of what the Bible actually teaches—individually we are to be living with a fire and integrity and from that platform, help them see that God loves them and wants to be connected with them while corporately, we are there to support each other through the many issues and challenges of life—loving and being unified.

I know this church in our example might also need to be reminded about the individual mission, which is all evangelism and service to others. They might also need to be reminded that they cannot become religious relics, frozen in their beliefs, judgmental to others younger or different from them. But on the whole, they are okay. They get it. Pastors get frustrated in that setting, mostly because they've never been taught what the true mission of the church is anyway. They don't understand the real call of a leader of the local church. That call is to shepherd that group, lead that group, train, release and encourage each person's personal ministry that operates out in the world. And don't forget that call is not toward one leader only, but that Biblical leadership and the task inherent in it is a group effort.

So to you who are in a church that exists in community—keep going strong. Don't fear when you let pass that latest and greatest plan. Just keep loving each other and being unified. And then let that unity spread to the other parts of the body of Christ in your area. It does us little good to sit in our own group, smug in our unity and community while at the same time blowing off other groups. We cannot expect anyone to accept that Jesus is love when those who supposedly call on his name won't even talk to members of other churches.

Do we get this? If we really hope to accomplish what God wants, we'd better. As I said at the very beginning, I remember when the Southern Baptist launched "Bold Mission Thrust 2000" back in the 1970s. They were going to win the world and our church at least focused on it. Well, the year 2000 came and went and the world is still not all saved. I'm not sure it ever will be nor that God expects us to accomplish that fact. But his word is very clear for the body what they are supposed to do. And, as we've said elsewhere, amazingly his plan for how church life should look (the mission of the church) links up with his outreach heart for the individual. We must have both. I wonder if my hometown church in 1976 had actually focused more on teaching and leading us to learn to love each other deeply, perhaps we might have actually gotten somewhere.

This is a hard teaching, I know, confrontive and perhaps exasperating. But we must recover the very things Jesus taught us to do. The Church in America must do this even if in doing so, we expose the 80% of our church people who are only "Christian" in name only and have never decided to actually follow Jesus and so now they abandon the pretense and go somewhere else. Don't forget that, in one sense, Jesus spent much of his time *running people away from his ministry and avoiding "success via numbers."* He was even very strict and disciplined regarding his most ardent followers. Many of us would have wilted under the penetrating gaze of Jesus as he challenged us with a "have I been with you so long and yet you do not get this?" We would probably all do well to strive to add this sense of challenge to our ministry, but it is hard when you know doing so will run people away.

are you ready?

20

Does it work?

The burning question you might have is "does this work?" I'm still out here on the front using this tactic, this philosophy of ministry, so to speak, so, I'd say "yes, it works." But it's not without it's challenges, not the least of which is the response of the modern church.

I was chatting with my wife's stepmother about this very book. In trying to tell her what I was doing, I used a phrase that might explain best the focus and, at the same time, explain a bit about why the response of churchmen, particularly leaders, has been lukewarm to cold. I said these letters were basically like a manifesto, a call to arms, a cry for revolution. You might think about them as a new 95 Theses.

Of course I am not going to claim equality with Martin Luther, but the effect is basically the same. I, like he, have examined the landscape of the current church and found it wanting in a few areas. Luther didn't really have Remember, though the title is 95 Thesis, in actuality, that means he had 95 flowing points. Were we to re-write his work, we would combine several of his points into single paragraphs. In the end, he had a few main ideas or complaints that he then supported with ideas and thoughts. Like Luther, I am not trying to attack the whole of the church in its basic sense of theology.

Instead, I am merely responding to the facts of our day concerning the state of the world, lost people, the church, church leaders, church members and the like. I have said again and again, I am not talking about some kind of stylistic change to a worship service. I'm not even talking about a leadership structure change—

a leader by one of several names is still a leader—though some change would probably be good.

We are talking about a philosophy of ministry, a functional approach to what the church should be doing and what individual Christians should be doing. If something is wrong with the church (and it must be unless the researchers are all wrong, unless all of the church leaders who are crushed and dismayed by life in the church are just confused about why they feel this way, unless those who say our society is sick and immoral are wrong), then we must look within to see what is going on.

When we look within, we see a lot of confusion about what to do and how to do it, particularly when compared to what we have written for us in Scripture. Consider the world—most people have no regard for the church. Either they think that "look, I'm in, so leave me alone, my life is not any worse than yours and you go to church" or more directly they cannot conceive that the message of the church is true. There just is no evidence to them, so why bother. So while many will say they are Christians (probably just to get tele-marketers and parents off their back), few actually live the life.

Where does that confusion come from but from within the church? Yes, of course, our great enemy, the father of lies and confusion, has had a hand here. Ultimately, though, the problem lies within. The church can no longer cast a critical eye at society as if it is somehow lost society's fault for acting at odds with God. We are the salt. We are the light. We are God's representatives. If the message has gotten lost, then it's gotten lost because the messengers have gotten lost.

Collectively, we are the body, the community of the called out ones. We are the family of friends. And He promises that through that community, others will come to Him—through the love and unity demonstrated in that community. Not through that community's great outreach program, Tuesday night visitation or the preaching of the pastor. Just the other day, one of my co-workers confided to me that he was attending a local church of some renown for the teaching of that pastor. The day before, interestingly enough, another person had asked me if I thought that co-worker was a Christian. I had to be honest and say I did not know.

When I asked for more details from the co-worker, I pressed to know if he was in community with others there. Sadly, the answer was no, that he just liked going because of the speaker. I'm not saying my co-worker is or is not a Christian. Nor am I saying that he is wrong to go that church, but the motive is wrong. Instead of going to pursue community, he is merely going to the place that fits his personal needs. The church ceases to be a community that you are a part of and merely becomes one of many service-oriented businesses and you choose to become a member or not. You remain apart from it—basically paying your membership dues, some occasional time spent there, but no real connection. The others around this person—do they know of his supposed strong convictions (how can this person be a Christian without strong convictions), do they know and sense his community? I did not.

So, I say we, the Church today, have a problem that cannot be solved merely by adopting some new style or allocating more money for evangelism training or the like. Our problem lies solely in the confusion about the role of the church and the lack of credibility in most Christian's lives. So, do these ideas work? Are there problems? How does leadership fit in? Doesn't all this talk about community smack of cult stuff or a commune? And how can you judge success? Purely on numbers? This is the rub, really.

Judge success of a Fortune 500 company and you really are looking at dollars. Maybe innovation in products, but really, it all comes down to quarterly earnings.

Judge success of a professional sports franchise and it all comes down to wins. Here dollars, while important, are not the key issue. It all comes down to the foundation and that is all about winning and losing.

Judge success of a lawyer and it comes down how she handles her cases. A Doctor? Saving lives or not. On and on we go and it's easy to determine a success formula, but when you come to God business, we hit a snag.

That snag is Jesus. In his teaching, he paradoxically laid out that true success for "his boys" would be an antithesis of what the world judges as success. A leader is a servant. The first must be the last. They are specifically forbidden from choosing to act in leadership like the world's leaders act.

Wow! Maybe that is not a big deal somewhere else in the world, but here in 2003 America, that is scary in its obvious "against the grain" approach. Now this does not mean that you need to burn all your John Maxwell's books by any means, but it really calls into question how we determine our success quotient.

Sadly, the normal church success determination is people. Go to any church conference, talk to any church leader and ask them about their church. The normal response will somehow relate back to the number of people who are there. If their number is small, then there is usually an apology involved, as if that small number somehow implies they really are not doing a good job.

And in this culture, it does imply that! But, the Bible does not say that; in fact, tied to various things Jesus said such as following him would lead to conflict or that the way is very narrow and few find it, it seems the Bible says the opposite—success is not in large numbers.

So where do we go? Are we being successful at Numinous, Inc? How do we evaluate success here? I think the answer lies in connection between the mission of the church and the mission of the individual. I think that our success will be clear in the depth of our community, as far as it connects with the larger mission of the community. As our churches reflect a depth of love and unity that is obviously missing in many places, that will be the correct measure of success, whether we are talking about a church of 15, 55, or 505.

That measure of success also must connect to how each individual is moving forward in their personal growth. In fact, one of the clearest statements of success and mission comes in Ephesians 4 and it is aimed at the leaders. Paul tells us that:

4:11 He [God] is the one who gave these gifts to the church: the apostles, the prophets, the evangelists, and the shepherds and teachers. *12* Their responsibility is to equip God's people to do his work and build up the church, the body of Christ, *13* until we come to such unity in our faith and knowledge of God's Son that we will be mature and full grown in the Lord, measuring up to the full stature of Christ. *14* Then we will no longer be like children, forever changing our minds about what we believe because someone has told us something different or because someone has cleverly lied to us and made the lie sound like the truth. *15* Instead, we will hold to the truth in love, becoming more and more in every way like Christ, who is the head of his body, the church. *16* Under his direction, the whole body is fitted together perfectly. As each part does its own special work, it helps the other parts grow, so that the whole body is healthy and growing and full of love.

There is a lot here that we should note, but before that, lets zoom in on the key idea that I alluded to. Verse 12 clearly says that the leaders job is to prepare God's people for fulfilling the work. What work? II Corinthians 5:18-20 is a great summary statement of that work, as we have already clearly lain out. Here, in Ephesians, we also see success when the leaders help each person grow towards looking like Christ, maturing, loving and unifying.

Beyond that, we have to stop. Anything more than that takes us dangerously close to the edge of the very area we are urged to stay away from—thinking like the world leaders think.

But "what about conversions," you ask in protest? I feel your pain. Obviously people becoming connected to God is important to God—it's all over the Bible. "What about the Acts 2 stuff that I wrote about earlier," you demand? I know, I know—it's right there in ink—people were added to their number daily. Sounds like a success statement if there ever was one.

Note this—if we are really doing our job individually as Christians, then of course people will be getting saved. There is just no other option there, but as we stated earlier, our sharing of our faith, and in seeing others decide to believe in Jesus, is dependent on the church fulfilling it's mission of love and unity.

What I think is that God maintains dominion over those saved. I think that salvation, i.e. numbers, are the sphere of God. All through the Acts and the Epistles, the picture is of authentic Christians living boldly in the name of Jesus. Others see and wonder and ask, hear and respond—all controlled by the Spirit of God.

Stated another way, I believe that it is possible for a group to be doing everything God said, and doing it well, in the areas that are clearly marked for us in the Bible and still be small in numbers.

We must judge our success or lack thereof solely on the Biblical injunctions and directions that we do have. They are not plentiful, but there is enough there for us to go on.

Before I leave this topic, let me direct your eye back to the passage in Ephesians 4. Did you notice the stuff that Paul says implies overall personal success? He could have said a lot of things regarding the church there. It is one of the very few times he mentions anything about leadership of the collective, so those statements would seem to carry some weight! So, what does he say? Not much about programs, nothing about numbers—just the same message that is inherent throughout the Scripture, the very things we've laid out in this book and the very things that we've said seemingly get overlooked with many groups—unity, togetherness, community.

Paul says the aim is to be fully mature. Then he defines that for us: not easily swayed in our theology, holding tight to love of truth, taking our position in the body as He lays it out and focusing on love and unity. Clear. Concise. Easy to understand. Not much wiggle room. Sounds like a plan as far as I'm concerned—how about you?

It is time for the church to make this change, to return to the narrow way, and live out church exactly as the Bible depicts. If we do this, I think we can begin to have a small sliver of influence on the culture and society today. I hope the writings in this book will inform you and inspire you to move to that spiritual existence. Maybe God is calling you right now, in the city that you live, to start gathering together in a true example of church. Maybe God is preparing you to share this information with your current church, to teach how to really bring your church into alignment with God's teaching. I hope you go for it. I think our country needs it, but regardless, we owe God that level of obedience. It's time to make this change.

are you ready?

A Theology of Community

Series of essays written for
Numinous n-print Newsletter

by

Carl E Creasman Jr.

are you ready?

Theology of Community

Recently, I was at a dinner with another of the church elders where she recounted a story of a working peer who, when asked about Christianity, discussed how she had moved towards a slow rejection of Jesus due to what she had experienced in the church. It is this story, and countless more, that continues to drive the passion of Numinous, Inc.

When my wife Kim and I started Numinous in 1998, the overriding purpose was to be used as a communicator about Jesus' love to a generation that had clearly and defiantly rejected Jesus because of the church. Surveys then and now paint a bleak picture of this generation, now aged 19/20 – 41/42, showing how a strong majority have rejected Jesus as an answer. These are the parents of today's children. The need to reach this group of young adults is great.

But how does one attempt, as a Christian and thus as a part of the body of Christ, make a connection with a group that has rejected church? For Numinous, it was to set out to re-define church. Or, to state it better, the answer lay in forcing today's "church" back to its historic roots in the Bible.

For the early church, the Bible presents a clear theology of community, of one-anothering. That is the foundation of the first church. For a deeper explanation of this, you'll want to read my book [section 1 of this current book], but in brief, it is clear from a simple reading of the New Testament, that Jesus meant the church to be a "home base" of sorts, a community of fellow journeyers. As I often say it, "we know the deepest need of every human is to be known by another; it's clear in the literature of almost every field, from biology to motor sports, gangs to the Internet, people long for feeling a part."

The word community or communal has popped up in so many places these days; it is clear that the world is hungry for this. But why? We believe they are hungry because where they should find community, the church, seems to rarely fosters that aspect. In

146

its place, the church has become a large institution of doing stuff (mostly good of course) that has lost its soul. To reach the lost world, we must return to the style and design of the Master—a theology of community. How that looks will differ from place to place, but at the core will be a heart for one another. Any thing less makes the church a mere business.

Theology of Community, pt 2

If the idea of community is central to the Biblical idea of church AND we see the concept of community present in the secular parlance again & again, "why" is the first question to answer.

As I wrote in the last newsletter, community is central to the church, but that concept is not a new idea that Jesus threw in at the last minute. Rather, He was rescuing a notion of "one anothering" that is inherent in the creation.

In Genesis, we see that from the start with Adam & Eve, God desired a close relationship with his creation. We were created to be in relationships, or as I have said, "created to know another deeply and to be known deeply."

Over and over again through relationships like with Noah, Enoch, Abraham, Issac, Jacob and others, we see the God of the universe coming across space and time, divinity intersecting with temporal. This desire of God is part of his character.

We know that one aspect of God's character is One-ness, unity (hence why He hates divorce and broken relationships). We also know another aspect of God's character is the Trinity picture, one God existing coeternally and coequally in three distinct persons: the Father, Son, & Holy Spirit. You guessed it—community.

This desire is a core aspect of our very being, thus it should be no surprise to see our enemy hard at work to cause division and competition, the antithesis of community. So, stay on guard and fight for the community of faith around you.

Theology of Community, pt 3

Why is this so hard? Or maybe better stated, why, if community is so important, do we see churches more like businesses? I have asked in other places, "why are some churches places you join, a thing that exists apart from you that you can leave when and if you choose?" That is much like choosing a different store to shop at based on prices? Why isn't the simple process of love and unity the way it's done in churches?

Well, part of that answer lies in the long history of the church which perhaps we will get to next issue. Based on the many historical inaccuracies of books like *The Da Vince Code*, my background as a historian can help us understand this. First, though, know that the deeper answer of why churches are not typically focused on community, on love and unity, lies within a reality of "the human."

One would assume that since God created us for relationship, we would eagerly seek it out and embrace it. Well, while many do seek, embracing it is a different story. Time and again connection is desired as long as "it remains on my terms." The moment the community needs differ from my own desires, we bail. Perhaps its our American DNA of individualism, but through our experience in Numinous and that of countless other groups and churches, it is clear that we are afraid of community.

Partially this crisis emerges due to past hurts and betrayals. That pain is known by most. Yet there seems also to be a concerted effort by someone, perhaps an enemy, to convince us that real community depends on "others" and they usually fail us and can't be trusted. Right at the moment when "I" must allow myself to be vulnerable, "I" instead run for cover. It turns out that allowing others to be devoted to me also means allowing them to exhort, even admonish me. Sadly, we seem to hate that part.

Don't run from "Invasive Community" (a term we often use to describe this tension, this fear of community). Rather embrace the love and unity.

Theology of Community, pt 4

The idea of community, of "one anothering" is not some new idea that Numinous has come up with. This strategy, as we said in part 1, is Jesus model. How, you may ask, do we arrive at this concept?

I started doing Biblical study on the idea of church back in seminary, in the early 1990s. I was drawn to this question both through the pain of what I had experienced from the church, but also with a hope for the body of Christ. Something clearly is wrong with the church if people like George Barna are correct; Barna's last study showed over 95% of those who claim to be Christians cannot actually explain it, defend it or choose to live like it—his conclusion is that they simply are not Christians. As a pastor friend of mine lamented, maybe it's just the people. Well, it is our contention that instead it is the thing called Church and the failure of that organism to train up others. If those who come from our churches aren't Christians, perhaps it's the training they got or didn't get.

As I looked for any teaching that would show Jesus speaking to the collective group of disciples, I was surprised by what I saw. We know that the Bible has wonderful teaching for how a specific Christian should live, irrespective of what other Christians do. Yet, as one looks in the Bible, a companion teaching is there for the collective, instructions for how a group of Christians should live. We call these the "one another" commands. These cannot be done independently of other Christians. They demand involvement with others. We believe these "one another commands" are based upon Jesus last words to us, this side of the cross. We'll look at these next time, but till then, you can read John 13-17 for the most full account of Jesus last thoughts with his disciples, the early church. It is clearly focused on life together.

Theology of Community, pt 5

As we said last time, our position on what the church should be is labeled "community." We realize this is a word thrown around a lot these days and as such can be devalued or not understood. Before, however, we attempt to define the word, we need to show the Biblical basis for this concept.

I told you of my search in the Scripture for the mission of the church. This is not to imply that famous "mission" verses like Matthew 28:18-20 have no value, but it is obvious that how we do what we do has become questionable, weak or without accomplishment. Too many people are going to churches and yet coming away unchanged. While that could have some relationship to those people's actions and choices, nonetheless the church bears responsibility here.

What I found was astounding. When you look in the Word, there are clear places where the command or verses are directed not at one single person, but at the group. As I narrowed my search to see specifically if Jesus said anything about the church, not surprisingly He did. Realize, he doesn't say much about the organization or gathering of believers. Yet, during the Last Supper, John reports two stunning comments by Jesus. The first is John 13:34-35. Jesus gives a brand new command to the collected disciples. "Love one another as I have loved you." Note this is not the command to love others, the outsiders; that is elsewhere. This is specifically for the infant "church" (who else would be the core of the church than the disciples?). Jesus then spends the next few chapters fleshing this idea out, answering questions of the disciples and introducing the Holy Spirit to them. Later, in John 17, Jesus prays before going to the Garden for his final test. In that prayer, he prays in three basic sections. First he prays for himself, basically chatting with God. Then he prays for the disciples in the room. But then, lastly, he prays for us. In that prayer, we see Jesus second key statement about the church. There, Jesus prays that we would be remain unified (17:21).

Now, with both of these ideas, commands, he offers a promise related to evangelism. This is not surprising since we know God's main goal is to lead people into a saving knowledge of Himself so that we can offer Him glory.

The point? In Jesus last words before the cross, he had one core notion in mind for the collected body. A mission, if you will— love one another and be unified. In this we can see the entire point of the church and yes, ultimately it IS about saving souls. Yet, his

150

strategy lies not in more evangelistic crusades or more church programs. Rather we get there through the promises of Jesus; if we'll just focus on his commands, he'll do the rest. Love and Unity!

Now, did the young "church" accept this command of community, of a focus on one another? We'll look at that next time, but you can simply glance ahead to Acts to see a hint. There, we'll see if the theory of Jesus could be transformed into practice.

Theology of Community, pt 6

So, we have seen that community and relationships are core to the entire strategy of God. It's been in us since creation and historically, humans have sought this out. We saw last time that Jesus made this notion the core of his strategy for his disciples. Realize, his disciples WERE the early church. Let me try to show you that in a simple equation using different metaphors about the collective group of disciples.

Church=disciples=believers=followers of Jesus=People of the Way=the body of Christ=the Army of God=the Aliens of this World.

What Jesus said to the disciples were statements to the church and in his few words about their responsibilities as a group, as a collective, He was very clear.

Love one another as He loved them and stay unified as He is unified with God.

If we do those basic (though hard) things, others will see our credibility ("know we are his disciples") and believe our message ("know that Jesus came from God"). However, as we look across the landscape of the church over the past 40-70 years, we don't really see a community of believers but rather a large Christian mall of activity and programs, a business of good works and activities. While those type of things are not bad in and of themselves, the clear result is a church that is hyperactive in stuff to do yet full of lonely people who really don't see any clear connection between themselves and others. In Carl's many travels and discussions with people outside of church, that message has come again and again.

But how do we know that what Jesus said, really just a theory, was ever put into practice? For that we turn to the historical record of the early church. Dr Luke, one of the top historians from antiquity, wrote a two-volume record of birth of Christianity. His second volume focused on the early church and its actions. In the section from chapter 2 to chapter 6, he lays out the actions of the very early days (the remainder of the work looks at the church expanded across the Mediterranean Sea region). In those first chapters, we see a clear picture that the early church was determined to put Jesus' theory into practice.

Acts 2, for instance, tells us "the believers met together constantly and shared everything they had." Acts 4 states "the believers were united as they lifted their voices in prayer." Later in that chapter we are told the early church "shared everything they had" and "people who owned land or houses sold them. . .to give to others in need." Chapter 5 shares that "the believers were meeting regularly." Chapter 6 shows us that Jesus' promise had come true and many had believed and thus were now a part of the group. It was so large that they added special helpers to continue the community ministry.

In essence, Jesus' theory was put into practice and it worked as He said it would. The "called out ones" chose to express love to one another and were focused on unity. As a result, others around them believed. Certainly the tactical action still involved individuals sharing about their faith to their friends, relatives and strangers. But as they shared, the point is that they had credibility of this new life, this community of believers.

What in the world has happened to the modern church? We'll look at that next time. To get there, we'll first need to see how the expression of community was taken or rejected in the new churches founded by the first church.

Theology of Community, pt 7

As we saw last time, Dr. Luke demonstrated that the theory of Jesus ("love one another" + "prayer for unity" = mission of church/community) was put into practice in Acts. From the start, the early Christians just did what Jesus told them to do and they were successful in every concept of the word.

But anyone with eyes can look at churches in modern America and see that the focus is on anything by unity and love. Oh sure, those ideas are of course accepted, but they are not the focus, the mission. In their place has emerged some concept of church as business or church as Christian Mall. Much has changed and much is wrong with the church; the product produced is clearly flawed and much of the blame for that has to lie at the organization.

So what happened?

As I said previously, it's a long and complicated story that I will get to, either now or next time. However, first, we should look at what happened in the next 40 years after Jesus was on the earth. To do that, we merely keep moving in the Ancient Texts to see the story.

Perhaps not surprisingly, these critical concepts of how the body of Christ interacts provide the core of what is written in the letters of the remainder of the New Testament. Obviously the core authors this issue of maintaining Jesus' directive was imperative. We can see how they talked about it through a series of verses that we call the "one another" commands.

We know that within the Bible we are told how to live. And there are many commands to that effect which are directed clearly at me the individual Christian—don't lie, don't covet, etc.... But these "one another commands" simply cannot be obeyed apart from another person. They DEMAND the community, the body, the other believers in my group, and they lay out clear direction to what Jesus meant by "love one another" and "be unified."

Fully 12 of the remaining 22 NT books (minus the Gospels and Acts) have at least one of the "one another" verses. The others almost all contain clear information about how the church, as a group, is to act that supports or matches Jesus' call to love and unity. Timothy and Titus' letters are clearly directions to a leader of the body about how the body should look. Philemon is an example of reconciliation within the body. III John talks about how we should extend the love and unity to the larger church body. Revelation has the 7 letters to the churches making a final plea of sorts to focus on each other.

My own study of the Bible suggests that only II Peter and Jude do not specifically talk about the church's interaction, but are teaching letters for the individual Christian. Yet, even there, both warn about false teachers coming to destroy the body.

There can be no mistake. The one major thing that Jesus cared about—the one new command He gave the body and his ONE prayer item for the church—love and unity was central to what the disciples taught all the new converts. As they established churches all over the Greek and Roman world, they came back to this point again and again!

Perhaps we, in the 21stcentury should consider that a hint.

Theology of Community, pt 8

Unity and Love. That's it. Of course, as one looks into the "one another" commands, the vast depth in those two things becomes clear. And of course, as we shall see later, there are specific commands of actions to individual Christians. Yet, Jesus left us with one core idea revealed in two things, commands or prayers—love and unity—but that is lost as we showed in pt. 1 of this series.

How did we end up in the 21st century with literally thousands of denominations, entire towns with several church buildings sitting side by side, sometimes not even speaking to one another? How did it get to this?

The answer lies in "church history." Obviously, to give all of that in detail would take many more words than we can give here. A snapshot can be given, though, to demonstrate that our enemy clearly knows what God is after—the overarching mission of God that all people come to glorify his name. And, our enemy knows of

154

the new command and the single prayer and the promises that accompany—promises that provide the link to getting to God's goal. So, church history to this point is a tragic tale of our enemy attacking at this key point of community, undermining God's efforts.

From the first century till the early 300s, the church struggled with a series of major theological questions. Not surprisingly, these questions forced division. Of course, on several points, it was very important for orthodoxy to emerge, but this division over theology was not the only place the church struggled. The other was in leadership.

Short story—the church had two basic ideas or types of leadership emerge. One was collective leadership, as exhibited by the early church leadership as described in Acts. The other, which emerged in the late first century, was the concept of single leader who then worked with others. It is from this that the concept of Bishops, and ultimately the Pope, emerged. By the mid 200s, the first version had basically disappeared and would not emerge for over 1000 years.

Still, compared to what followed, the church was mostly unified in its purpose and the ideas of community remained. It had to as general persecution reigned for 300 years, with some periods of intense persecution arising. Enter Constantine in 313. While much could be said here, the simple concept is that from Constantine to the mid 400s, the church emerged from a focus on survival, moving to become the legal and dominant religion in the Roman Empire. Clearly, the church was now part of the machine of the Empire.

By the mid-400s, the church had less focus on love/unity and instead was institution based. And, perhaps not surprisingly, the first Reformers emerged in the monastic movement. The monks like Anthony were the first to declare becoming "legal" and turning into an "institution" had corrupted the true mission of the church. No longer would we talk about the church, the called out ones, though who had seen the Truth. Now, it was "The Church."

Here we see the modus operandi of "The Church" when it faced reformers—either co-opt the movement (sometimes for good, sometimes for ill) or crush the movement. In the case of the monks, it was to co-opt their efforts and legitimize what they wanted. Much good, of course, has come from the various monastic movements, but their early focus of reform for the Church would be silenced for over 400 years. Then in 909, the Monastery at Cluny became the center of challenge to the Institution with a heart for reform. They too would be co-opted, however, as The Church would rise to the heights of its power in this time.

The Church, from 1000-1300, thus was the dominant power in the West. However, during that time, the Crusades, greater corruption, and a major church split (Eastern church from Western) would begin to show the cracks in the foundation. With increased power came increased corruption that finally broke open with the Avignon Papacy, also called Babylonian Captivity, which led to the Great Schism where three different men were supposedly the one leader of the Western Church.

This crisis time-period brought out new reformers like Peter Waldo, John Wycliff and Jan Hus. All men left a spirit of reform in their respective areas, calling the church back to its simple beginnings. All three men were killed or imprisoned, and The Church heavily persecuted their followers.

Thus, in the early 1500s, Martin Luther standing on the foundation of Wycliff and Hus, called for change. The Protestant Reformation began from his preaching and writing; sadly, the end result was again division, not love and unity. Worse, within 12 years of the famous *95 Theses* (posted in 1519), Luther would split with the other leading reformer, Ulrich Zwingli over a point of theology dealing with the Communion. Thus, even though the split with the official Church seemed unsalvageable, the reformers could have led the way in calling for a return to the Bible, to simplicity of the community based on love and unity. Yet, sadly, they could not maintain a unified front.

Within 50 years, the Western church had 6 major divisions (Catholic, Lutheran, Zwinglism, Anabaptist, Calvinism, & Anglican). From that moment of breaking faith at the meeting with Zwingli, the Christian church has today, by some estimates, over 30,000 denominations (I have read about counts of higher numbers, though I don't know how that could be possible; 30,000 seems crazy-large on its own). Even if a more conservative number is used, the number is certainly more than 500, which is a long way from what Jesus prayed for.

The point of this very quick look at Church history is to see that the church was attacked and challenged at this very point of the simple command of Jesus and his prayer. So, today, we come full circle. Our hearts are not to complicate things, but move resolutely back towards a more simple (not simplistic) view. Rather than focusing on lots of various "activities" or "programs," why don't we just try to do the very clear thing that Jesus asked of us?

Theology of Community, pt 9

In the time that I've been speaking about this issue of the mission of the church, one consistent complaint has been uttered by the critics. The objection centers in the fact that I have, apparently, undervalued the notion of evangelism. For years, in many denominations and churches, one verse has taken center stage as the supposed mission of the church. Indeed, its been given a title, The Great Commission.

Of course that title is no where in the Bible itself, but over the years, the words of Jesus in Matthew 28:18-20 have stood as a good starting place for a Christian, or, as the thinking goes, for a church. So, by claiming that the mission of the church is something internal (love and unity), the argument is that I have blown off Jesus' last words.

Let me be clear—connecting people to God is at the heart of what Numinous, Inc means and strives for. While we may not use the churchy theological word of evangelism, that idea is an important issue for us. We just don't see eye to eye on the point of Jesus words.

For me, Jesus' words (and similar commands in Acts 1:8) are binding upon each and every Christian. It is our task to clearly tell others about God and his path to life through Jesus. So, where's the rub?

In our view, that mission belongs exclusively to the individual Christian. Yes, the Bible is written to all people and as such, one can claim that every verse is "for the church." But we also saw that some verses were aimed quite intentionally towards the group and others were not. I can do Matthew 28:18-20 on my own and, the thrust is, I MUST do it even if no one else does. I CANNOT do John 13:34-35 on my own (love one another); the sheer wording demands another person to do this correctly.

Thus, as we look at it, God gives each individual Christian a mission to accomplish. This is, to us, the point of the famous verses in the Sermon on the Mount in Matthew 5—we are the salt and light. Each of us. Individually. Where I live and breath, my work or neighborhood. I must be salt and light there, even if I am the only Christian.

Paul says much the same thing in II Corinthians 5—we are on mission as God's representative. Each of us. Individually. Where I live and breath, my work or neighborhood. I must represent God there even if I am the only one.

When the church takes over the individual mission, what we have seen happen is that people simply quit doing their work. If questioned, typically the answer is "my church does missions" or "my pastor does evangelistic visiting." Pitiful, but understandable. If what "I" see in my church is that the church as an organization does the work and all they want from me is my money and possibly a tiny bit of time, then "what exactly am I supposed to be doing?" Why "waste time" trying to do it myself?

This is a huge point! And when you see the connection between the individual mission and the collective mission, it all starts to make sense. For that you'll have to read the next installment, but note we must get this right. We need an army of passionate believers who are out there in the world being salt and light, leading people to Jesus, baptizing and discipling, going into all the world. If we don't have that, the church dies.

Hmm, since our whole premise is that the church is very messed up, confused or simply wrong, perhaps this is why.

Theology of Community, pt 10

Last issue, I said this: "We need an army of passionate believers who are out there in the world being salt and light, leading people to Jesus, baptizing and discipling, going into all the world. If we don't have that, the church dies." Yet, how do we go here? Obviously what has been tried (guilt, programs, more guilt, money, and a few dedicated people) has simply not worked.

Not only are more people clearly not saved (reference more of George Barna's work, www.barna.org) as evidenced by their actions, but churches are more dead than ever. It was Ezekiel who prophesied about the glory of the Lord departing the Temple before the Babylonian destruction. Could that same idea be present in the church of America?

We all want to see our friends get saved, that is clear. We all seem to want a strong moral country. We want our churches to be strong and healthy, what Jesus wants. So, what is the problem?

That issue emerges when we get the two missions confused. We've spent the past 9 issues of *Numinous n-print* building the case for a theology of community. Or, to say it another way, we've been showing what we believe to be how the Bible expects church to operate. What we saw back in part 5 was that the church, the collected body of believers, has a specific mission and its not the so-called "Great Commission."

Then last time, part 9, we saw that each Christian has their own mission. This is where Matthew 28:18-20 and Acts 1:8 come in. As long as we keep the two goals in their proper order and setting, God's plan works out fine.

Jesus showed us this when he gave the church its mission. As we saw back in part 5, we turn to John for this part. In John 13-17 we observed Jesus last moments before the cross with his disciples, the embryonic church. There he lays out his dream, his goals, for the "called out ones." In chapter 13 he gave a brand new command to love one another as He had loved them (a step up from the "Golden Rule"—love as you love yourself—that rule is how Christians are to operate in the world, but this new command is exclusively for the church). Then in chapter 17 he prayed for one thing—that the body remain unified.

Now, don't miss the follow-up. With both ends of the church's mission, Jesus gives a promise. He said if we love one another as He loved us, "then the world will know you are my disciples." Later, with the prayer, he added this thought, that if we must remained unified so "the world will believe that you [God] have sent me [Jesus]."

When I share my faith with others in the world, typically the resistance comes from one of two areas---either they doubt the message about Jesus or they attack the consistency of the disciples. There may be a few other areas skeptics go to, but these two areas—validity of the message or messengers—are the key attack.

So what does Jesus do? He provides the answer already through the body. Do you get it? If the church would simply do its job, complete its mission to love one another and be unified (and remember, THAT IS IT!!!), then as Christians pursue the individual mission of being salt and light, their efforts are supported. The two key questions of non-believers get answered.

It is an amazing fact to grasp. Far too many churches usurp the mission of the individual all the while failing to do their own mission (honestly, we all know several churches were there is little love or unity). In that failure, the very thing they want to accomplish (evangelism) gets thwarted. We must get this. You must force your churches to focus on their God-given mission. Those churches must support the individual believers being salt and light, their God-given mission.

If we will just do that, we will impact the world in a way not seen in many, many centuries. Will you do it? Will you join the revolution?

Theology of Community, pt 11

So, where do we go from here? To be clear, one option simply would be to follow the millions of other Americans who just quit church altogether, hoping that God will be cool with that. Last week I had the following exchange with a missionary who is soon to return to the US: "I would love to come hang out with [Numinous]. . .I am nervous about coming back to the "American Christian Culture" if you know what I mean. So I would love to see if I could get more involved with you all."

I replied that I knew what she meant, that to my peers in the faith, many who have known him over the past 10 years, "I am like a lost, black sheep. While I once had many connections with the "ACC," I no longer do." The reason why, I told her, was "Numinous is so "out of the box" in our functional theology."

What does that mean? It means that we've taken what I call the "Acts Gamble." We are willing to gamble on our "success" (or the American version of Church success") by doing church the way of community.

For the past 2 years, we have taken space here and online to explain the Biblical concept of community and what it means for the church. After 10 years of ministry with Numinous, it is still my firm belief that there simply is no other choice for Christians looking for Biblical Church. In these pages I've shown you how this concept of community is the expression of Jesus command the embryonic church. And we've demonstrated how important the role of the group, the community, is to fulfilling the individual mission of sharing the faith, being salt and light.

Now we face the critical question. Will you work to make this a reality where you are? Will you demand your church return to a Biblical expression of life for the called out ones? Or, will you merely snuggle deeper in your safe, tame church that really is nothing more than the Christian mall?

Will you join the revolution?

The need for revolutionaries within the church, FOR the church, is greater today than in any time in the past 300 years. There isn't space this time to really flesh that out, but it is clear that the years ahead of us are tumultuous. In those times, only real communities of faith, where people have invested deeply, are known and know one another, will make it through.

There is a telling story in II Kings 20 where King Hezekiah had made the poor decision to show the nation's wealth to envoys from Babylon. The prophet Isaiah came to him and upon hearing this news, told the King that due to his shortsightedness, God would allow the Babylonians to return in future days and destroy the nation. Worse, some of his own descendents would be taken into captivity and have horrible things done to them.

The King's reply is shocking and yet typical of the shortsightedness so often seen in America today in her churches and in her leadership. King Hezekiah said "at least there will be peace and security during my lifetime."

Realize this is the same king who had withstood the siege of Jerusalem by Assyrian King Sennacherib and had also been miraculously healed by God. Yet, rather than immediately throwing himself on the mercy of God for his descendants and his nation, he merely took the road of appeasement and immediate self-gratification. He had no concern for the future, only for his own satisfaction, his own sense of ease.

We must return to Biblical one-anothering, to real community, to churches that are not known for their size or for their program offerings, but are known for their love for one another. Future generations are counting on us. Now is the time.

are you ready?

On Mission 507Confident

A Chronological Journey in the life of Numinous, Inc.

Theological Emails from Carl
2000 - 2012

by

Carl E Creasman Jr.

are you ready?

Part I

Several years ago, perhaps back as far as 2005, one of the group asked me to publish several emails that I had sent. One of our more creative people, Vernon Schmidt, had started calling me the "Eyebrow Ring Bearer" in a sly nod to my favorite book, The Lord of the Rings *as well as the fact that I had gotten my eyebrow pierced early in the life of Numinous (a somewhat rare, and perhaps controversial move in the life of a spiritual leader). Vernon often would announce my longer emails with a "The Eyebrow Ring Bearer Speaks" kind of statement; later he used that analogy in his storytelling creation about "Numinaria"—his take on our collective spiritual existence. In any case, that desired collection of emails never saw the light of day, but as 2012 came and I felt a strong push to put these many writings into the hands of not only those who are a part of Numinous, but others who are interested in what I think, I began to collect those writings.*

To start, though, I wanted to share one more summation of my theology for the church written in late 2011. This shortest rendering of my theology about church emerged as I dealt with major questions in the body, brought on by the loss of two of our more core members. That development, quite naturally, shook the church and led us on a yearlong journey of investigation, study and discussion about the entire purpose of Numinous.

In retrospect, I had sensed the development of these questions, perhaps a challenge to our purpose or maybe a concern that we had lost our way, as far back as late 2007. Then, with the onset of our national financial crisis in 2008, Numinous faced external and internal challenges; the financial strains within our families brought community strains as different people chose to stop being on the journey with us. This first email, then, is a written response to one of our group, a leader for sure, who was asking for clarification about how we were applying our theology. I used that question as an opportunity to write the following summary of our theology.

Theology recap in 2011

The entire thrust of the Bible's call to the ecclesia (the term I will try to use the rest of the way rather than "church" because it IS what the Bible calls it), the call to "those called out" is to be in such an intimate relationship that it is binding, intimate (like sexually), deep. I know your business; you know mine. As I write in a chapter from my book about Numinous (written with Gaz years ago [the first writing in this large compilation]), our culture has lost this concept. Fifty+ years ago, no one would have thought what we ask of each other as strange, and few, if any, people would cavalierly just leave their ecclesia.

Alright, where to start.

1. The Bible gives a lot less about how the ecclesia is to act or be than most would wish. This is important—if there isn't a lot in there, then what do we do? Good question. That was where I started years ago. I have only taken our focus as a group based off of my search for "what does the Bible say, if anything, about a collective group of Christians."
    Remember my journey---if it were up to me, we would not have a collective point—I would just go to work, I would have some Christian friends from whatever spot (from work, from the neighborhood, etc....) and I would mind my own business. When Christians gather in groups, typically it becomes painful [like now, due to your choices, and for you because of something that others have done to you] and they make a big ol' mess and it's no fun (both my experience and supported by history). So, when I started this journey back in the mid-90s, I didn't WANT to find any support for the ecclesia.
2. But, in the term, is the clue. We are "the called out ones," so what I need to examine in the Bible is not every place the word "church" is, though that is useful. Again, as I have told you before, DO NOT TAKE MY WORD FOR IT, but go and search on your own. So, when I want to see what the Bible

says, if anything, to the collected group, then I go looking for all of the places where the focus shifts from "me" to "us." Thus, when I read in the Bible places that Jesus or others talk to the group, I can assume that those words and ideas do play a role in my understanding what we are to do.

3. There is a lot more in the *"Baptist Faith and Message"* or John Calvin's *Institutes* or the handbook of the Methodists or the Catholic *Book of Common Prayer*, than there is in the Bible. The Bible gives only a little. BUT, it does give some. And, for Jesus, the some while little is critical---first we see that the collected believers must stand on the confession that Peter gives (first place Jesus talks about ecclesia, I believe). You can find this at Matthew 16:13-20, with v. 18 specifically mentioning the ecclesia.

4. Next, we see that Jesus was concerned about their collected journey together after He would leave them, so we see the whole new command thing (John 13-17; John 13:34). Again, please note, I would PREFER to decide that Jesus was kidding, that it wasn't called a "new command" and that really He meant to just love everyone. But, with study, anyone can see that He had already said that—that everyone is to love everyone else—the Golden Rule. So, what's the point of this statement in John if not to raise the stakes for the believers, that they had to go beyond loving just as they love themselves (the rule for everyone) but love one another deeper, as Jesus loved?

5. As you know, that then connects to the unity prayer point (John 17:20-21)---he didn't pray for us to have better Bible studies, more success with teenagers, a special children's choir ministry, or even better 24 hour prayer rooms---all valid and useful things to do. He prayed for our unity.

6. The ecclesia has historically been understood on two levels: the universal (or often called "invisible") and the local (or "visible"). These terms are not in the Bible, but do match clearly what the New Testament shows us. Certainly, we are part of the ecclesia along with everyone who holds to

the same confession as Peter. There is a call for us to extend that "Platinum Rule" level of love to anyone who claims His name, so when I meet for prayer with Christians on my College, I need to love them the same way I love you. And I need to work towards our mutual unity. We are part of the invisible church, and where "two or more are gathered," so is Christ. YET, the teaching of the Bible, and the natural application of the rest of the New Testament, is that things happen on a local, gathered, level. Of course, before the Reformation, we had an easier time, not only because there weren't different denominations but also because cities were small. The largest cities would typically have less people that Altamonte or Winter Park. But, even then, the Catholic Church understood that the "city church" would really be split into parishes and there was a clear understanding that an individual Christian would be a "part" of that smaller, local, visible body of Christ. There would have been no understanding of someone deciding that they could just leave and either float, or go join some other body.

So, there is what Jesus said—you know, just on that ALONE, we could state that when your communal group asks for certain meetings, the call to love one another and the prayer for unity would bind us.

BUT, there is more. As I have said it, in real time, Jesus' words were merely theory. It wasn't till he left that we would see what the ecclesia actually did or does. So, we turn to Acts to pick up the story after Jesus left.

1. Acts 2:42-47 shows the local ecclesia in all its glory. We see what they did (devoted themselves to the apostles' teaching, to koinania [a deep intimate level of community equal to the idea of a marriage—one of the experts I look to for a better understanding of Greek words said "a favorite expression for the marital relationship as the most intimate between human beings"--wow!!], to the Breaking of Bread

(some experts see this as only the Lord's supper, hence worship, while others see it as the Lord's Supper [hence worship] AS WELL AS normal meals in houses), and to prayer. But that's not all—let me list it all that the early ecclesia did and was devoted to (key word there)

- apostle's teaching
- koinania (relationship like the marriage state)
- breaking of bread (worship, with perhaps also normal meals in homes)
- prayer
- meeting together in one place (so a large gathering meeting—they had over 3000 members)
- sharing everything they had
- selling their possessions for others
- sharing the money made with others in need within the ecclesia (maybe shared with outsiders too, though the force of the phrase and context of Luke's writing here does imply only within the ecclesia)
- worshipped at the Temple EVERY DAY
- met in homes for dinners (again, "EVERY DAY" is implied in the Greek)
- shared the meals with great joy (as like when Kim and I shared our recent meal with you, hoping to do another 48-72 hours later)
- praised God "all the while" -- for those who dislike praise and worship, this verse really nails it how the early ecclesia handles it

That's a pretty impressive list, is it not? Now, obviously, one could argue that the above would also be true for the universal, or invisible, church, but really, could we honestly admit that we could or would do everything on the list for random people who just happen to be Christians (the universal church)? Luke was describing the local church in Jerusalem—sure, it was the only ecclesia at that time, but it still was a localized group of believers. It was our example for any and every ecclesia where it meets locally---it is really only locally that I can do the things listed above.

2. They were together every day. Here is the one place you could nail us, but I doubt you will because of the implication. We are NOT together every day. Rather, we ask for 3 hours, on two different days. Add in driving time and you get 5 hours. That is five hours out of 168 over a 7-day period. Are we guilty of asking too much, or too little?

3. They were devoted. OK, the Greek here is a really long word, *proskartero,* which means to "continuing steadfastly" or "to adhere to, persist in, attach oneself to, be faithful to someone, hold fast to, continue in" and of course "be devoted to."

3. Digging into the rest of the New Testament leads us to the rest of the "one another" commands. I won't bore you with the entire list, but I have attached it for you. Please look at it. Again, we can affirm the idea that much of this list does connect me to the universal invisible church. No one has EVER said that they didn't. I have NEVER said, nor has anyone else speaking for Numinous, ever said that if one of us tried to do any of the one another commands with a person outside of our church, that the Numinous person would be wrong or evil! But, as with the Acts passages, the thrust of the other "one another commands" rest on the concept of intimate relationship. As I have said before, no one would accept admonishment or even exhortation from a stranger. When Paul talks of excommunicating someone, kicking them out of the body (I Cor 5), he does not tell the Corinthian ecclesia to do so to a person from Ephesus! The level of one another gathering DEMANDS the local, visible church.

So you were asking for the theology about "invasive community." Well, I have given it to you. Yes, it is a term I made up as a broad explanation of the above, believing that people didn't want to sit for 15-30 minutes hearing me repeat all of that. But, it is not in the Bible, so maybe I need to say all of that again and again---the Bible's call for ecclesia is like a marriage, it is intimate at the deepest levels and it requires "all the time" and "every day" expression. It is on that last point that we fail, though you would be even MORE unhappy if we tried to do it every day and all the time.

But, before we go deeper, let me restate this. No one has ever officially said that someone spending time with others [outside of Numinous] is bad. What has been said or at least suggested is that if someone who claims to be a part of our body does not spend time with us, then regardless of what other time they spend with other Christians, they clearly are not being devoted to us (remember, the idea of deep intimacy, like in a marriage). It has never been "us or them" but it has always been "us and them." What happens though for many is that they want to have it as "my close friends, AND then you guys when it's convenient for me."

At almost every instance of this kind of complaint, the person upset cannot point to a time when they were told, "you can't hang with those friends of yours." (Ok, some might have been told that in reference to not hanging with a person that the Numinous person was committed a sin, such as having sex out of wedlock, getting drunk, doing drugs). What they are told or urged or admonished is **about choosing to spend time with the "other" during the 5 hours we ask for each week.** That is five hours out of 168. What you are told or exhorted about is to find some other time in the remaining 163 hours. You work 40 (usually), so that leaves 123 hours. You probably sleep 8 hours, so that's another 56, leaving 67 hours unaccounted for. That is about 2.5 days of time in which someone can spend as much time as they wish with whomever. Again, if Numinous is out of balance, then it is **BECAUSE WE ASK FOR TOO LITTLE!!!** But I don't think we ask for too little, or too much. I think its just right, though I have always been open to figuring out a way to squeeze the 3-5 hours into 1 meeting on one day; so far no one has really had a good idea for that (or they've never told me).

But, we would NEVER dream of saying that, for instance, someone is wrong for going to a family gathering over the July 4th weekend. In my own life, I have missed Bliss or fluid to speak for God, to work, for funerals, for weddings and for family gatherings. If everyone remembers well the rest of our theology, we WANT YOU TO SPEND TIME WITH OTHERS. How else will people know about God's great love?

I don't think I've left anything out....wait, yes I did. How are we so bound? Meaning, on what do I have the ability to admonish anyone on this issue of obeying the clear commands of Jesus? It is supported by Jesus' statement back in John's Gospel that A) a Christian must remain in Jesus (John 15:1-8), AND B) a Christian is one who obeys his commands (John 14:15, 14:23-24, 15:9-10).

Ok, so there, I think I've covered everything. I'm sorry it doesn't match what you want, but you, like I had to do 10-15 years ago, have to bend your own will to God's. The theology of the Bible is NOT Numinous' alone; it is God's theology, His plan.

PART TWO:

Let me back up a tiny bit first, though, to make sure we see the context. As I hope you remember, my entire purpose as I see God's calling on me is to be a small part in changing the world. I have believed that God called me to participate as a communicator for him to help the lost world see Him and come into right relationship with him.

So, my drive, my passion, is to share the real Jesus with the lost world. Along the way, though, what I kept bumping into was the fact that so many Americans believe that they are saved, when it is clear that how they live their lives does NOT match what the Bible says. Worse, you see this most clearly in the church, with "church people" saying one thing with their words and actions on Sunday and something else the other days. And some even act horrible on Sunday: greedy, prideful, arrogant, arguing over things that are pointless...all the while the lost world around them was dying (and many of them in the church pews being just as lost). It is that "church" that angered Crystal so much; it angers, frustrates and saddens almost everyone who is Numinous, by the way.

As God started pushing and prodding to the point that Numinous went from being my ministry to being His church (where I was just His apostolic voice, working with other elder leaders, working to bring others into their own works of ministry (Eph 4) like you and Crystal), I knew that He was hoping to have us build a model. Or, at the very least, it was my intent that if He was going to force me to do this (remember, I didn't want to do this; it is God's church, not Carl's), then I was determined to start over from scratch. Forget everything I had ever read or heard or seen about church and start from ground zero.

That journey, that theology, I laid out in yesterday's email, so I won't reiterate. But, note, my focus and my hunger HAD NEVER changed. Just so you can see it, here's my mission statement that I wrote in early 1998: *"My mission is to know and glorify God and to be known by Him and through that relationship, communicate His love for others in a relevant, thought-full, and thought-provoking way in my speaking, my music, and my writing."* Later that year, I wrote this about my new venture (Numinous): *"Numinous' vision is simple: to change the world--one person at a time, innovatively impacting culture. We want to see the day when all types of people will connect with the Eternal One, the One True God."*

In 2000, to coincide with some deeper insights as to what God was doing in Numinous, I tweaked that vision statement about Numinous to say this: *"Numinous exists to provide relevant ministry to a post-modern generation, seeking to introduce real people with real issues to a real God who wants to have a real relationship with them."*

I show you all of that to set the stage for this "Part Two" of the theology, and hopefully give you even more insight (or it should be a reminder) as to WHY I push community, why I press people to value it so deeply that grief is a word I use about it. The entire point of what we (Kim & myself, joined early by D and Matthew) were doing was trying to reach lost people, the least and the lonely, for God!

This dream is the "Revolution" that I constantly talk about. To me, the options are join the status quo or be a part of a revolution. There is the status quo seen in many churches around the USA, and the Western world, where church is like the mall or worse, the Christian gated community, a closed set where people could pretend to be holy. All the while, both inside and outside of the church, people were dying and going to hell. Or, there is the revolution, raging against that status quo, going to confront that thing and be a part of bringing a revolution: a revolution about who God was, what Jesus wanted, how deeply they love. A revolution about the church, what the purpose was. As I said at our first fluids, "this isn't a game, this isn't church as usual."

Recently, Kim, the girls and I, saw the *Lord of the Rings* trilogy again. At the end of *The Return of the King*, there is the tremendous moment when Aragorn has led 7000 soldiers to the lands of Mordor, to the Black Gate. After an initial verbal discussion, Sauron, the evil one, released his army. Tolkien wrote that the numbers were "ten times and more than then times their match would ring them in a sea of enemies." So, over 70,000 of the enemy surrounded the 7000. In the movie, Aragorn looks back at his friends, knowing that they should soon all be dead, but believing that "Greater is He that is in me than he that is in the world," and says boldly, "for Frodo" and begins to run AT THE ENEMY.

This is how I perceive the journey that God has had me on. Maybe it is too grandiose to suppose, but I feel that way. I am sent like Aragorn, to die if necessary, to rescue any and all that I can, with

Numinous, marching against the black gate of the enemy. Though surrounded by ten times our number, or more, rather than quailing in fear, we march boldly toward them. Numinous is launching a revolution, to participate in rescuing the perishing, to be a safe place to build up the faithful as the body of Christ, the family of God!

OK, so now with that context, let me go back to the theology. Some would say, "well Carl, if your entire focus is helping people meet God, get saved, then why isn't the mission of the church the famous 'Great Commission' verses?" That's a fair question. Matthew 28:18-20 says "Jesus came and told his disciples, "I have been given complete authority in heaven and on earth. Therefore, go and make disciples of all the nations, baptizing them in the name of the Father and the Son and the Holy Spirit. Teach these new disciples to obey all the commands I have given you. And be sure of this: I am with you always, even to the end of the age."" Luke tells much the same story in Acts 1:8, when Jesus says, "But when the Holy Spirit has come upon you, you will receive power and will tell people about me everywhere -- in Jerusalem, throughout Judea, in Samaria, and to the ends of the earth."

I agree with the theologians that those verses indeed give a mission to each believer. But, that is the issue---those are mission statements to each individual Christian. It is not a "one another" command to the collected group. Instead, each Christian can and must do this, regardless of what another Christian does.

Now, then, back to community.

1.   We have already seen that there is a collected mission given to the ecclesia—love one another AND be unified.
2.   Individual Christians also have a mission, to go share Jesus with others. Other verses that support this mission include Matthew 5:13-16 and II Corinthians 5:17-20.
3.   Obviously, though, the current USA/Western church has failed

miserably on this, though not without trying. For many churches, this issue of "evangelism" is all they ever do or talk about, yet as we have talked about, clearly the church in America and the West is failing terribly. Why?

4.   Look back at the "new command" that Jesus gave us in John 13:34-35: "So now I am giving you a new commandment: Love each other. Just as I have loved you, you should love each other. Your love for one another will prove to the world that you are my disciples." Do you see it? WHY are we to love one another? Not so that we each feel good about ourselves. Not so we'll have a "nice" church. Not so others will leave their church for ours. One reason only: "will prove to the world that you are my disciples." WOW.

5.   It gets better—look at the unity prayer—John 17:21 – "My prayer for all of them is that they will be one, just as you and I are one, Father -- that just as you are in me and I am in you, so they will be in us, and the world will believe you sent me." Again, why the prayer for unity—just so we won't experience betrayal, abandonment? So orphans can find a home? So others will agree that we are very nice and all seem to get along? But that is not the reason Jesus gives, instead He says one reason only: "the world will believe you [God] sent me [Jesus]." WOW.

Do you get it? As I said, my passion is to help people get saved, yet by 2000, it was clear that God was putting me into this position of leading a church. He even pushed me into with the Luke 5 verses that said "push out into deep water" so that we'll catch even more lost souls—"fishers of men." So, here I am in this 1997-2000 period doing research on what God wants for his church. If I am going to have to lead one, then I want it to be a model to others. I want to do it the right way.

To my surprise, for I HAD NEVER SEEN THIS, nor been taught it by someone in seminary or any other place. God had given the church a mission IN ORDER TO COMPLETE HIS DESIRE—that everyone come to be in right relationship with Himself. **The idea of community, love and unity, is to ENABLE EACH OF US TO TOUCH THE LOST, THE LEAST, AND THE LONELY.** I won't belabor the point here, but I did say this at the retreat. If you ever actually try to share Christ with others, they typically have two basic argument groups from which an outsider opposes believing in Jesus. Either, they argue, the message is flawed in some way, or, they argue, the person(s) making the discussion (if not you directly, then "the church" in collective) are wrong.

They will talk about how the church is broken, full of hypocrites, only there for the money, power, or is so sinful (priests with little boys, adultery, gossip, hatred towards gays, etc....). Or, if they can get past that, they'll talk about how the Bible isn't true, that many other gospels exist, that there are many paths to God and so forth.

God KNEW that would be their argument, so he wanted the church to provide the answer; but note, NOT an answer verbally, through intellectual argumentation, but through a living, breathing model. Our love for one another would prove that we indeed were disciples of Jesus. Our unity, especially unity among people who clearly were not of the same ilk, would prove that Jesus came from God.

This is why community matters so much! This is why I will push on simple things like attendance, whether attending an organized meeting like fluid or Bliss OR attending a non-organized meeting like going to a hockey game, helping someone move or sharing life through social events, even as simple as eating a meal together. We must build UP the community life. And, as we saw in the other email about our theology, perhaps our great sin is that we don't stress community ENOUGH!

But, the individual part is still critical. Why do you think I've spent the last 6 months pushing us on maturing spiritually, individually? Because of what I want to see happening—revolution, change, lost friends coming to Christ. Why do you think I spent a year pushing the 3r3 concept? Why do you think, then, I also push for people to connect with each other? The 3r3 or spiritual mature people reaching the lost WILL NOT HAPPEN without the love/unity collective. Can't you see why I am so passionate about this?

Look, for me, I also look at other national churches around the globe. My friend Bailey is always trying to encourage me that all is not lost and that the church universal is strong. I believe him. When you consider the Chinese church or the African church or the Korean church, the church in Islamic lands---they are strong. I don't know all of the reasons why, truly, but I have some inkling based on what Bailey and others have told me. In those places, the Christians are so aware that they must rely on each other, that they must be a true Christian community, fulfilling the one another commands. And, in all those places (except Korea), the ecclesia faces extreme persecution---you have to be serious to accept the faith knowing that you could easily be killed for the faith. Again, that completely plays into God's hands and ideas—you have to be deeply intimate with each other, sharing life, exhorting, admonishing, caring for one another—otherwise, the person who just "comes to visit," who shows up when its convenient for them— that person could turn the rest of us in and have us all killed.

Well, I know this is a lot, but like Aragorn, you are worth it. Deep things of God are not simplistic to be shared in only pithy statements. I pray that you will read to this point. My hope is that you remember that we've covered this ground before, and that you have agreed. You were at retreats when I have asked "are you with me?" You have said yes. I believed you. I think deep in your heart, you are still with me. You still agree, yet you've been wounded. Come meet with us. Let me help bring healing to you from this grievous wound.

But, if not, then go with the knowledge that our stress on community is not some random concept. It is what the Bible describes for the ecclesia. There isn't anything else in there, and I have looked and looked. Wherever you go next, that MUST be their focus too, if they are a true church. If they are a true church, then get ready for them also asking hard questions of one another.

Part Two

So, as stated, there have been prior requests for some of my thoughts, first shared in email, to be collected. These writings from "The Eyebrow Ring Bearer" have not been edited beyond mere grammatical work and appear in chronological order.

There are, not surprisingly, a lot of emails to choose from. Not only were their writings to the entire group, but many deeper theological emails to our leaders or to specific individuals. In most cases, I have only provided the group emails because it is too tricky to present emails to individuals without major editing and/or giving the context of their email.

What follows then, after the first few pages, is a chronological journey in the life of Numinous. Along the way, I believe you can see a strong pattern emerge of a consistent theme of my passion for community, for church, for God's plan for the body of Christ.

Remember, these are emails, so at times the verbiage or the grammar is tricky. I have only edited them enough to ensure clarity of thought.

A Consistent Call on Community
Emails from Carl to the body

June 7, 2000

Life is a complex deal. The longer I go through it the more I know that I just don't get it. Even those who seem to have it all, are still questioning beings wondering about the deal. Often they are still wanting for more to satiate the longing inside that can only be filled one way and by One Man. But then as he tells us in the Word, that coming of him is not as individualistic as the West has made it. We have made the God thing such a personal issue that "I don't need you" is our mantra. But in true Eastern family style, Jesus preached that He would only be found in a unity of love that comes from us together. Well, as more and more Americans reach for the brass ring, they get more and more isolated and alone. Then they become shells of what they could have been. Instead of prioritizing community ahead of everything else, it gets put further and further back, all in the name of getting ahead. And my experience is rarely do we actually use well the 2-3 hours that would have been given to community.

I know for me, what really matters is you, Matt, Kim, the girls, D, Jason some other friends--that is all that really matters. Together, with all of you, I find God and He works in me and makes me a better man. I am more and more convinced that such is the totality of life.

I guess what I am trying to say is that I want community with you over success in my chosen field of life. I mean, I don't really want to keep sweeping floors, but in the end, if somehow that is where I stayed for 10 years, would it not all be worthwhile as long as you and I got deeper and others got connected? I think it would. So often, instead of that image, we each make our choices in isolation (What is best for me, regardless of anyone else). **I long for the day that we are so connected as a group that decisions of life become**

180

common property. **To that end, something like fluid or Bliss, rather than being just this event that I come to, becomes the totality of my life because that is where my community is.** Of course, as we have said, our personal community is much wider than that with our other friends, the places that we work, etc... But the place that I am well known and share intimately through my life and struggles is this place.

June 19, 2000

We've talked about it, but I have not put a more specific time in front of you for this retreat idea. So here we go. The idea would be for us to spend time looking at scripture and other works that would help us understand more about being the church in the 21st century. We would also spend time sharing the vision of Numinous and how all of that relates. In the end, it would be a very spiritual as well as practical time together. More details will come out as we decide exactly when to meet.

Help me do this for us. Remember, "its an us thing." I need you!!

Without you, what is the point [of Numinous] other than "it's just a Carl thing" and who needs that.

Kim and I love you guys and are honored to walk with you in faith. The encouragement we need is knowing that this matters to you and that you have taken ownership. It's a vision of a church that works for our generation, done solely the Bible way, not the traditional way that has been in place for 400 years. We are doing it now!! Wow!! Be encouraged and get excited to get your friends connected, maybe for the first time ever, to a God that loves them. What a great time to change the world, when the world more and more has no idea what it really means to be a Christian, to be a part of the church. And as one of my spiritual heroes, John Maxwell, says, you will never accomplish our vision without a committed team beside you. God has given me this vision for us, but its not my vision, its God's and now its been released to you. Can you see it? Can you see your friends that you hang with, or live with or work with who have no connection with God, being intimately connected with Him? I can. And Numinous (Bliss, fluid and other parts that you don't even know about yet) through you as the minister of reconciliation is the vehicle. Pretty cool, huh?!?!

July 12, 2000

I feel this struggle [over my] desire for a more committed group of followers. If what we are doing is not a church, then why should I expect them to be more committed or give money. If what we are doing is not a church, then everything that I have believed about church is suspect or wrong.

I am returning to the issue of what makes a church successful. Is it only when you have a certain number? Or when everyone gets paid a certain amount? By all means, I want to get paid a good salary to meet my needs, but I think that becomes selfish and self-centered to think the success of the church is in that. And who is to say that you must be a certain size to be culture-impacting. Look at the power of one person in George Lucas or Steven Spielberg or Prince or Jordan. I'm not saying that we must aspire to that kind of life or power, but we can change the world and culture even from a small number.

But I can't keep doing what I am doing if they are not committed. And committed to what? At its heart, **committed to a life together as a community and that is a church by any other name.**

The dream was simply to touch my generation, to be one of those who is committed to taking God back to the people in any method possible to fulfill II Corinthians 5:11-6:2. That "evangelism" was at the heart. . . to see them connected to a church that makes sense.

Anyway, what makes the church "right" or "make sense" is striving for the simple version of church that is inherent in the Ancient Texts. I know that questions come out of this (how do you teach them if there are no classes, for instance), but I just feel like the church has become too institutional, too much focus internally on the business of church instead of externally on living life as a Christian, too structured. It seems as if that stuff just was not the issue of the early church. Maybe we got here due to church history, but the free-flowing stuff of the early church is just so appealing to me. That does not mean no commitment. It's kind of like **"Look, we aren't asking for 4 meetings a week, so the one or two that we set up ought to be easy to prioritize."**

September 11, 2000

Man, was God on fire tonight or what. Watching the 30+ of us moving in harmony and concert together in praise of Him to the dance that Kim taught us brought tears to my eyes. That is the body!!! It was so cool. If you missed tonight, we so sorely missed you.

God is moving in so many ways in our body. Be encouraged and get excited as lives are being touched through our ministry together. And remember, when I say our ministry together, I don't just mean our Sunday experience together but the literal expression of community that we express 24/7. I also know that things are happening because I am seeing opposition come our way on individual basis. Different ones of us are experiencing tough times, so be praying protection and support for one another. Everything from school issues to job issues to personal "at home" issues are surfacing. Lets face them together.

Keep being Salt and Light, touching people, impacting eternity. This is so thrilling to see. Next week we continue our overall series on "postmodern Christian living" and zoom into a new part of that entitled "Resource Management." Over the weeks to come, we will look at how does a Postmodern Christian live simply, really without going into debt or living in a box. We'll see the Godly principles of giving, sharing, and living well with our lives that honors and worships Him with our time and resources. Man, this is going to be cool.

March 1, 2001

Whatever each of you decides or I decide, know that our love for each other is deeper and stronger and will hold firm as long as we commit to each other. Please continue to value the commitment to one another. Don't grow weary of community and pull away into self and self's things.

I am more and more convinced that the enemy has attacked us there more than anything else. I think that many who have chosen not to come with us at this point are confronted by such an invasive love in community that they cannot handle it. And I think that level of community challenges each of us. In the end, will I choose community or self? That does not mean that you never have self issues or do things for yourself, but it means that the few (and never forget they are few on purpose) community gatherings we have do take a place of precedence in your life. You choose to join the community, so participate in that.

September 11, 2001

As I have been telling you, we are alive in a momentous time, unprecedented from over the past 500 years. The days we live in are perilous and should awaken us to the very real war that we are engaged in spiritually. And we should see from today how this war spills over into the physical world.

Pray. Pray for the survivors, the victims, the families. We will not know the total cost in lives for many days--it will be horrific. Consider giving blood this week.

Some of you, like Kim, may have had family in NYC. Her step-brother works in a building literally connected to the WTC by a walkway. Today, he was at his dentist, thank God. Kim's sister's brother works uptown. Her sister is somewhere in the city. You too probably know somewhere up there. Keep them all in your thoughts.

Again, though to some of you I may seem over the top or bombastic, we are alive in a time of crazy events. If you can not see the connection between your spiritual life and this horrific event, pray for eyes to see. My friends, its not going to get a lot better-- our need to live authentic lives of faith that can provide answers and hope. Be prepared for conversations of faith and spirituality over the coming days.

I was driving in my truck to an assignment, listening with an ever-growing anger at these attackers. And I was reminded by God that He is still in control. He is, my friends, He is.

February 19, 2002

Get ready for some next level stuff. We are taking it deeper, funner (yes, I know the correct stuff there, but that's so boring), and higher!! God is like all shiny and stuff. :) fluid, as good as it gets, is getting better so get ready to pay attention. Bring your friends so they don't miss out on all that God is up to.

I was reminded even more Monday night that my face and heart are set toward the lost of our generation in Orlando and will continue to move resolutely in that direction. Pray that I find the right path, for me and for Numinous.

And hey, in case you missed my big announcement two weeks back, we are taking a serious turn for some serious fun in our Numinous future. What the heck is the body gathered if not for fun? We've got some fun stuff planned, others are planning even more fun stuff, it's just fun to be alive with such a great group of friends. If you are reading this, and yet you are missing this fun, well drop the charade and come on back and hang with us and have some fun. If we have not seen you in a while, we miss you.

Remember, the spiritual life is a wild ride in a wilderness for hardy adventurers following a mysterious stranger, but a stranger the soul somehow knows (and a stranger who likes to rock, roll, laugh and play

May 11, 2002

God has been moving so powerfully at fluid over the past 4 weeks. I want to encourage you to be there. The elders met last night and we talked at length about fluid and what it means. A lot of prayer (and I mean a lot) has occurred by the elders, together and individually, in regard to fluid—what we do there, how it happens, our attitude, etc.... I wanted to share with you just that the elders are again calling us to dive deep into God via fluid. Statements were made of "gaining a stronger focus on God," "we've been experiencing the power of real worship," a call to "de-emphasize the social element and re-emphasize the vertical aspects," and I could go on. A phrase you are going to hear a lot over the next months comes from John Aedo who, with Chris K and D are heading up our planning for axiom in the Fall. It rang out last night and reverberated in connection with fluid and it is a cry of our hearts as elders FOR OURSELVES and for you as well.

"May God run wild in your soul!"

186

So, make your entire week roll around fluid, as it is a cry for worship, not for Numinous, it's a cry for God, not for a man, and it's a cry for the Spirit to touch us as only God can, not for religious ritual. All else pales in the light of that opportunity to actually touch the face of God.

August 26, 2002

WE ARE GOING SOMEWHERE WHERE FEW HAVE TROD AND THE TRAIL IS VERY COVERED OVER IN THE BRUSH. WE NEED EACH OTHER TO SHOUT OUT THE WARNINGS AND THE ENCOURAGEMENT!!! THAT IS WHY I BEG YOU TO USE THE EMAIL TO SING GOD'S PRAISE. OR FOR PRAYER NEEDS!

We are in the midst of a revolution fighting for the lives of our non-connected friends (even the ones that think they are connected, but their lives clearly display a lack of any evidence, or fruit).

are you ready?

October 2, 2002

I have heard and noticed certain things over these past weeks that concern me so I wanted to remind you of our purpose. I hope that I am clear about these things, but I forget that we all need to be reminded. Here it is in bullet points so as to not ramble around.

- The mission of our gathering is to be community; to love and be unified with each other.
- The strength of that lies in servanthood, service, esteeming others more highly than myself, selflessly giving others my time and energy. The "one another" commands specifically are done "for" each other and they cannot be accomplished alone.

- Servanthood is done in a manner that happens regardless of how you personally are feeling.
- Community IS NOT merely an acknowledgment that we are friends. There is intentional action directed toward one another. It is action that does not quit, even if I feel I am the only one doing it.
- That action IS NOT merely phone calls, emails, IM and personal house visits. It is those things, but I am not at liberty to make it ONLY that. As I said Sunday night, were it up to me, I'd probably never go to any group meetings. However, from Jesus' implications through the Acts all the way to Hebrews and the Revelation, there is a clear DEMAND for the corporate gathering. If you bail on that moment, the large group, then you bail on the teachings of the Word.
- Don't withdraw. If I let it, then community does die. In essence, as I start to sit on the sidelines and not participate, then I do find myself alone. Participation leads to relationship and thus to connection. It's not the other way around. True, it does loop—connection guarantees that I'll find participation in others with me.
- This is the hardest thing I've ever done!

Thus, in closing to you, I want to remind you to love on each other, to care for each other, to tend to the weary, to lift up the wounded. Carry one another's burdens. How can you carry another's burden if you don't know what that burden is and how can you know unless you spend time together? **Don't think this means neglecting your non-connected friends, it means taking them with you.**

Reach out in love to both the non-connected and the connected. You are one body. Should you choose to move on, then sadly you do so and our relationship changes. You are in another city or connection and giving your limited time to other people—it has to change. We remain part of the global body of Christ surely and that is wonderful; we can even remain casual friends. **But the depth of** relationship inherent in the teachings of the apostles cannot be accomplished by casual time or the occasional IM or email or even phone call.

Reach out to everyone, stay involved in their lives. We are on this journey not to change the world. We are on this journey because this is the true calling of the church. I will remain obedient to God's orders. You are hungry for the same. As we fight for this, fight through the pain and the opposition of our enemy, we are providing a healthy church that can literally change the world.

are you ready?

December 8, 2002

As I've been studying and praying, I felt that we needed to be reminded some of our purpose and reason for gathering. We are only under attack as God's people when we are actually close to the front lines or getting close to something our enemy wants to keep us from. When we started Numinous in general, the heart of Kim and myself and leaders like Matthew and D were all about helping our generation connect with God. Little has changed since 1998, nor indeed since 1984/85 when God first started moving me into spiritual leadership. We exist to be a gathering of believers, called out together, towards love and unity. Through that, in accordance with Jesus' own last commands to us, only to be accomplished through that love and unity, we are actively, individually, working on mission as God's representatives. (II Co 5, Matt 5, etc....).

Meaning, in the end, our hearts are about others hearing this wonderful news about God. We do that because our ultimate aim is to stand around the throne giving God glory. That is the #1 goal. And God wants us to do that, but He wants us to bring others with us. So he gave us individually that mission. And to accomplish that mission, he wants us to corporately demonstrate this crazy little thing called love and unity. We do that and He will work to help us accomplish the individual mission. Amazing!

So, I have 5 things I want you to start praying about and to plan on making part of your prayer on the 22nd. This is nothing more than a re-stating of some of the things we've taught and said for all these years now. This is not about bigger churches, more money or more fame. We will continue to decrease so that he will increase. We will go lower so He can be seen higher. This is about fulfilling the desires of our hearts. I want to see my disconnected friends see God and go to Him. I know you do too. So as we are fasting through the 22nd, calling on God to move, let's be praying and asking these hard questions about ourselves to see if perhaps we might be blocking what God really wants to do in and around us.

Apostolic Increase
(based on material from The Gift of the Apostle by David Cannistraci*)*

Increase comes from investment—pray for God to acknowledge the investment we are making individually and corporately. Ask "Am I truly investing my life, my time and my finances into ministry and the lives of the unconnected around me?"

Increase rises through faith—without faith, all we have is a lot of activity and noise. Pray for God to increase your faith in Him, His word and His promises. Ask "Do I really believe and am I willing to take further steps into the unknown in faith?"

Increase follows effort—pray for God to encourage you in your hard work. Ask "Am I working hard or just living my "normal life" with no concern for the hard work of the Christian life?"

Increase come through synergy—pray for God to increase both our unity in the local gathering and the unity in the larger gathering. Ask "Am I really seeking to be unified with those I am journeying with or am I content to fly solo even though I know that is the way of death?"

Increase is a reward for obedience—pray for God to sustain your obedience, especially in the face of trials and tribulation. Ask "Do I obey God's word, both the written word and the word brought forth to me by his communicators?"

January 2, 2003

Way back in the Spring, I called the body to demonstrate your love for each other, to pray specifically with another, preferably weekly, and to pray for your lost friends, leading to action on your part in helping them get connected. At the retreat in July, I reminded you of these things:

1. We need to be doing the things He has clearly told us to do. (James 4:13-17; Joshua 1:16-17a)
2. We are to desire to grow in Christ and through that reconcile our world to Him (Eph 4:1; II Co 5)
3. As the body, we are commanded to love and be unified (John 13 & 17)
4. We are committed to keeping it simple, not complicated.
5. We are committed to keeping in Biblical and not adding to that. There is no reason to try and add stuff to what the Bible says when we aren't doing the Bible part right yet.
6. We are committed to "letting it be what it becomes."
7. We are committed to being before doing.
8. Finally, in the only new thing on this list (yep, all that stuff was reminder of what God has led us to over the past 4 years), but not a totally new thing as it wraps up a lot of the above, especially #s 4-7, we are committed to what God said through the prophet Micah. I'll leave you with that.

I pray that you will continue to love God deeply and know that for all of you that we don't see often, know that we still love you and pray for you and all of us who are active together wish the best for you, including your physical connection.

In November, I called us to spend 5 minutes each day on the phone with another person from Numinous. Just 5 minutes, actually putting our beliefs into action ("be unified" -- point #3 above, point #1 in Jesus commands to the church).

In December, I called us to actually specifically be intentional about speaking to our non-connected friends about our God. It was and is to be your best Christmas present to them. See that as a gift you can give through the New Year.

Finally, December 29th, I gave a New Year's challenge and call: God is calling us to "live" in Philippians 2 for a while.   First, realize that Paul obviously thinks this is critical to their "success." He actually thinks that for all of the body and if you read his main letters to churches, you'll see unity mentioned over and over again— apparently Paul got the message Jesus was trying to communicate. Back yourself up to Chapter 1:27 to see his lead into the letter proper. He's been talking about his own trials and how he feels about it before that. In verse 27 he finally gets to it--"no matter what happens to me, live worthy." Man he says this statement over and over again in his letters, again reflecting only what Jesus has already said. And his lead point to living worthy? Being unified. Lastly, please note that Paul did not write this letter to this church (or the others) because they had it right, but because these things are a struggle for every human. Look at Chapter 4:2—this gathering had it's fights too—every church and group does—we are human. The real question is how are these barriers to unity handled. Continue, all of you (and me) to "fight" for unity. Look at 4:3—be the teammate and helper to unity that Paul calls upon to help others get over whatever differences they have. And if someone tries to "help" you get over yourself and help you submit to the other person, even to another person who actually hurt you, please let them.

April 9, 2003

However, the key [for personal spiritual growth] is not a meeting and the like, the key is internal in our hearts. I challenged everyone to study the Luke account of the "Travel Narrative." This is the section in Luke from 13:22 — 19:28. You should actually start in Luke 13:1. Just read a couple of chapters a day and be challenged as Jesus really begins to press home his message on his way to the critical week.

Today, I was again floored by 14:7-24. There, in two different stories (called pericopes [pear-ick-o-pees] in Biblical studies), Jesus challenges our natural bent to strive for personal honor. He demands that caring for the freaks and outsiders is part of being his children. Man, that is hard for me, even though I know I am a freak and weirdo. The problem is that I want to believe that I am the cool one. :) He goes on to tell another killer story that tremendously shoots holes in the idea that us saying that we know God--that we are Christians--is not enough. In fact, Luke's account already, in 13:24-30, demonstrates that Jesus teaches many will actually want to be Christians (gain access to "the door to heaven"), but they simply are not allowed in as God speaks those terrifying words "I do not know you." In the Message, it is written this way "You'll protest, "But we've known you all our lives! only to be interrupted with his abrupt "Your kind of knowing can hardly be called knowing. You don't know the first thing about me."

Chilling.

Back to Luke 14—Jesus is trying to drive home the point to me (and you?) that I must not walk around arrogant, but must be humble and "content to simply be myself." In doing so, I can find myself comfortable to invite "the misfits from the wrong side of the tracks" to dinner.

Prepare your heart!

July 17, 2003

I wanted to write and encourage you to the deep validity and need of our gathering time. This last 3 weeks of Bliss (my first attending since work so rudely interrupted that time) has been outstanding. I certainly have been at Bliss more or at least as long as anyone in the group. If anyone was thinking "I don't need to go, I know all of that stuff, all of those stories" well how wrong you would be. How sad for anyone to rise to that level of arrogance and isolation to think they know the deepest parts of one another. I can guarantee you that there are MANY stories in my life that no one knows, not even Kim. Yet I long for you to know me deeply and that comes through this interaction.

Oh, of course such knowing comes through many avenues— stamping parties, LAN parties, dinners together, crying together, "5 Minute phone calls" and the like. Make no mistake—Bliss (nor fluid) is NOT the "be all and end all" of being a Christian or being "in community" together.

There lies the rub for some—they want one or the other. Yet the Bible DEMANDS allegiance to the whole story—we are to gather together for the sole purpose of Bliss (fellowship/teaching) and fluid (worship/prayer/teaching). **AND** we are to gather daily in small groups of phone calls, IM'ing, email, lunches, dinners, helping with issues, dropping by, sharing dinners, etc.... Do these sound too many, too much, "I won't have time for my other friends?" Nonsense—God wants you to incorporate your other friends into this life. Do you think that the Good News you know of God's love, of his relationship, of his connection, is for you alone? Have you so

194

soon forgotten that You are God's representative and He wants you to use your new family, your new community TO connect your other friends. Not to exclude them, but to INCLUDE them.

Yet, how can you include them if you have forsaken the gathering of the community? And this is particularly true for anyone who has been here for a while. You (me) are particularly susceptible to the LIE of our enemy that "you don't need this." He'll whisper lies such as "you are too tired" or "you are too busy" or "they'll ask the same lame questions" or "you'll hear the same lame stories" or "you can connect at other times." Oh, he'll do anything to keep you from deeper connection. Then, when you are not watching, he will use YOU to poison the water. A newer person will hear you speak disparaging about the need for coming together intentionally and they'll think "well, if he/she doesn't need it, perhaps I don't too." Before long, we dwindle and separate to our own little lives and the power of our unity is broken. Again, having been there the longest, most tenure so to speak, I know that ONCE AGAIN at Bliss I heard new powerful stuff—stuff I could not hear anywhere else, not in that grouping.

Oh I could go on in my defense of God's glory. "God's glory," you ask? "I thought you were discussing Bliss." But I am dear ones. Our gathering is the representation of God's unity and through it, one of the key ways that we get to demonstrate truth to a disbelieving world. In that, we reflect God's glory. So, yes, I will vigorously defend God's glory and beg you to not forsake the gathering. Don't think too highly of yourself my friends. Oh, how can I humble myself more to get through to you? I know I am speaking crazy now, but if humiliating myself before you will remind you of your deep need for one another, both time spent during the week AND our unified gatherings, I will do it.

Perhaps Douglas Coupland, an erstwhile bard of our generation, says it best:

*My secret is that I need God—that I am sick and can no longer
make it alone. I need God to help me give, because I no longer
seem to be capable of giving; to help me be kind, as I no longer
seem capable of kindness; to help me love, as I seem beyond being
able to love.*
                   -- Life after God, p. 359.

Insert Bliss where he has God. Says the same thing. Insert "godly
relationships" where he says God. Says the same thing. Why?
Because that is the way God set it up. He wants relationship with
us. And then, through Him, he wants us to have radical, loving the
unlovely, caring for the least and the lonely (people the world
would say "reject") RELATIONSHIPS. And we get them in MANY
WAYS, but at the core, Biblically stated, is a unified gathering—we
do that at Bliss and fluid.

August 12, 2003

So, today I was reading I John 5 and was just overwhelmed with
God as I read and then even more so as I meditated on what was
there. While there are many thoughts in that chapter, the thing
that God kept bringing me back to was this thought: "I show or
prove that I truly love God by keeping what he commands of me."

So right there, I looked stunningly at the fact that his commands to
read his word and meditate are the proof of (or lack thereof) what I
say I am---a God lover. Thinking more, I realize that the opposite is
quite damning and must be confronted---if I refuse or simply DON'T
DO what God commands of me, then I DON'T REALLY LOVE GOD.
Jesus touched on this in many places too like John 8:47 where, in
the midst of being confronted and tested, he hammers the crowd
(a crowd he might need to keep him off the cross, I might add) by
saying this "anyone who claims their Father is God, that person
GLADLY LISTENS (obeys) the words of God." Wow—similar idea,
intent and fact.

196

I know that many of you may think that the commands of God are too numerous and too hard, but really they aren't (something John quickly adds in Chapter 5). Jesus boiled them down to two, yet even as we look throughout for the various commands of God, seeing them define those 2 commands of Jesus, we can see they aren't too much. I won't list them all here, but note that most of them deal with our relationship with each other (which, as an aside, John connects to our supposed love for God--"how can you say that you love God, who you have not seen with your eyes, when you hate (don't love) your brothers and sisters, who you have seen?").

So, when you blow off Bliss and fluid, you are in direct disobedience to God. When you don't encourage your brother in Christ, you are in direct disobedience to God. When you don't pray for each other, well, you get the point.

Does this sound hard? Are you thinking, "I thought being a Christian was easier than this?" If you are, then you are confused. When you have time, glance at John 6-8, look at Luke 9, especially verses 57-62. Jesus minces no words—NOTHING COMES BEFORE GOD and HIS MINISTRY. We Americans way too quickly put other stuff in front of God. Oh sure, at times, some things come up. You remember that I just had to miss 8 weeks of Bliss due to work. I chose to do that—no one made me. Perhaps I was very wrong. Yet, I thought it okay because I knew it had an end, a short time really that would come to an end. But those times in our lives when we DON'T do what we know to do should be FEW. It should be rare. Or, to say it another way, if when we show up at fluid or Bliss, our ONLY organized community times (in accordance with God's commands), people are surprised that I am there, rather than the other way around (surprised when I am absent), then that is a clear sign to me that I have gotten something out of place.

Let me be clear, in Jesus world (and do we live in any other?),

NOTHING comes before God or obedience to him---not family, not work, not death, not religion. Certainly we fail and we sin (I KNOW I DO), but it should never be our intent. When I willingly stay away, fail to call my brother, put an idol in front of God (Diablo, Buffy, guitar, religion????); slipping is one thing—willingly going there is another.

As I said at fluid and Bliss this past week, once again I had that honor of traveling the country for God—from Georgia to New Mexico. Once again I saw those desperate for him, yet unwilling to consider him due to the church. And again, I saw many who call on his name yet are desperate, sad, crushed due to the church, even as they lament and settle (THEIR WORDS) for the best church experience they can apparently find. And, in each face and in many voices, I heard a cry for what we have right here. I am amazed by that, and humbled. We have something that, unless they are liars, 100s of people I have met wish they had. Rejoice my brothers and sisters for God has blessed you with both the ministry of His through Numinous, Inc and through the relationship of Numinous the church. Rejoice and forsake not the gathering of the beloved, the called out. Rejoice and rush out to tell your friends around you.

I love you dearly and miss seeing many of your faces. I hope you are well. Email me and let's get together so I can rejoice in your presence, encouraging and being encouraged by you.

August 20, 2003

Hard to believe sometimes since I look around and I see you guys so deep already. :) But He seems to be desiring to take us even deeper—of course his longing is not so we are special, better than others, but that we are exactly how he desires all to be—pure in his sight.

I was reading Ezekiel 16 this AM and, whew, that is some tough

198

stuff there. Won't give you the blow by blow, but its basically God calling out his people, calling us sluts and whores for how we so quickly run away from him. In there, God reveals how hurt he gets when I sin, when I run after other things. And that he will punish and spank his children! Man, it is intense! Reminds me of what I read yesterday in John 15 how he once again commanded that I love each of you as He loves me. But here, unlike in John 13 where He first brings this up, he defines what he means---that I lay down my life for those that I love. As I meditated on that, it hit me that though I probably won't be asked to literally die for one of you, I am asked to die. In fact, the whole point of Jesus call (see Luke 9:23-27 or 14:26-27) is a call to death. Death of self, death of the old way, death of fleshly ambition. So, since I am dead already, there is nothing I can say "I won't do that" for one of you. This is a hard teaching because it cuts against the grain of everything we are taught as Americans. If you need me and I want to practice with my band---hey, I'm dead, I have no rights. If you want to borrow my truck and don't even ask ahead of time, just assuming it's okay and I won't need it---hey, I'm dead and I have no rights. You need some money or you need to talk to me or you just need to come over---hey I'm dead and I have no rights. Or, I'm tired and I don't want to come to Bliss—hey, I'm dead and I have no rights. On and on I could go and at every juncture, remember, this is not about just having to do something---this is about me PROVING TO JESUS that I REALLY do love you as he loves me. Because that proof shows up in my dying for you. He later, in John 15, states that love is also connected to obedience to him. So, this ties in to 1 John where he says the same thing and thus, back all the way to Ezekiel. If I claim to love God and yet I don't obey him (the one another commands, the spiritual disciplines, the way of truth), then not only am I a liar (I John) and I certainly DON'T love you (John 15), I am also a prostitute and worse than a prostitute, according to Ezekiel.

Wow!!

Makes me take a deep breath before I casually proclaim that I am a man after God's heart and then defiantly disobey him in one area or another.

I love you all and pray for you, particularly those of you who I don't get to see very often. I pray that, if you are local, you will be deep with another community of faith (since you obviously are not with us) and, if not, you will start to seriously consider what to re-arrange in your life so that you can begin to get back deeper with God.

Remember, don't accept the lie that says you and God are great while you are disobeying his commands. It is challenging I know, but no one ever said being a Christian was easy—in fact it is the hardest path to choose, according to Jesus---very narrow, very twisting, very hard, a way that many attempt but only few accomplish (seriously, read his words in the gospels—he says that very thing---don't accept the lie that says being a Christian is basically easy—say a few words, attend a few meetings, give a few dollars—WRONG). So, strap up, pony up and realize that what you awoke to in the real world was a cold hard floor of a ship, eating not necessarily the best gruel, but you were ALIVE and you had PURPOSE. It is only a lie of our enemy that says, "you should have taken the blue pill."

September 16, 2003

Wow—Bliss was incredible last night. If you missed, it was a sad time for us and you. We truly missed seeing your face. But more so was what Stephanie shared from Ezra. I won't steal her thunder, but her suggestion that we read Ezra is a good one. Her words to us were a call for us to move past "community only" to a "holy community." And, what she meant was one were we long for each other, where sin in one another causes us to cry like Ezra and where the loss of one person break us. And that is so powerful.

200

In fact, Greg just sent me a link to a research report that confirms what I've been saying---we need community and healthy deep relationships for good mental health. The study looks at children and reports that even though poverty in America has gone down over the past 30 year, mental health issues in children over that period (meaning, our generation to current kids) has skyrocketed. Why? Mostly because children (us and our peers) have been raised with only one parent, unhealthy parents and poor connections. It goes on to state that the need is not just for a good parent, but an "Authoritative Community" to undergird the development.

I pray that you will continue to beat back the thoughts that lie to you, that tell you staying away is a good option, that you are just too busy for this spiritual stuff, that we don't really like you or that we just want to control you. I pray that you fight every moment to keep your schedule free for that singular moment in time when you connect deeply in a holy community. It is Bliss that allows for the other connections that happen during the week. Without Bliss, I slowly move to where I only chat with those closest to me, those most like me—With Bliss I am forced to deal with a dude who sports an eyebrow ring or who is a geek or who likes music I hate. And that provides the foundation that Jesus was talking about and the early church went and lived out. I pray that you continue to move to the place where you are indignant that someone would suggest you miss Bliss; where you would refuse to work OT on Bliss night; where you would say to the in-laws "since you are here, come with me to Bliss" rather than staying home.

December 30, 2003

It's a brand new year—2004—and time marches on. If you've been travelling with us for a while, you know that God has taken us on the most remarkable journey. Heck, we weren't even supposed to "have" a church anyway, yet here we are 6 years later with our ministry still thriving, but thriving alongside a wonderful community of faith.

The upcoming months promise to be ones of a thrilling adventure. Certainly, in one aspect, the journey of life is mundane—get up for work/school, meals, pressure, routine, friends, TV, wash, rinse, repeat. The community thus is there to be partners in the journey as we go along; to keep us from being alone. The chief end of the creation of man is about relationship—to be known deeply and to know others deeply.

But in another aspect, the journey of life is anything BUT mundane. It is an adventure, fraught with peril and danger and wonders and battles and scars and victories. That is what we have been discussing at fluid and Bliss, and in reality, every day as we make the journey. I wanted to remind you of the overwhelming call from the Bible to cling tight to each other. At fluid, we've been looking at our "Hearts Alive." We will be picking up that story as January begins. I pray that you will find yourself there. At Bliss, we've been looking at more aspects of community, of how we do this thing together---none of us gets this fully and each of us is in a continual process of getting to know each other. I've been married to Kim for over 14 years now and there are still aspects of her that I am learning, so no one who is a part of our group can somehow feel like they've "heard all the stories before." And Bliss is on a special journey that will become even more clear over the months ahead.

In sending you this New Year's message, I want to leave you with something that I said at fluid back in November. It is a call to remind you that "things are not what they seem" and that "you are part of a wonderful, deep story." I'll see you soon.

> In the end, our lives are Frodo--We are hunted, yet we've been given a quest. We were minding our own business when someone, some great angelic spirit, arrives and tells us that the insignificant thing in our life actually is part of a

powerful story and that we are called upon to deal with it. SO, off we go, hunted by a great enemy who desires to destroy you.

In the end, each of us is Frodo. And yet, at the same time, each of us is a Sam, a faithful friend who will go the distance with the Frodo's of our lives. Or, we are Aragorn, a powerful friend who steps into the fray, not really part of the story (or is he?), but willing, with our sword and our life, to defend Frodo. Or, we are a Gandalf, a strong spiritual advisor. Maybe we are a Pippin or Merry, close friends, not as close as Sam, but still in there hanging with our Frodo friend. Perhaps we are just Farmer Magee, able to lend a happy meal and place of refuge for one night. In the end, though, we are all part of the tale of each of our lives--this speaks to the aspect of community again, the true and foundational calling of the gathered body.

We are part of a grand tale. Don't lose sight of it!

March 16, 2004

Over the past 15 months, I have been watching God move and prepare us for new steps, fresh changes. I started walking the elders into this change, and along the way, saw how many of you were already sensing something like this. These are EXCITING times for Numinous as we move beyond the familiar into the unknown. It's a great time of new things, new beginnings. Most of you weren't around in the exciting early days of Bliss and this is your time to re-create that special magic.

Last night as we looked at the facts of Acts 2 and noticed that we were eagerly involved in all those things in places obvious like fluid and Bliss and places not so obvious like meals at Lenny's, LAN parties and random phone calls, one piece of news came out. The early church had a clear sense of awe, of a "sense of something deeper, spiritual, electric, in the atmosphere." As John then remarked, "a numinous feeling." Nice! Well, I had not really thought about that aspect when I had studied Acts 2 and so was drawn to that comment. As I meditated while you guys did some leg work, I was reminded and struck by HOW OFTEN I have sensed that feeling at Bliss, fluid and in the chaos of life in which we are together. Man—what a huge testimony to God's hand on our endeavor.

And he will remain so with us as long as we stay focused on the core issues of what we are about. Today, I was doing some reading today and was struck profoundly by some stuff in a business magazine that Greg turned me onto. In an article about IMB, the author wrote this:

> During the years between [the old CEO and the new one], IBM lost sight of the key dynamic of an enduring great company; adherence to core values combined with a willingness to challenge and change everything except those core values---keeping clear the distinction between "what we stand for" [which should never change] and "how we do things" [which should never stop changing.

I think that sums up my heart on the matter of Bliss and indeed, church itself. And that is what I have been preaching, modeling, driving towards and dreaming of from day 1. It is what we are and, by golly, we will never forget that Numinous is Numinous. We do things differently and in keeping tightly with what really matters. We will change anything and everything except the core values (and if you are not sure what those are, please ask me and I will tell you again)!

Thus, to that end, as I announced last night, starting in April, **Bliss will move into three groups meeting in three locations.** There is obviously a ton of thought and prayer behind that concept (15 months) and perhaps there are still some pitfalls that we have not seen in the 15 months of prayer, but we know God has given us at least this next step.

During this time of prayer, I was struck by some simple concepts drawn from the Acts 2 info and the theology of the "chaos of life"—:

- Love and Unity were aggressively pursued; intimacy was chosen over isolation.
- Small groups are the place where real intimate community occurs.
- Unity occurred (continued) across large numbers (shared resources, and there is no picture that they had exclusive small groups where people did not know others).
- Church SHOULD see new people come to God, thus growth.
- Growth should be on a regular basis, but then growth becomes counter-productive in the life of small groups— (we meet small, have intimacy, real community, thus people know we are disciples/Jesus came from God, thus growth,-- uh oh, we aren't small anymore)
- Intimacy is NOT forced to happen in ORGANIZED settings. Or, community is MORE than just any organized meeting.

Of course there are dangers and fears. Trust me, God and I have wrestled with these concepts fearfully and fitfully. Kim and I and even many of you and I have conversed about these things (and you didn't even know I was listening with a deeper purpose to our chat). But I know God has led us here. As I said last night, the only other options are to NEVER grow (refuse to let new people in) or move to a huge new building (but then we fail at part of the Acts direction and we just simply reproduce the program-driven church that we've all left). Thus, those ideas have led me to these conclusions that will help us make this exciting move.

- *We need Bliss.*

- *Bliss is too big for one house.*
- *We must split Bliss.*

But what about our unity?

- *Unity is maintained in the "chaos of life" (the phone calls, fluid, dinners together, LAN parties, stamping parties, lunches, emails, Bible studies, TV watching parties, and on and on and on).*
- *Unity is maintained through a larger worship gathering (we will NOT split up from the command to worship together).*
- *Unity will be maintained by having intentional quarterly gatherings (like local parties—Christmas sock exchange, Easter party, Memorial Day, July 4th, Labor Day, Thanksgiving party, etc...). All of our traditional parties and gatherings will continue as ONE group—if there are too many of us to have the Labor Day party in one house, then we'll rent a boat dock, but we will be together.*

In the end, Intimacy occurs on at least 2 levels:

- *Intimacy, at one level, occurs in the chaos of life.*
- *Intimacy, at a deeper level, occurs in my Bliss group.*

Be excited. Look at this energy as an impetus to obey what Crystal was telling us at fluid 3 weeks ago—be passionate for others (a core concept of Bliss: a safe place for new people who are discovering God and re-discovering the church to find community, love and acceptance). Look at this energy of change as an impetus to obey what Kim told us also at fluid—be passionate for the body of Christ and see this as a chance for even deeper intimacy with a tighter group [remember all the relationship experts tell us that intimate small groups are best at less than 10 people]. Look at this energy of newness as an impetus to obey what Nick told us at fluid last Sunday---be passionate for serving others within the body and that such service is rarely contained at some organized meeting! Our unity, to be maintained, WILL occur mostly in the chaos of life.

Heck, for many of you on this list, I rarely get to see your face, yet you still want to be in our group by staying on this list; we are already striving for unity via the chaos of life. You should, also, see this as a great chance to step back into Bliss. Come find a new home and start fresh.

Finally, look at this energy of God stuff as a risky venture. All that Numinous has stood for could implode if we fail to do what we know the core concept is. And that concept of being Passionate for Risk Taking is exactly what John is going to be telling us at fluid this week! I urge you to be there!!

April 14, 2004

Not sure why God led me here, but I think we all need to see this too—was listening to a praise song yesterday that had in the chorus a bit about God loving a contrite spirit rather than sacrifice, so I went looking for it. I've loved that concept, but had forgotten where it was.

Jesus mentions something about this in Matthew 9:12-13. He's speaking to religious leaders who were being quite haughty and arrogant and had no desire to be around people of low position (They called them "scum" in my translation). Funny, as I'm typing this, I remember that we are talking about this very thing in Bliss! Amazing. And unplanned, I assure you. Or, unplanned by me. OK, so Jesus then says "Now go learn the meaning of this Scripture--'I want you to be merciful; I don't want your sacrifices.'" Boom.

OK, now that passage come from Hosea 6:6. The prophet is speaking for God who is calling Israel (and through Jesus, us as well), to repentance so "we can live in his presence." Though they are not being pure, being mean and ugly to one another and towards any that God sends, he says to them "I want you to be merciful; I don't want your sacrifices. I want you to know God;

that's more important than burnt offerings."

Micah says something similar, also in chapter 6, verse 6. There Micah reports that the people of God are asking what they should do "to make up for what we've done [the sin in our lives, how we have turned from God]?" And then they list the usual from humans—sacrifices of things, even to the point of listing "sacrifice our firstborn children to pay for the sins of our souls?" Wow! Pretty crazy. Remember how a lot of people want to paint the God of the Old Testament as somehow a mean God, a killer, a cold hearted law judge? Well, that type of God would probably say "yes" to that idea of sacrificing the children. And, if you think about the opposing gods of our day (consumerism, favoritism, MTV, malice, etc....) you see how that is exactly what they want and what people have done and are doing. But our God says (through Micah) "No, O people, the Lord has already told you what is good, and this is what he requires: to do what is right, to love mercy and to walk humbly with your God."

The Psalmist gets this clear enough in Psalm 51:14-17--"Forgive me. . . .You would not be pleased with sacrifices or I would bring them. If I brought you a burnt offering, you would not accept it. The sacrifice you want is a broken spirit. A broken and repentant heart, O God, you will not despise. (that's where the song chorus came from).

So, what does this all mean? Well, probably tons, but first off if we remember what we've started discussing in Bliss this month about "live in harmony with one another," we can see that to do so demands a humble spirit (as Peter and Paul both said). But to get there, we need to recognize that it does not take religious activity or sacrifice, but something internal in our spirit.

Second, as we deal with the various things of our day, our world, our lives and we find ourselves dealing with difficult situations, sometimes what is going on is the loving chastisement of God. No, we never want to go here for that means I've somehow messed up and as typical Americans, we hate to think that. But, rather than running from it (usually as we bitterly complain about our situation), we should quickly move to submission and again choose a contrite, humble spirit. And, again, its not sacrifice that He is demanding. It's not "come to more fluid services and that will make it all better."

Third, look at what the prophet Isaiah says for this is most cool. 57:15 and following--"The high and lofty one who inhabits eternity, the Holy One, says this: "I live in that high and holy place with those whose spirits are contrite and humble. I refresh the humble and give new courage to those with repentant hearts."

WOW!! Race all the way back to Jesus in Matthew. What is he saying there? If you want to be with me, you can't be religious snobby or arrogant. That is precisely what God says in Isaiah. And, we know that for now, the Holy Spirit (or God) resides where? Within us. So, he resides with those whose "spirits are contrite and humble." See it? As we move to be the kind of people that are commanded in the New Testament ("live in harmony with one another"--just one of 20+ commands about how to pull off love another and be unified), we find ourselves accomplishing the very thing that God wants (humility, contrition, mercy) so that we can live with Him. Not just later in Heaven, but today now.

Do you feel as if God is far from you? Do you feel cold about spiritual matters? Do you wonder why some hard things may be coming your way (and just so you know, I had to face one on Monday—one of my first questions was "why Lord" and I made sure that I was okay with him, not being punished or chastised—I wasn't , but I was being allowed to grow more into His image through a hard thing, a $$$ costly thing, a thing that we will demand sacrifice from me, something I personally won't like)?
    Well, if you find yourself with these thoughts, race quickly to your prayer spot and humble yourself before Him. Look for those of

"lowly position" or "scum" that you can be with, minister with or to and be merciful to. Look for ways to serve others, even if you feel as if you are the poorest or have nothing. Get your eyes off yourself and onto the very others that God loves. I promise, the more you do that, the more your own issues will grow strangely dim. As you demonstrate mercy, humility, contrition before your God and toward others, especially those that the world deems scum, or lowly, I promise you will notice something wonderful! You will discover that you are in the very present of The Holy One who lives in that high and holy place with those whose spirits are contrite and humble for He will not despise a broken and repentant spirit for He desires not sacrifice but mercy. I love you all. Have a great day!

April 17, 2004

We are at a wonderful, slightly critical junction of our ministry and existence. From here, we can continue to be on the journey that has touched all of your lives. In one manner or another, you were outside the church, perhaps cold to God, distant, wondering if the church had any relevance or concern in today's world and then you discovered Numinous. God brought you to Kim and me. It will be people like you who enable us to take the next step to helping others see this too. Or, the lack of leaders like you will condemn us to a slow death. OR worse, to a place were we end up looking like the very thing we set out to leave. :(In one manner or another, I've been praying for you while I've been praying about Numinous over these past 15 months. I've been working hard to understand God's steps for us and while I certainly do not have all the answers, I can promise you that we are staying very close to the One who does have the answers. And his steps for us are exciting. And to get there, leaders like you, people he rescued and brought to us, will continue to be the buzz leaders, continue to be the owners who see their own life in us. Heck, through us, some of you have seen how you can be an adult, continue your education, pursue a

210

new job, leave the bitterness of the past, find a mate, experience family and wholeness. You know that you are "alive" because of Numinous, so I know you are totally psyched to continue the journey, leading others to that same wholeness.

Never forget that I need you. Not only are you my friends, but also you are my partners, walking in this exciting experiment in changing the world. Thank you.

April 23, 2004

Remember what I've been telling you---there is more going on than it seems. No, we don't want to start thinking there is a demon behind every tree, but make no mistake, the enemy of the Lord will target his people as a way to get back at him. Jesus told us don't be surprised if the world hates you; it hated me first. As his servants and followers, of course we'll get the same stuff thrown our way!

And, it should be no surprise to anyone who has been around us long to see that we are doing things differently than the norm. Now work with me here---let's assume one of my basic concepts is right, that much of what is ill in the USA today falls solely at the feet of the church, its failure to actually do what the Bible asks for "church" (the called out ones) to be—in love with one another and unified with one another. Assume I am right there. Now look at Numinous—we are doing exactly the opposite of what the current church does and exactly (and only) what we see the Bible demanding of the "called out ones." Yes there are other really good ideas and programs that happen in the name of God (Sunday School, Precepts, Awanas, Upward Basketball, Christian Line Dancing—ok, maybe not that last one) and each of us can be involved in as many of those type of things as we wish. But as an organization, I have led us to be single minded and focused, as a group, on the core issue that Jesus laid out for us, as shown to us in Acts 2-7 and simplified in the word "COMMUNITY."

Now, all that being true, it is not too hard to see that those who are chasing after God, devoting themselves to him and His word and the very things he asks of us, specifically for the group, for the "one another," will find themselves front and center, in the crosshairs of the enemy.

So, stay vigilant and watchful as Paul urged us in Ephesians. As Peter said, our enemy prowls around looking for someone to devour. His intent, as stated by Jesus is simple, to kill, steal and destroy! Our defense is a simple one---pray, pray and pray some more. Pray in all manner and types of prayers.

June 27, 2004—email to elders and certain "other" leaders

I was reading my new favorite author, Seth Godin, who writes monthly for *Fast Company*. In his last article, he wrote about the power of what he calls "off-roading." The point was that to really succeed in business, often you need to be bold enough to take the "off-road," using your Hummer to make a new trail. About 5 years ago I used a similar image to describe our path. I said, "I feel like I'm in a long line of travelers on a well used path [traditional church] and yet I can tell it seems to be really ineffective and many, many people won't come along. But as I look around [studying the Bible, looking at where God is moving], I can see the faint trace of an old trail. So, now I'm off the beaten path clearing this trail and happily I can see hints that others had been there before, long before. The name Paul carved into a tree; hints for the next journey by someone named James and so on."

Godin says "the irony of off-roading is that the farther away from the [normal trail], the easier the journey." And you can't be just sort of off-road; you really have to go full bore into the wild. Then he said this and it made me stop reading, put down the magazine and pray for God's protection for us. "Most people who think

212

about following this strategy lose their nerve at exactly the wrong moment. They get through the hardest part, then realize just how bold they appear to be [and then bail, freak out, head back for the normal road]."

We have made it through some hard roads. The last year has been critical. I've obeyed coming down the escalator. Each of you has stepped up in leadership. The new birth prophesied last summer has come true in spades. We are in three Bliss groups with many people floating around us. We are at some sort of a tipping point, but which way will we tip?

You hold that answer. We've gotten here by off-roading, following the counter cultural position of the Bible (counter to the traditional culture of most churches). I'm not sure where the next turn is; what the next hurdle to come our way will be. But I do know that we will make it largely on how well you lead. How well you stay devoted to the calling, to the body and of course, to God.

Now is not the time to get lost "in our own little lives" but to see how my little life is part of a grand story (much bigger than just Numinous, by the way). Realize, this will probably never make us famous and certainly is not the sexy road. We aren't out to impress anyone; we're just determined to do this Christian thing, this community thing, the way God said to do it. Godin ends his article this way—he tells of seeing a Hummer all tricked out on the interstate. He says the owner was seemingly making a statement of how "big, strong and brave he was" even though it was obvious this truck was never going off-road. "There are companies (and people) that think this is the way to go off-road, but it's not. It's just annoying. Far better to be a lot less showy and a lot more bold."

And that is exactly what we are going to do---not worry about being showy, but concentrate grandly on being even more bold. Are you with me? Of course you are! So, are you ready?

June 27, 2004

Well, it's been a furious couple of weeks, has it not? I've spoken to enough of you to know that I've heard the same story again and again---pressure in life, issues at work, my things breaking, no time. And within it all a clear sense from most of you that there seems to be a clear minded opponent at work here. Welcome to life on the front lines.

Smile for you are clearly showing the world Whose side you are on! I missed seeing each of you tonight so I wanted to email you a "letter from Carl" to encourage you. There is so much I long to tell you, dreams God shares with me, thoughts that flash through my mind, warnings that emerge, fears of mine, hopes for the future.

I was praying today asking God "what is next; where do we go next?" I haven't got a clear answer at all, but I did get one thing back. Everything hinges on you. Yes, on you and you alone. How so—let me show you 3 things.

First, the concept of ownership emerges clear again as the issue. We are shouting a counter-cultural message because it is so Biblical. In a typical setting, there are a select few who run the store, maybe a few volunteers who are just above average go-getters and the rest of us sit back soaking it all in, like good consumers. However, that setting simply is not Biblical. Instead, we are told that all of us have the same job description, having seen the light, to tell others.

Secondly, our future hinges on you and on you knowing our path. Many of you are new. I think many of you have come to us BECAUSE we are off-roading, blazing our own trail. Good, but that's risky if you don't realize why we are out here and why we do what we do.

You can help yourself by finding out the "why" behind things. If you don't understand why we do it that way, then before long, it just becomes a "that's just the way we do it" kind of motif and we don't want that. Again, it all hinges on you and if you don't know why something is done a certain way, then you can't help. You can't be an owner because an owner knows these things. There are too many things to list here, but know that there are no secrets, no elitisms, no "cool people only" spots. I need each and everyone of you. Our future all hinges on you.

Thirdly, our future and the success of this experiment of God hinges on you because you are the "other" of the one another commands. Remember his teaching, success in the individual mission (mentioned first above) is grounded on the foundation of one another. Love one another. Be unified with one another. Stay devoted. Stay committed. Remember, as an owner, if you aren't there, then how can it go on? We need each other in the organized side of our circle (Bliss, fluid) AND in the chaos of life (the phone calls, emails, dinners together, prayer together, Bible Studies together). And, each OWNER (that means you—remember our success and future hinges on you) must be the person who takes the lead here.

Of course, if you really think that your job is to be a computer programmer, school teacher, coach, engineer or whatever, then you'll never see that fact. You'll always be really busy with "your life" and you'll just "do your best" to find time for "that church stuff."

I love you! Each and every one of you. I need each of you. God has taken us this far, but we are bigger. That means new challenges, bigger things to deal with, more chances for us to careen off the road quickly. But if we stay devoted to His Word and what He commands there, seeing myself as the owner, that it all hinges on me, we can take this next step as he gives it.

June 28, 2004—email to elders only

I still don't know where we are going, but God is sending messages in and I'm listening. In the same magazine as the Godin article that I mentioned was an article about Starbucks--yes, the coffee company and they are seeking to become an even more powerful force. Behind their success are some ideas of their Chairman and chief global strategist, Howard Schultz. As I read these I thought each of you need to hear this.

1. Customer loyalty is not an entitlement.—Of course we don't have customers and we are doing all we can to destroy the consumer mindset within the church. But his core point that the people who are with you "are fickle" is big. He adds, "our success is based on their continued trust in our people." Well, "our people" are the elders. Please never lose sight that God has tapped you for this much bigger challenge of leading. I don't know why. I wouldn't have. I wouldn't have chosen me. But He did and we can find confidence in that. But stay alert—obviously first (I think) to your Bliss group, but always to the entire group. Though you'll never be super close with everyone, you are an elder for the entire body.
2. Great brands aren't built on ads or promotions.---we've never focused on that aspect of growing church and we won't start now. I have used the UCF paper a little bit and want to again, but not at the expense of our ability to minister well within the group. God forbid the day come that we can't meet someone's need because we owe some promotion house money.
3. It's no fun being a pioneer.—I could have told him that. Do you think I like being out here off-roading? I don't, but this is where God is, what the Bible says and I am determined to stay true to that. But Schultz's point is also good in that you

216

should attempt to surround yourself with people, groups, other companies that have experience in areas you may not have. I hear unity in that and a unity that goes beyond just us. But, within us, I have surrounded myself with you. Now you help us surround ourselves with others who build up the body.

4. Stay humble! There is no room for arrogance.---Amen. God help us from ever becoming arrogant. Keep us on our faces before you, in awe that you would use us, clearly acknowledging that You have the knowledge—we don't. We trust you; help us follow you well.

July 19, 2004

Well its been an incredible 3-4 weeks of fluid (6 if you throw in our normally fun 4th Sunday and then the extra fun of the holiday) and we've been looking at the very important (a top item on the list you created and handed to me about issues we needed to look deeply into) topic of the Holy Spirit.

We've discussed who He is, His nature and His role. Last Sunday was powerful to consider how important, critical, He is to "my" personal success as a Christian. I was reminded of that again today as John and I had a wonderful lunch together. We discussed many topics and the issue of "Hearing from God" came up. We talked about how the Apostle Paul was so clear that a core, perhaps most important, way we hear from God is the gathered body together. Certainly, we celebrate that we, individually, can and do hear from God in our personal study and prayer. And we hear from him in Bible Study's we attend and things like that. But Paul was insistent that we hear from God in the group, in the gathered body—it is no mistake that the writer of Hebrews hammers this point also saying "forsake not the gathering together" (and that's near that other powerful verse where we are told to submit to our leaders—perhaps already there was an issue of people thinking they could make it alone without the body and this writer wanted to alert them to continue to submit even about when to meet, where and so on).

Anyway, while we (John and I) were talking, I was reminded what we saw about the Holy Spirit two weeks before that He exists not only within us personally but also, critically, as a part of the body gathered. In all of us WHEN WE ARE TOGETHER. Powerful stuff. Well, think about what we heard last night at fluid—it is the Holy Spirit that teaches us all things. You may have thought I was only rambling on or perhaps waxing poetic when I say that we EXPECT to actually HEAR from God at fluid, but that is serious stuff to me. And how does that happen? VIA THE HOLY SPIRIT. Thus, if I'm not there, a critical moment of God's speaking to me is lost by me. Amazing stuff—the power of the Person of the Holy Spirit and his job.

Another point I wanted to make for you, one we didn't necessarily cover is "how do I do this?" I mean, I could see some of you walking out of fluid perhaps wondering what step you needed to take. Well, its simple really---if you are a Christian, then the Holy Spirit is already there. He is in you. And his being there in you (and in the body gathered) is an issue you take in faith. He just is there! Praise God! And you know that as your day goes by---you read your Bible and sense God speaking—that's the Holy Spirit. You are at work and a co-worker shares a need and you say the right words to minister---that is the Holy Spirit. You are busy with your day and then a friend, family, Numinous person comes to your mind to call or pray for them---that's the Holy Spirit. You get tempted with a sin (perhaps you fall)--that sense of conviction or protection---that's the Holy Spirit. He is with you!! You can, however, block his connection with you by how you live your life. You can, as the Bible states, grieve or make sad, the Holy Spirit. Primarily that is by sin. You over come that by confessing your sin to God asking for his forgiveness and RECEIVING IT (man, that is good stuff there—grace abounds), thus getting back into right relationship.

218

See it? The issue of praying and (as part of the prayer) asking God to "forgive us our sins/debts/transgressions" is not just to get a clean slate or something like that. In fact, as we saw last Fall, when you became a Christian, you got the clean slate then! What the forgiveness does on the daily basis is keep us moving forward toward the ultimate end of being like Christ. And how does that happen? A daily sense of God's guidance. And who does that? The Holy Spirit. And if I can't hear him, if I have allowed sin to block my access to him, if I've shut down the place where he speaks (like at fluid/Bliss), then I am alone. Directionless. So daily, I take time to center down, shut out the noise and just talk to my Father asking him to (among other things) clean me up SO THAT I can hear him speak via the Holy Spirit.

Jan 9, 2005

At the core of what is at stake is each person's clear desire to walk with God. Over the holiday, while we were on the road due to my grandmother's passing, Kim and I talked at length about some of the many issues within our group. The overriding theme that kept coming to me as we chatted was "why doesn't [insert name] just obey God, just walk with God? Their answers would come if they would simply obey. My heart aches for them to just draw near to God."

Yet, so much of the time, we are blinded or confused; we think we are okay with God as we make choices that are clearly not in keeping with His word. We blow off worship (corporate and private), we rarely speak to God, we rarely read his word, we selfishly pick things that take us away from community, we don't live simply and rarely share our resources---on and on and on. I started to cry as I thought of my heart's wish for you.

My New Year's Grown Up Wish for you is that you WIN. Win at life! That is accomplished ONE WAY---becoming like Christ. So my prayer is that your life's prayer become--"Father, help be become like Jesus."

How does that look in my life?

- Think about God often---does God and his will and his glory cross your mind often?
- Talk to Him often—do you find yourself in fairly constant communication with God?
- Worship Him—do you play worship music; do watch the skies and worship; do you stare at the ocean or stars and bring Him glory; do you value your private and corporate times of worship above other things?
- Remain in constant community—do you find yourself thinking about, praying for, hoping for "one another?" Do you seek to rarely miss the times of communal gathering.
- Look for ways to share Jesus/God with others—do you find yourself praying for, worried for the many others in your life, thinking about how you can interject God into your conversations?
- Complete Obedience—do you constantly check your actions against God's word and ways? (there is a difference between my sin where I slip up and my sin that I choose to cling to, KNOWING I am in sin)

March 25, 2005

One of my favorite business authors, Seth Godin, wrote an article back in December 2003. I've had some of his quote clipped out on my Mac desktop to remind me of what we are doing, where we are going and what its going to take to get there.

His premise to the article is that there is a shortage of things that are scarce. "Scarcity, it seems, has a lot to do with value." But if nothing is scarce, if we can get anything as a knock-off, a cut-rate deal, then nothing has value. "So how do you deal with the shortage of scarcity? Well, the worst strategy is whining. . .whining is rarely a successful response to anything. So, what is scarce now? RESPECT. HONESTY. GOOD JUDGMENT. LONG-TERM RELATIONSHIPS THAT LEAD TO TRUST. Ultimately, what is scarce is that kind of courage [to offer those things]."

Its Easter weekend, an Ember Days Weekend. Time to reflect and ponder, plan and celebrate more life. I've been digging around in my old notes from the early days of Numinous, looking over some stuff Gaz and I bantered back and forth. We still hold firm to the original premise that God is real, but the church has done a poor job of pointing others to Him. And if we (the church) can fix this issue, we must return to the basics of what He said He wanted for us and not much else.

Which led me back to Godin---what we should have in spades are those things on Seth's list, particularly the part about long-term relationships. And here, at the 5-year mark for us as a church (6.5 years as a ministry), we ARE DOING IT. We are not, of course, perfect, but being perfect was never on the list. What we are doing is offering real life to your real friends who wonder, deep inside, if life matters at all and what, if anything, religion (hate that word) has to do with it. We've prayed in recent weeks for those friends of ours. Maybe today or tomorrow, you need to give them a call or drop them an email simply inviting them to risk a little BASED ON THE STRENGTH OF YOUR LONG-TERM RELATIONSHIP WITH THEM and come to fluid Easter Sunday night.

It will take courage and, as Seth said, that is something that is scarce. Be the risk taker; be the person who actually decides to live life like a Christian, like Jesus. It's bold. It's gutsy. But it's scarce and thus, its valuable. I wrote these words to myself back in January 2004. Maybe you need to read them now and decide from this Easter forward, you won't allow His sacrifice for us to be wasted while you sit timidly on the sidelines of life, lost in your pet sins or confusions about obeying or not.

> WHAT COULD BE DONE IF YOU ARE NOT TRAPPED BY ANY SUPPOSED LIMITATIONS ABOUT "HOW IT IS SUPPOSED TO BE DONE?

> THINK LIKE A DISCOVERER!! YOU ARE OUT ON THE HIGH SEAS, MARCHING THROUGH WILDERNESS. YOU DON'T KNOW WHAT YOU THINK YOU KNOW, SO DON'T BE LIMITED. PUSH THROUGH TO FALL-URE, GO TO THE EDGE!!

> WHAT IS SCARCE is considered VALUABLE--HONESTY, TRUST, REAL, COMMON SENSE, COURAGE, CRITICAL THINKING, CHRISTIAN SPIRITUALITY WITHOUT THE CHRISTIAN BUREAUCRACY/INSTITUTION.

> I'M SPENDING SO MUCH TIME TRYING TO FIGURE OUT WHO I AM, WHAT I AM, THAT I AM MISSING THE NOW OF JUST BEING WHOEVER I AM!!! SO LIVE BOLD AND OFFER YOUR SCARCE (& VALUABLE) LIFE TO OTHERS.

August 8, 2005

From last night: Respond to God's passionate love and mercy on you. Our actions POST-CONVERSION don't come out of fear or threat, but out of relationship, a desire to respond to His love for us.

But that produces change. No change would imply that "I" think "I'm fine just as I am." Well, according to God, that's not true for any of us. Thus, part of my passion for what God has us on right now is wanting to see even more spiritual change in us (I've seen a ton already in me, in others, in us), but we need to go deeper. "Push out into Deep Water." *Fluid.*

Where I've been recently is in Colossians and part of that journey---in there Paul says 9 times, in one way or another, due to Jesus loving gift of getting on the cross, his death, blood and resurrection, YOU ARE DEAD IF YOU ARE A CHRISTIAN. "You have died with Christ, so it is not you that live, but Christ living in you." This relates to the above because, I at least, feel week sometimes and wonder why it is such a struggle for change, or why it takes so long. I can't explain all of that in this email (partly due to length, mostly due to it being the mystery of God), but part of it is me realizing (believing, back to faith as Greg was teaching last month) that I am dead. I can QUIT trying and just allow Christ to live in me. The Spiritual Disciplines help me here by allowing God to shape me as I allow His Spirit to live in me, to operate out of me. I don't live; He lives through me. So, part of the journey comes as I allow Him more and more to live in me.

Related to Bliss: So, all of that (the above, the stuff we heard last night as fluid) comes back to how I relate in my new life, as a "called out one," one who has heard this marvelous mystery, TO OTHERS. I must be here, I must be engaged, I must be intentional. Of course that MUST happen in (as we call it) the chaos of life; it just happens via phone calls, band gigs, Disney Adventure clubbing, stamping wedding invitations, dinners, emails, etc.... BUT AT THE FOUNDATION ACCORDING TO GOD, is the intentional gathered moment of Acts 2. For us, under the authority of our elders and the direction of the Head of our church, Jesus, that happens at Bliss!

This month, we are looking at a key "one another" command—honor. You know, this is a hard concept in our day, a day of massive incivility. Heck, I read an article recently that said saying "Ma'am or Sir" was insulting to people. Imagine that? Are we in need of any more evidence that today, black is white, up has become down, and lie has become truth (check out 1 John for some scary reality from that point). A statement of respect, of honor, has now become a statement of insult to someone. Amazing. In our Bliss groups, we are going to dig around in a variety of ways to understand this one another command. Feel free to meditate on Romans 12:10 yourself before tonight to see this concept in the Word.

Kim and I were preparing for our group and she looked in Webster's---something there really caught our eye and I wanted ALL of you to hear it or see it. In the synonyms section, honor is related to reverence, and "reverence implies a profound respect mingled with love, devotion or awe." Further, honor also is related to deference, and "deference implies a yielding or submitting to another's judgment or preference." WOW---respect, love, devotion, awe, yieldedness, submission, allowing preference to another---MAJOR KEY POINTS OF A CHRISTIAN LIFE.

As you prepare for Bliss tonight or this month of Bliss, think deeply about how you relate to others. Are you clearly in the "me first" or "my issues take precedence" group or do the actions of your life show that you honor one another? Of course, kind of hard to do this one another command (or any of them) if you aren't here, aren't present. I pray that you will eagerly come to one of our three Bliss groups.

November 16, 2005

Yesterday I had the honor of sharing our story with another weary traveler who is tired of "the junk at my church." When we were done, I think she was emboldened to try to make changes at her church (yay!). While we were talking though, the concept of ownership came up.

So, allow me to challenge and exhort you to remember that we embrace an "Ownership Mentality." Perhaps I am a fool to believe this. Perhaps the reality is that only a few people will actually care enough or that the system of the west, with few owners/leaders who dominate, simply overwhelms our ability to try new things.

But I am certain that the Bible actually presents this notion--that we are all called forward. And in the end, that means each person can/should think like an owner. An owner realizes that "its up to me." That the doors won't be unlocked if "I don't go." An owner sees the problems (carpet issues, people issues, supply issues, emotional needs, and more) and then moves to meet the problems head on. An owner does not expect "someone else will take care of that."

In specific, a person with an owner mentality will listen well to the main leader (Jesus/God) and move as He directs, quickly.

Are you listening?

Dec 12, 2005

Sometimes one's zeal for this can sound harsh in the ears of another, yet that zeal must not be mistaken for anything other than simply zeal. Would that we all have the same zeal for the Lord, the kind of zeal, as we saw, that would brook no opposition in casting out those who would cheapen worship (the very complaint of Jesus as we saw in John 2). I would also remind that it is ONLY the Holy Spirit that brings conviction, so if you took someone's zealous statement and were offended, then the Holy Spirit is obviously doing His job on you. If you read any of those emails and, thinking "I've been late" or "I've had to miss" and you know you were somewhere appropriate, then I doubt you felt guilty about it and obviously thus there was no condemnation. See, in that case, the Holy Spirit certainly wasn't speaking to you, thus no reason to worry about it.

At the same time, no one on the earth is able to cast judgment on another. Only God knows and, trust me, He does know. He knows where we each are in relationship to Him. He will not be mocked. We, however, walk through life a bit in the dark, so we do well to acknowledge that issues come up, things happen, and stuff can't be avoided. If you were there last night, Kim certainly was not at fluid. Something came up with our girls that caused a schedule conflict. Is she condemned? Obviously not. Does her zeal for the Lord remain? Certainly. Things happen.

I think a simple way to look at this is to consider "my patterns." If I am rarely away from worship or community, then my rare moment away makes me personally sad ("I hate to miss"), but I don't worry about it. I won't be judged. My zeal is clear through all my actions. The rare reason I would bail on the community must be impressive in scope, otherwise, I wouldn't go there. However, if it is my pattern to be careless with God's things (worship, community, others, etc...) and I find myself consumed with things of the world or things the world places above God, then my continuous habit of missing is a signal about something.

We must worship. We must worship together (or the Bible is false). We should admonish and exhort one another to be faithful to that calling. If we failed to do so, we would be guilty of not loving one another. We must also accept that each person will stand before God and God knows, so if Kim can't make it to fluid, then in the end, she and she alone will answer to God. In the end, God may not be happy with Kim's decision, but it is one she made to the best of her ability. Her hearing (from the body) that she was missed is important. And, if you thought Kim's commitment to the body and to her calling, as seen in something like fluid was weak, then your LOVE for her would COMPEL you to exhort her ("you really need to be at worship") or admonish her ("stop missing so much; I love you too much for you to grow distant from God"). That is best done directly as Marcia suggests and with love, as in the tone of Elisabeth's email.

226

April 4, 2006

Some of you will remember Eric and his friend Sam who ran with us for about a year, a former student. So we ended up having a great connection again. Previously, when he had left us, he had taken the typical way out for people who leave our group---silence, avoidance and no explanation. We finally had some closure, but it was frustrating. Well, a few days ago, we were able to have a good chat on "his turf" and as the day went along (time spent at hospital—only 2.5 hours, not that bad) he and I chatted about a ton of things.

In that time, he asked about Numinous and I told him how we were. I then got to ask about his church; he had been one of the few to leave us to return to a former church, totally a good thing. Here's where it really gets good—he tells me that due to work and life, he really hadn't been in a while. Well, I could have guessed this because the reason he came to us in the first place was that he wasn't really feeling connected there at the other church. But I had prayed things would work out the second time (something I had told him when we "cleared the air" over a year ago). So, however, now he's telling me he really wasn't in the fellowship or community at all. So I got the honor of telling him that he's always welcome to come and just hang out. You should have seen the smile on his face. I did not act like he needed to "leave" his other church—as you all know we NEVER imply that and have said openly that if "you" want to go to 5 different churches and their services each week, well knock yourself out. We don't "own" anyone. I did remind him that if people really want to run with us, that we'd like a sense of commitment to that journey, but if someone like him wanted to just come around when work kept him from his other church or he just wanted to hang at Bliss, he was always welcome.

June 6, 2006

Look, we've never said that we have some new theology, that we've found some new secret---that would be Gnosticism and the Bible is strictly against that kind of thought. The basic theology is the same as you'll find just about anywhere. What is different is our expression of it, the actions and attitudes of the leaders, the idea of group ownership and our honesty in what is expected---everyone in, all owners, each adds to the atmosphere, fellowship really matters and so forth. This is what I call "functional theology." What we've found is an old thing---they were together all the time, sharing their love, their resources, their meals and their lives. Church NOT as an institution, not "the Christian Mall," but real life and real lives, actively engaging one another.

Often when I am asked about how to do this and should a certain church go there and stuff like that, I merely ask the pastor "do your people like being together? If you put on a game, Super Bowl, or party, would everyone come and want to be there?" Invariably, the answer is a sad no. Sure, some in that church get it and go for it. Yay for them; I applaud them and pray for them. But the rest miss it and sadly don't even know its important or even what I am talking about. THAT is the problem—the mission has been lost. But here, we DO love being together and we see that hanging in the waiting room with Josh (remember that??—he does!), playing volleyball together or watching The Super Bowl.

So, pray over Bliss and over the body. Let me leave you with these words from Vernon written June 8, 2006 as a reminder of who we are:

> *Imagine that you have a theology so rare that most Christians don't know that it exists! Imagine further that this theology is so dynamic and demanding that it's effects cannot be fully controlled.*

228

To complicate matters, imagine that you brought this unknown, dynamic and demanding theology with an acceptance of people regardless of who they are, their spiritual maturity, or even their ability to handle the theology.

Welcome to the revolution. Welcome to the extreme.

Welcome to Numinous.

July 4, 2006

Wow—what a great day of community together. 8 years ago, Kim and I were walking into the unknown at this time, a few short weeks from embarking on the journey that would be Numinous. We were scared and a bit nervous, yet confident in what God had shown us and willing to risk it all for that vision. We knew we were called to use my communication gifts for Him to attempt to connect with a generation that I firmly believed desired a spiritual connection with the Eternal One but were put off in general by Christians and the Church.

Seven years ago, then in the Spring of 1999, we headed to England to see the Awakening that we believed clearly was happening there among that specific generation. What was saw was not some program, not some building, not some worship style, but something so much more basic---people actually living life together in a spiritual community of faith.

In my (then) 34 years of Christian living, I had never seen that, not really. I had certainly seen good churches as I defined church. And in those churches, I had seen some hints of community in groups like the choir, a youth group, a Sunday School class. But in general what I saw was what the modern church had become—a business, the Christian mall, a place with activity, things to do, programs, but no real deep connection. In the process, my generation was finally willing to say "no more" and walk away (I am convinced that many generations before Gen X, people felt the disconnect, but were afraid or unwilling to say it).

We flew back aware of the task—no great thing to start, no building to buy—just being. No real doing. Just being.

Being.

Interesting that this is a hard thing for many of us, we Americans who usually must be doing and are always looking ahead to the "next great thing." Now, 8 years later, I tell you that this is the hardest thing I've ever done. It is easier to run with just my friends, those just like me. It is easier to just focus on my own needs, dreams, issues. It is easier to come occasionally to worship and rarely, if ever, let my mask down. It is easier, when I come, to smile blankly, sit on my side of the room, and know no one. It's just easier...and yet, it is death.

Being, but not being alone. Never alone. They were together all the time, true in England, true in Acts.

Now, as we experience our typical Numinous summer of pause (taking July for togetherness in the outdoors, the retreat, vacations and trips), we again set our focus to that calling—to love one another as He loved us.

Being as one in faith.

Simply Being.

Be aware that most Christians you know are probably a bit afraid of that, needing the comfort of lots of programming. OR they need a place where they can do some work so they feel as if they have earned their place. Instead, we say "you are just accepted. Come and be."

Be aware that most non-Christians (if you can find anyone to actually admit that fact) are equally afraid or perhaps a bit ambivalent, having made their life separated from God. To risk letting the mask down and admit that there is Something or SomeOne bigger than them and that they NEED that someone. . .well, that is a lot to risk.

I tell you those two facts (or remind you) because we still eagerly invite the world to His table. We invite them to 4th of July celebrations like this one. We invite them to Bliss. We invite them to fluid.   Keep the coffee warm in your heart for all of those around you who need this. Keep inviting them. Keep praying for them that He will open their eyes and hearts. Keep sharing our secret, sharing the revolution---"Letting it be what it becomes."

Being. Community. Love one another as He has loved, is loving, you. Be unified as He is unified with His Father.

August 30, 2006

You know, we never really have any promises of tomorrow. We should live more in that view—not scared of course to leave the house, but with a tender sense of love and devotion to one another. Yes, with that view--perhaps, I might not see you again. Not being morbid here, just accurate. Are there people in your life that, if you found out they had died, you would be sad because you knew that you had last spoken to them or thought of them in anger?

I love you all. I am still stunned that you follow me. I am honored that you journey with me and Kim. And I am humbled that God would choose to actually have people respond to the simple words I share, words that come straight from Him. Please live your lives boldly. As I said long ago, "welcome to the Revolution." Keep living your lives in that tension, knowing you have the answer that the people around you really need. Even as we roll, often undercover, never forget the task and willingly take his yoke, accept the suffering that comes with it, and glory only in the cross.

December 29, 2006

I was watching the DVD extras for *Cars.* That movie really spoke to me and one of the songs became a theme song for our August vacation. On the extras, the director confirmed what I had thought about and that was he wanted to try and touch a memory of the America that used to be.

Once, long ago, we used to be so much more in tune with the rhythms of the world and our place in it. This idea is, of course, a connection back to a time before the massive urban cities, back before most people left the land for various reasons. We were reminded of that this holiday as we spent Christmas with my sister and parents in the mountains of Tennessee. Very remote area where we stayed, very country (cheap land and houses), yet close to Gatlinburg (basically an I-Drive in the Mountains) so full of tourists, noisy and crowded.

As the Church expanded through the early centuries and then came to take hold of a Europe no longer connected through the power and protection of the Roman Empire, the church took pains to give form to the rhythms of the seasons. Most people, whether Christian or not, could appreciate the turning of the seasons and many cultures celebrated those moments. The Church desired to take those periods and connected them in a deeper way to God. Hence, the Ember Days.

The idea was of a 3-day celebration, fasting and feasting, giving individuals a specific time to reset and replenish the soul in

232

response to the dawning of a new season of life. The word "ember" refers not to coals or fire, but is a corruption of the Latin *quattor tempora* (four seasons) or the Old English *ymbren* (periodic or recurring). For us, we no longer really connect to seasons, but to our cultural holidays (which are close to the seasonal swings).

The New Year period (really Christmas through New Year) is our last of the '06 and first of the '07 season. So, my email to you is a reminder as you head into this weekend that you take time to stop and pray. Reflect on the last period (back to Labor Day)--rejoice on the many things God has done for you; consider areas where you were a champion; reflect on those things you could have done better; note areas where God is trying to show you something or change something in you, and more, just remember the time.

Then, turn your attention ahead—pray through what God may be pointing you towards; place your spirit in a submissive heart and attitude for the challenges He has ahead of you; remind your spirit about Prov 3:5-6; reaffirm your desire to be His slave, a slave to righteousness and set your face like flint to move resolutely on the narrow path; and more, just prepare to rejoice for each day as yet another day of life. It is His gift to you!

I know this period, for many, is to goal set for the year. That's fine of course, but I urge you NOT to spend too much time on some yearly goals. Most of those get far away from us and we then feel bad for failing or think goal setting is a waste of time. Instead, just think about the season ahead between this Ember Days and the next (Easter, this year late, April 8). Do write down a goal or two in connection with time spent with God in fasting and feasting over this weekend.

January 15, 2007

Last week, I meant to show this to you all. I was reading Oswald on the 11th and was blown away (again) by his words. I am certain that God is deeply at work in us, both individually and collectively, on the very large issue of obedience and walking with Him and the cost of doing so. As I've told some of you, I am studyin 1 Peter during January and in this book, God speaks about suffering a ton. The verb 'to suffer" is in the Bible 40 times. 10 times occurs in this book. Wow! More so, Peter goes on to speak about the concept using other words.

Anyway, in that vein and on the larger topic of really living in this thing we call Christianity, here's some of what Chambers wrote on that day:

WHAT MY OBEDIENCE TO GOD COSTS OTHER PEOPLE

"They laid hold upon one Simon . . . and on him they laid the cross." Luke 23:26

If we obey God it is going to cost other people more than it costs us, and that is where the sting comes in, the pain begins. If we are in love with our Lord, obedience does not cost us anything, it is a delight, but it costs those who do not love Him a good deal. If we obey God it will mean that other people's plans are upset, and they will ridicule us with it - "You call this Christianity?" We can prevent the suffering; but if we are going to obey God, we must not prevent it, we must let the cost be paid.

When our obedience begins costs others, our human pride entrenches itself on this point, and we say - I will never accept anything from anyone. We shall have to, or disobey God. We have no right to expect that the type of relationships we have with others should be any different from those our Lord Himself had (see Luke 8:2-3, 19-25).

Stagnation in spiritual life comes when we say we will bear the whole thing ourselves. We cannot. We are so involved in the universal purposes of God that immediately we obey God, others are affected. Are we going to remain loyal in our obedience to God and go through the humiliation of refusing to be independent, or are we going to take the other line and say - I will not cost other people suffering? We can disobey God if we choose, and it will bring immediate relief to the situation, but we shall be a grief to our Lord. Whereas if we obey God, He will look after those who have been pressed into the consequences of our obedience. We have simply to obey and to leave all consequences with Him.

Beware of the inclination to dictate to God as to what you will allow to happen if you obey Him.

That last line is what really blew my mind. I've walked these past 22 years with one basic mantra—not my life, but yours Lord Jesus. I have no "say so" in the matter of my own life. Yet, that is not easily lived out, especially when my choices cause others to "suffer." And currently, with the choice about Valencia West Campus (should God open that door), I again am confronted by my own boast. Will I obey and merely follow or will I try to dictate to God what consequences I will allow, connected to my relationship with Him?

I choose to obey. So, in all things, whether that is if I read my Bible, if I speak a blessing to others (you are in Bliss right now, aren't you, running in 1 Peter 4:9????), if I come to worship, if I help the poor, if I witness to my office mate, if I share my resources, if I admonish properly---in WHATEVER He has stated is HIS WAY for me to walk, I will choose to pursue obedience based on HIS SCALE, not mine.

God is deeply at work! Relish in it. Share with others what God is doing in you and in us. God is breathing a fresh breath on us in our walk and our witness. Do not grow weary in well doing. Do not shut down because it costs someone else. As Greg read to us last night from a couple of places---lay aside every weight that hinders you and press on, not that any one of us have attained perfection, but press on, forgetting what lies behind, what failures or frustrations you have experienced, and fix your eyes on the prize and run the race set before you!!!

I love you all and am honored to walk with you in these days.

April 11, 2007

Well, as we survey the scene of our group, again and again we seem to get the same story—people suffering. Sometimes, it appears it could just be "rain falls on the just and the unjust" (so no great eternal issue here) and sometimes it could be self-inflicted harm. But underneath it all, it does feel like a sense of attack. Perhaps that is just the lot of the Christian or maybe it has something to do with the stand we take in the spiritual (and natural) world. In any case, the fact of our many issues (dentists, struggles in pregnancies, struggles in marriage, struggles in dating, work, health, finances, backs, did I mention dentists and teeth) continues to raise the point of "when does it all end." Or, "when do I get my way," "get what I want in life?"

I've been doing a study of The First Epistle of Peter (part of my ember days goals from January), written to the scattered crowds of followers throughout the Mediterranean World. I was a bit caught off guard to find, just as we saw in Paul's letter to Timothy, this issue of suffering. Again and again, he calls for the disciples of Christ, the called out ones, the followers, or, as we would say it today, the Church, to pursue or accept suffering. Let me attempt to break it down for you.

To start with, Peter makes the strong connection between the goal of the Christian (to become like Christ) and the fact that Jesus himself suffered. Jesus, of course, had already alluded to this when he was with Peter and the others when he told them that if the people mistreat and hate the master, certainly they would also mistreat and hate the servants or followers. Seven different times Peter reminds his readers that Jesus suffered and in 4:1 lays out exactly what Jesus said—"**4:1** So then, since Christ suffered physical pain, you must arm yourselves with the same attitude he had, and be ready to suffer, too."

Peter makes the point that Jesus suffered for a reason, or really several reasons: suffering is part of the salvation event (1:11); to be an example to us (2:21); to show us how to trust God (2:23); to show us to NOT retaliate (2:23); to heal us through his wounds (2:24); and to bring us safely home (3:18).

Peter further explains why we suffer: to purify our faith (1:7); to test our faith (1:7); to please God (2:20); because God calls us to suffering (2:21); to gain a reward (3:14); to help us become partners with Christ (4:13); to gain the Spirit of God (4:14); to gain the privilege of being called by God's name (4:16) and because its God's will for us (4:19).

Lastly, when we read through, we see that Peter makes some pretty big promises for those who suffer and in doing so, lays out some strong demands on us. First, the promises are rich: stronger faith (1:7); praise (1:7); honor (1:7); glory (1:7); God's pleasure (2:19); a good reputation [as long as you are suffering for doing good or God's will] (3:16); the attitude to stop sinning (4:1); partnership with Christ (4:13); the chance to share in the glory of Jesus (4:13); the glorious Spirit of God (4:14); the privilege to be called by God's name (4:16); and after we suffer, the promise of restoration, support and strength (5:10).

The demands, though, are just as strong. Suffering is no picnic. Peter makes that clear. He makes the point that suffering is painful. He calls it fiery. He also states that it will be unfair. One would think we'd all understand that instinctively, yet how often, upon starting some kind of suffering, do we cry "unfair." Yet, Peter calmly reminds us that ". . .it is necessary for you to endure many trials for a while." Of course, the clincher for him is that Jesus suffered, thus we will too.

I realize suffering is painful. I too bear those marks on my body and mind. Some of you know the depths of my own trials; others of you do not. To you, I may just be this guy who has shown up on your radar and (I hope) in some way impacted your life. But my wounds are deep and the trials connected to those wounds are still in my memory and mind. Yet, in the end, the secret to walking through those moments unscathed is to recognize that this is the path to greater depth of soul and spirit. God is with us in those moments. We should happy, glad. Peter says it best (4:12-14)—"Dear friends, don't be surprised at the fiery trials you are going through, as if something strange were happening to you. Instead, be very glad – because these trials will make you partners with Christ in his suffering, and afterward you will have the wonderful joy of sharing his glory when it is displayed to all the world. Be happy if you are insulted for being a Christian, for then the glorious Spirit of God will come upon you."

I'm not sure I have all of that yet, but I am working on it. If we can continue to walk together, we can bear one another as we journey. At times, you are holding another up; at times you are being held. Yet, always we are together.

So, tomorrow, enjoy sticking out like a sore thumb as you navigate through your world. And, if suffering comes or you are still in the midst of it, just smile.

April 22, 2007

This so gets at the entire point of Numinous---not a religious group centered around some religious activity, but rather a family of friends who are all on the journey, all equally dealing with successes and failures, highs and lows, all holding one another.

Last night, Matthew and I saw the movie *300* which is a fairly accurate movie about the city-state of Sparta set in the 480-ish B.C. Period. There were many excellent points one could draw from this movie, but related to Numinous was this simple thought—**we stand together and we die together. The strength of the group IS THE STRENGTH. If someone tries to go totally alone, they are, well, alone and more easily picked off.**

Note this, as I've said many, many times, cuts both ways. Meaning, we each have to protect the atmosphere of love and unity. We each have to reach out and, when reached out to, respond with acceptance. I call some people. Others call me. When I haven't seen or spoken with another in the group, I call them. Others should think the same thing--"hey, I haven't personally spoken to Carl in a few days; I think I'll email or call him." As we do this, we are moving forward on the journey together.

So, I hope you came when invited (and at least 2 major things today were a very open invitation). If you didn't, then you honestly cannot say "there is no community in Numinous" nor "no one ever calls me or reaches out to me." What you can more honestly say is "I really don't value community." I hope then you'll re-evaluate what the Bible says at this point. I hope you'll check your spirit. And I hope you'll reach out to others and, next time, accept the open invitations. Everyone is welcome. Everyone has a home here. Bring your friends; the more the merrier.

June 11, 2007

Love all of your hearts. The essence of community my friends. Please realize how precious this is which (as an aside) is one reason why I push so hard on this and why I get so sad when people leave (particularly when I find out later that they are not in community anywhere later)---people literally kill for this (what do you think gangs are all about) or do horrible things to their bodies (fraternities, anyone??) to find some sort of community.

And, apart from God, most other communities are merely Posers and leave people hanging. They typically can't make it very long and leave a cheap taste in the mouth.

What we have is so incredible; I am so glad God thought it up (community AND Numinous the church). Anyway, when you have those moments of the fragrance of heaven, just breathe as deeply as you can.

My family will meet for a family reunion this July. Some are coming for a week (I'll just make the weekend). Regardless, it won't be enough. No matter whether its mission trips, summer camps, retreats, reunions---those times (no matter how long) of real community are intoxicating and leaving us wanting more. They leave us wanting heaven.

So, sure, dream of the weeklong Numinous retreat. Realize you are dreaming of heaven.

In the meanwhile, understand we CAN create a 365-day long retreat or at least something close to it. 5 minute phone calls. Meals out (even a simple bagel together can be fun as you experienced this weekend). Story time (sad I missed Creation with Vernon). Sharing time. Don't you see? Its not just the "get away" part (yes, that is a part and that is harder to replicate), but its the being together part. Today I was sad, missing all of you—I was at

240

VCC all day, alone, just as many of you were alone. But, I had 5 minutes to glance at my n247 email. 30+ emails and most were retreat thoughts, some were prayers, others were needs. Made me smile BIG!

Just remember this feeling, capture it, share it with everyone on this list (which of course means all of you who we missed a LOT on the retreat are included and all of this applies to you), and just keep experiencing the moment! This is that memorable, "little knit hats on bottles" conversation thing of value that others WANT—let them know you have it!!

July 30, 2007

Remember, you ARE A VITAL PART of what we do at Bliss. First off, you obviously contribute to the body of Christ that meets in your little group. Secondly, you bring you, your stories and the experience of God around you to the group. Thirdly, you are responsible for sharing bliss to others. Bliss is, to me, the safest place to help people make the connection to God. Yes, we want them to also make the connection with worship at fluid, but Bliss is a very safe start place. So, each week think, "who can I invite to come with me to Bliss?" I mean, all you tell them is "come with me to have dinner with my friends—we eat, we tell stories, we talk about our lives in connection to a larger story of God." There's no real Bible study; not really intended for there to be prayer (though you certainly can bring out the Bible or pray). There's no "Christian" stuff to freak someone out or worry them. Just food, fellowship and community. Most people are very hungry for that. So, you have the great and awesome responsibility to be God's representative in opening that door to others.

So, with this week being our "first week" leading us into the rest of the year, it's a great time to help people make the connection in deeper.

Kim and I love you all so much and are so proud of the depth you continue to move to in spiritual matters. Continue to make Bliss a priority in your life as we all learn more about what it really means to be in community, sharing deeply and openly about our lives and our issues and our questions for/about God. Thanks for staying true on the journey!

October 15, 2007

Interesting thing came in my private time with God this morning.

Look what He showed me and, while you read, think about our conversations from fluid last night:

> "Don't look for shortcuts to God. The market is flooded with surefire, easygoing formulas for a successful life that can be practiced in your spare time. Don't fall for that stuff, even though crowds of people do. The way to life—to God—is vigorous and requires total attention. Be wary of false preachers who smile a lot, dripping with practiced sincerity. Chances are they are out to rip you off some way or other. Don't be impressed with charisma, look for character. Who preachers *are* is the main thing, not what they say. A genuine leader will never exploit your emotions or your pocketbook. These diseased trees with their bad apples are going to be chopped down and burned. Knowing the correct password—saying 'Master, Master,' for instance—isn't going to get you anywhere with me. What is required is serious obedience—*doing* what my Father wills."

Jesus went on from there to describe what I believe is the most horrifying picture of the end times and a passage that has driven me for all these years in his service. You go read it yourself along with what I typed above—Matthew 7:13-23.

242

Driving home I told Logan how hard sharing last night's message truly is. I told her at times I feel like I should apologize to her for bringing strict, for being a Daddy who pursues God to become like David, a man after God's own heart. It would sure be easier on her if we just lazed around, few rules, playing our computer games, watching TV, and having no spiritual basis for life.

But, I went on, I think about the need for a godly foundation. In essence, I think about what God showed me, reminded me of, this morning, and thus I refuse to apologize for what He said. I am determined to pass on to her and her sisters what was passed on to me by my father, and to him by his father, and so forth on back in my godly family heritage. Yes, it probably means that we are the weirdoes, not caught up in the world's stuff, fixations and idols. Collectively, it will mean that our church may remain small in these latter days as I (and you with me) remain steadfast to tell the truth. But to bail on that is to invite the horror of Jesus vision (vv 22-23) into my reality.

Yet, I do not hang my head in resignation ("well, I guess we'll just be the strict group, the serious group, and all the other "cool" churches will grow with their "tickle the ears" philosophy"). Instead, I think back to my times as the Student Minister with Chris, D, Jennifer and Matthew (and equally I think back to my swim coach days; I was the "tough guy" then also when other coaches played at swimming).

When I was the Student Pastor, this [fact of me pushing for spiritual honesty over the great cost of following Jesus] came up again and again. Here was my experience, for a positive spin. Though some kids left, turned off that we focused on serious spiritual issues, we also worked so hard to build community (though that was LONG BEFORE I ever used that term) and had fun together that it really was the idea that "even though it's hard, I love this community of mine that I will move eagerly towards whatever comes my way." I mean, we went on mission trips and youth camps and I heard from adult after adult---"those are your kids? What are you doing? You guys [the students] all seem so close, so fired up, are leaders, hungry for God." I would just smile and talk about empowering the students ("everyone's an owner"), treating them with respect (D and Kutcher became my closest friends then, when they were late teens), and always telling them the truth about God/Jesus (we did Precept Bible studies, dug deep into God's word, had our own worship service, never held back).

So, maybe it comes back to community. Though your friends and mine will think we're crazy, when they can see and taste the love we have together, see the real community connection, I think for some that draws them in EVEN THOUGH they know it's some sort of radical call to "come and die."

That's my prayer at least. Now I just have to figure out how to better express that community love from within my work—how can I let my students know the truth so they can at least "come and see" the joy of community."

So, as we work through more of this life with Christ, hang tough. Remember Jesus' own words that I showed you above. Know that I am always here for you (and want you to be still be here for me). Grow deep. Get passionate for Jesus. Share openly about the love and depth we have together and entice your friends. We'll tell them the truth, as I have told each of you this "hard" truth, but we'll show them our deep love that sustains us as we run forward in life. . .together.

November 3, 2007

Perhaps I'm too sensitive; perhaps I worry a bit. In any case, I always worry that we drift away from our purpose into some banal religious thing. I wonder sometimes what others think when they show up at fluid. What is it that they see? A religious thing? Something to do rather than a boring Sunday night? Some weird

244

freaks who are like a cult? Or, passionate people of God who carefully keep a balance between the vertical and the horizontal aspects of living life as a Christian?

We attempt to walk this fine line. We believe that in our lifetimes, the church has largely failed in many aspects, yet we love the "gathered ones" (which is the church) and we desire to live our lives as He commanded, in love and unity. So, we tentatively step out to try and find a way to do this thing of church without just ending up in some religious trap. We look then for instructions, which are not many. Of course, the less instructions is probably better for us; keep it simple. So, in this list of instructions (Acts 2) we understand that there are these 4 key things the church should do: fellowship, prayer, worship, teaching.

In my experience, as you know, fellowship is the one that really gets hammered and overlooked. We have Bliss for that purpose where fellowship gets center stage, and stands alongside teaching (and some prayer). So, prayer and worship?

That's fluid. God seems to put an emphasis on us giving him glory in all of our lives, but in also having specific times where we stand apart from culture and gather to give Him adoration. We believe that in that moment of worship, he teaches us.

Please remember these things. This is not an email about "hey you should come more often"--our group pretty much comes all the time. Rather, this is a reminder to me and you about WHY we come. When I forget why I come, then I start to judge the thing that happens. The actual action of what happens there is much less important than my heart about coming. It's kind of like going to a friend's house for dinner; dinner is rarely the point and if the food is less than stellar, well it doesn't really matter. The communion between me and my friend is what matters.

So, as we come back to fluid and head into our last weeks of 2007, please keep these things in mind:

--put your heart into the deep devotion of your Lover, your Friend, your Father for those short 90 minutes

--hearing His voice is what drives you for 7 more days

--some are there desperate to know that you know they are there; take the time to speak love to them (no one should leave feeling they weren't seen)

-- nothing brings more security than being totally surrendered to the will of God.

-- you cannot be told, you must experience this reality firsthand, so be bold in sharing your secret with others.

-- in the community of worship, you discover who you really are.

-- nothing should be louder than our silent awe in the face of a holy God.

-- it's not a religious event, but an experience in touching the Eternal One and having Him touch us, but our friends (and some new people at fluid) do not know this.

-- there is nothing more than Jesus and He longs to share this short time with you.

December 7, 2007

Over the past few days, I've had the chance to speak to some students about what we do here at Numinous. Both were very intrigued about the ideas of community, the focus on loving one another and on protecting the unity. As I shared, I once again saw clearly the important need in the world today for community.

But, for it to really work, it has to be protected and cultivated. This is not a new idea, of course; we've been saying this from the earliest moment. This call of the church, to "one anothering" each other, is a hard thing to do, however. Reading the New Testament in the light of the mission of the church, I should not be surprised at how hard it is since I see that the very first churches were wrestling over living this thing out. To love one another simply is difficult.

246

It is far easier to walk away. And therein lies the danger. I've seen this in others who used to be in our group or who only casually come around. They want (or wanted) the connection, but were (are) often unwilling to pay the price. Yet the secret to the success of community is actually a small thing.

Investment.

Vernon said at our elders meeting, if everyone really, truly got the notion of what I mean in the "5 minute phone call," in the simple small way of calling to invest in a person, our group would be revolutionarily changed. He is right.

And it simply is not hard.

Our community is strong.

It can be much stronger.

For it to be stronger "I" have to quit waiting on others to do stuff and "I" have to quit being so focused on my own life and start investing in other people. I promise you, that is the secret of a happy and whole life fully connected.

January 8, 2008

I have to keep reminding myself about what I am doing in this walk of faith. I have submitted to the Lord as my King, among many other titles. He owns me and I willingly submit to his leadership about what life means and how to walk within it. As such, I am not at liberty to redefine what a "disciple" or "Christian" looks like or what they do.

What are those things: 4 simple ideas. Be devoted to the teaching of the Bible (happens at fluid, Bliss, in your quiet times, in your small group Bible studies, over coffee, over dinner, at work, and wherever you can break open the Word). Be devoted to the worship of God, the fellowship of the Lord's Meal (happens typically for us at fluid). Be devoted to prayer (happens at fluid, in your quiet time, in your small groups, within your small family). Be devoted to the deep fellowship of the community (happens at Bliss, at movie trips, at group gatherings over coffee, somewhat online).

Note these are not options to choose from. I can't say that since I pray at fluid that I am devoted to prayer if I never speak to God any other time. I can't say that I am devoted to fellowship if I gather over coffee or see movies together, but blow off Bliss. As we have said in previous times, it's a both/and—I do the more corporate things and I do the more private things. Regardless of how you feel about fluid, if you blow that off, you are failing at 3 of the 4 main ideas of God about church. Regardless of how much you love Bliss, if you blow off emailing one another, sharing dinner together, calling one another, then you are failing at a key aspect (fellowship) and maybe 1 other (prayer). Do you see it? All of it is important, as we walk through the mundane day by day life of the community. Note again, this is not Carl creating what I think we should do nor what Carl thinks is the best thing to build a church. Rather, this is us using our disdain for the failure of the current institutional church to look back at the Founders Thoughts and attempting to do those simply.

Fourth, those 4 ideas are based upon the corporate mission of the disciples as given by Jesus: Love one another as He has loved you AND be unified as Jesus and God are One. Maybe you should re-read the Founder's Mission this week as a start to your new year. Head over to John 13 and read through John 17. You'll clearly see his brand new command and you'll see the single thought of his prayer.

April 21, 2008

As I was riding my motorcycle to work, having more quiet time with God, He was reminding me of last night's talk He had through D. We got so much great stuff last night; I am still chewing on it all. For me, one of the most powerful things that stood out was the part right at the start.

Simply put, do things God's way, no matter how weird, stupid or silly it may look. Better, do it His way and he rewards you. Now, I know what some of you think, that you never have gotten the "hook up" that Daniel and his friends got for your faithfulness. Remember, however, the rest of the book. Daniel clearly shows that God's promise of blessing does not counteract the reality that Jesus taught us that the world will HATE you.

Not only do his friends have to face the fiery furnace, but think about the Lion's Den episode. Now that happens many years later and Daniel was probably about 75-85, but don't forget how that happens. His co-administrators got jealous. Now, think back to chapter 2--Daniel saved the lives of all of the King's advisors. Certainly between chapter 2 and chapter 6, some, maybe most of them had died, but if Daniel was still alive, then I have to believe that some others were alive. So, it stands to reason that possibly some of the same guys who conspired against him to throw him to the Lions were the same people who he had personally saved many years before.

Do things God's way.

I know so many Christians who blow it on this point and then wonder why so much junk happens in their lives. This "God's Way" thing includes all of life--how we think about each other, what we do with our time, how we treat the poor, how we fulfill our mission, what we do with our money, our acceptance of submission, our willingness to embrace simplicity, and many other things.

Yes, there are other reasons why "hard times" come to Christians, but in my experience, I can promise you that a large majority of the time it simply happens because God is trying to get someone's attention. In other words, as C.S. Lewis explains, "pain is God's megaphone." And usually, He is trying to get the attention of a believer who has chosen to NOT do things God's way.

Funny how God works--I don't know about you, but often I find myself wondering why God doesn't do more in the punishment realm to non-Christians, especially those who rape the world and seemingly have no care for anyone but themselves. The Psalmists as well as the writer of Ecclesiastes wondered the same thing. Yet, I should not be surprised. Jesus told us that punishment would start in the house of God. In other
words, God is a good parent. He focuses on the upbringing of His children and will use effective chastisement to continue to bring his children into alignment with Him.

Do things God's way.

He wants us to pray, so pray.
He wants us to read His Word, so read.
He wants us to share our money, so give.
He wants us to share our faith, so speak.
He wants us to reject the consumerism of this world, to be merciful, to love peace, to reach out to our neighbors, to love the unlovely, to turn to wise counsel for decisions, to break bread together, to worship Him as a community, to . . . well, the list goes on doesn't it.

Thanks D, for reminding me of this. I have already, today, refocused myself in an area where I had grown lax and had sort of slid away from God's way on the matter.

Do things God's way. It's really for your very best. And, if you are finding yourself challenged in some hard thing of life (not enough time, illness, relationship issues, not enough money, etc...), make your first investigation on the matter to see if you are doing things God's way. Remember, no one is asking for his way to make sense. It made no sense for Daniel to refuse to eat the food. If you are his child, do things His way. So, don't say you don't have enough time, you don't have enough money, you don't have enough whatever--- just do it His way and have faith.

July 1, 2008

It was a great time, wasn't it?

Some 9 years ago (Sept 1999) or so, Kim and I started Bliss on the hope that this would get us close to what the Bible discusses about the church. It was our desperate attempt to bring home what we saw in England when we went over in Feb of that year. It was there that we saw in depth that the secret to the renewal that God was breaking out over there was not some cool band, not a hip speaker, no cool programming, no big building. Rather, what we saw and finally understood was that these people were building relationship and community in a way that I HAD NEVER SEEN IN AN AMERICAN CHURCH!

When that reality was put, in my head, in to context with what I was studying about the church, it all clicked. This was it. The first church, for centuries really, was NOT about programming or about preaching per se or about mere evangelism, but was about being on the journey together. Without the "together" part, it was all just religion, just as it had been all my life. So, we brought it home. I mean, it was in England that we saw we had permission to just hang out, to have a meeting without forcing the Bible into each meeting, to not HAVE TO pray just to feel spiritual, that it was okay to spend the entire night in PLAY since our Father loves us as children and what parent doesn't like to watch their children play! Shoot---it was there we saw the name Bliss and thought, "real church is BLISS so why not make the name as reminder of our aim?"

As we enter into our 10th year of all of this, I pray that you get it, either for the first time or on a deeper level. Bliss is where it is at. And as I have said MANY TIMES, if you are forced to choose, Bliss is more important than fluid. While clearly the need for corporate worship is core in the Bible and Acts 2, at the end of the day, if I have to choose due to life, work, family, or illness, I can worship ON MY OWN! However, I CANNOT FELLOWSHIP ALONE!

Please, make Bliss a priority for your own spiritual health. If you have work issues, please speak to your boss. If you have family pressures, tell them about your desperate need for this time. If you are tired, get more rest Sunday night. If some of you think "well, I don't know all those people," remember community connection runs both ways—its not just you waiting on someone to come talk to you or include you, but it is ALSO YOU STEPPING UP TO INTERACT WITH THE BODY.

Man, last night we had it all going on—people chatting in the shelter, walking for health, volleyball, tennis, playground. If you were ever alone, then that was your choice.

Remember our story—Bliss is not just some religious service, but it is us living life together, learning more about community and how to go deeper in this walk.

August 19, 2008

Have you noticed yet?

Slight, perhaps oblique, and tad bit "under the radar". . . But still there.

Maybe having the retreat later made, for me, a deadened sense of things. Perhaps no one else saw it or felt it. In any case, after a series of things in our collective lives, I wanted to sound the alarm.

252

Not an alarm for panic—we don't panic, for to panic would be to assume control of things has been lost. It hasn't. The One who maintains control still is in charge.

But an alarm calling us to attention, calling us to action, calling us to one another.

I won't try to list everything or everyone, but suffice it to say, once again Numinous is in the cross-hairs of our enemy. Today, while at a prayer gathering with Bailey, one of the missionaries we support, I saw some other acquaintances who I spoke with. As they asked about Numinous, I replied that we were doing great. I went on to say that as I understand the Word, what we are doing is as close to what the early church experienced as I think possible. Sure, I said, it's all in a spectrum with different ones of us getting it better, going deeper, but in general, across the board, on every possible measure of a healthy community, we are moving forward well.

And that's when it hit me—it is that fact that our enemy hates. He hates it that we read the Bible, unlike most who claim to be Christians. He hates that we are devoted to one another. He'll hate it that many of you will do all in your power to help Gwenda pack, perhaps even in the rain and wind. He hates our attempts to become more like Christ and allow His Spirit to live within and through us.

So, as he has done historically, he attacks. He brings conflict in work. He can bring pain in health. He can move to ruin relationships. He can bring monetary set-backs. He brings doubt. He tempts with things perfectly suited to hit you in the right spot.

So, please stop right now and offer up a prayer for the body. If you know of specific things, certainly speak to God about those. But in general, you can merely lift up a prayer asking God to continue to protect us and to guide us through. Remember, sometimes, God likes to use our enemy's efforts against him by ALLOWING us to persevere THROUGH the situation, thus growing stronger. So pray for God to give us the strength, grace and patience to make it through.

Be of good faith my friends. . .remember, greater days are yet to come, greater things are still to be done. . . .

August 29, 2008

This past week, I saw Katie and Ricardo at school and was reminded why I love worship. Even though in both cases we didn't have a lot of time to chat, the heart of worship made the connection between us. Of course, I look forward to seeing both Sunday at fluid. . . .

But what happens at fluid? Really?

For the past 9 years, we've worked really hard to break with molds from the past that we don't think fits the picture of worship. Of course, the Bible gives us a very limited view of what worship was for the first church. A couple of images appear, but they don't seem (to me) to be dogmatic about it. So, we've tried to make our way through.

Of course, 9 years is a long time and with that, even with our best efforts, there are some things that happen often and seemingly in the same place. Perhaps there is no way around that. We know the early church worshipped. We know that the early church heard or talked about "the teaching of the apostles" (not necessarily a "sermon" but certainly someone teaching, others listening and reflecting, perhaps responding with questions or ideas). We know they prayed.

In a 1.5 hour session, there are just so many spots to put things without falling into some routine. We try very hard to keep things fresh and up to date. We do art nights of worship. We've now just had a "science night" of worship. We've met in silence. We've spent the time reading the Word. I hope this is all paying off in giving us a fresh look each Sunday night.

But I do sense one thing continues to remain lacking and I want to draw our attention to it. The one picture of worship for a local body comes to us in I Corinthians 14:26-33. The key thing in that passage, to me, is to be reminded that "its' an us thing." Or, "everyone is an owner." I think we have produced a faithful attempt at trying to build all of that example into what we do---we invite others to speak (not just me as in most churches), we have multiple worship leaders, we invite others to lead "prepare your heart" (I hope you have gotten with D to get your turn) and we do things like "worship through art" where we want everyone to speak or show the word. We gather often in prayer, in 2s and 3s; we allow others to share, and when we teach/speak, we don't shut down others from asking questions or interjecting.

YET, as you already are thinking, we don't do those things much and the interaction of the others could fairly be described as limited, both in when it is allowed/encouraged, and in when people are willing to do it! So, my email to you is to call this to our attention. I suppose the biggest thing I can tell you is to look for ways to bring your experience of God during your week into worship. Look for times during fluid when you can contribute. Sometimes that might just be something you throw out during the pause between a song, or maybe you'll be asked to join in with some testimony of what God has done.

I don't want to tell you more than that for fear that we start to "program" the action, feeling something specific must happen at a certain time and then, well, its not really us just worshipping.

All in all, its a brave idea that we actually allow the Holy Spirit to lead and guide us. Most of us have had no experience in this, or very limited at best. We have some cultural religious baggage with us also. And, we want to be "orderly" as the Bible also tells us.

Just, don't be afraid. Maybe what you want to bring will catch the leader, me, someone else, off guard. Maybe it won't even "sound" right. Just know that I want you all to continue to "own" what we do. Yes, that starts with setting up. Are you certain that the building will be set up in time for fluid? How do you know? Aren't you the owner? Shouldn't you make sure, possibly by coming early to make sure its set up? But it also extends into our collective experience during worship in ways that God leads us.

September 17, 2008

I'm listening to a recording from Seth Godin, who you know I value as a excellent voice about life even though his focus is marketing. He is talking to a group of leaders of non-profits, so that caught my attention.

He just got a question from a small non-profit saying that they are only a small "household" name and how can they "get the word out to spread our story?" Now, he really already answered this earlier by saying that the key focus is to shift from thinking "spam email and direct mail that no one is reading" to "releasing your current supporters to holding a megaphone about what you do."

However, Seth launched into this reply that was strong: **"How dare you be a household name? We don't need any more house hold names. We don't need more than 50,000 households to know who you are or what you do. The goal is not to colonize North America. The goal is to find a very small, tightly knit, loyal, obsessed community that cares deeply about what you do. If your organization can get to 30 people, who care that much, then the question is can each of you find 30 other people, one person at a time. If you can, now you have 900 people. If you can do it** one more time (each person getting 30 more people), then you are up to 27,000."

Did you read that well?   I find this amazing.

Now, please understand, I am not now, nor have I ever been attempting to suggest we should "grow the church" or that "only strength is in large numbers" or that "being a mega-church is something to attain." In fact, those of you who have been around me for a while knows already how I feel about all that large church stuff.

Leave church out of it and think strictly about "who we are and what we do." We are passionate followers of Christ with Good News about life. We are this in a world that has rejected Jesus and/or think "his people," the "church" are whacked and not really folks to hang around. So, we see ourselves as called to be his representatives to a generation (45-under specifically---GenX and Millennial) that has rejected Him through rejecting the church, and yet are deeply spiritual. So, "what we do" and thus care about, are helping people find the truth and learn how to live that out.

I don't know about you, but I would so pumped to know that the 30 of us (yeah, we have a few more but these numbers work easier for me) led 900 people to Jesus, or at least had 900 people "more in the light" of who they are and what it means to be a Christian (even if many of them now realize for the first time that they really are NOT Christians---at least that truth gets them started to a better conclusion later).

900 people.

Let's leave the "large church" questions alone, remembering that we are faithfully holding the notion that "Jesus is the head of the church." If he feels free to give us 900 new people, we'll let him take the lead in figuring that out, just as he has led us in figuring out what to do with 30 people.

BUT, let's not let any sort of fear or worry about his plans keep us from the calling. We certainly are "a very small, tightly knit, loyal, obsessed community that cares deeply about" what we do collectively, about our mission.

Are you already working on your 30 people?

Sure, exciting someone about a non-profit about putting new shoes into the homes of the poor is less challenging that sharing about Jesus. I mean, he already admitted that when he said that "I have come to divide" (Matt 10:34-35). People reject Jesus, thus they reject our mission. But, can we at least admit that we brought it up with 30 people? Can we stoke the fire of our passion so that we don't quit? In other words, rather than merely seeing our existence as something for ourselves only, we understand that we are "the obsessed" that "cares deeply" about Jesus and helping people just like us.

Man, I hope this fires up your passion for Jesus and what he has saved you for. Remember, we've never hid this part or downgraded this aspect of being a Christian. Quick reminder:

--Your purpose in life is to glorify God
--Your goal in life is to become like Christ
--**Your mission in life is to be God's representative**

Of course, we know our corporate mission—**to love one another and to be unified**, but also remember that Jesus tied those goals directly to our individual mission.

How about it? Between now and next summer, we collectively tell 900 people? I really think this is a challenge I want us to undertake—each tells 30. We'll let God take care of what happens; that's his business anyway who gets saved and what they do and all that stuff. But honestly can many of us state that we have had strong spiritual conversations with 30 different people expressing our Good News?

All I know is that when he said "The goal is to find a very small, tightly knit, loyal, obsessed community that cares deeply about what you do." I thought, "that is Numinous." Let's not squander what God has given us or asked us to do. So, "If your organization can get to 30 people, who care that much, then the question is can each of you find 30 other people, one person at a time?" Well?

December 14, 2008

My take remains, I believe, the same as through the years. We must continue to take steps towards a deeper walk into the real life of faith. Not pretend spirituality, not rigid fundamentalism, not lackadaisical libertarianism---but the real, deep walk of obedience as a slave of Christ. Some seek signs, other seek freedom, still more look for the law---Christ has called us into the MORE risky narrow road where real faith is demonstrated in our every day life.

Do I really spend time reading the Bible?
Do I really spend time in prayer?
Do I really spend time in fellowship with the body?
Do I really devote myself to one another?
Do I really share all of my resources with one another?

That last question is where the rubber will seriously meet the road. When we consider all the things where we can and perhaps should put our financial resources (like the various requests I read tonight; or stuff in the video; or giving to others to have clean water or food), those resources will only come as I break the hold that consumerism has on me. If I were to ask each person or couple in our group, I believe that you would honestly tell me that you don't think you have enough to get by on as it is. . .and once I saw your budget, I would agree with you.

HOWEVER, if we really want to go deeper in the areas of simplicity and how we live, going into real deep belt-tightening will be a part of that. We will give more when God is given more by each other. None of us will be able to give more until we decide to break free into simplicity and simply buy less---less eating out, less junk food, less stuff.

I know for most of us (all of us??) we probably think we are giving as much as we possibly can. . .yet we all have cell phones and most of us have extra stuff on our phones that we know we don't NEED (like data service). I know, I know, I can go into all kinds of areas (TV, clothes, computer, Internet, gaming, cars, CDs, and so forth) and I am not a saint, I am not perfect. Kim and I battle this all the time and covet your prayers that we TOO go deeper into simplicity!! Some of us, however. . .are we ever giving? Are we willing to take the stand of the widow giving all (Mark 12:42-43)? If we aren't giving to the body, how are we even being obedient in this clearly defined command of God?

Sorry for going on---when I really "saw the Lord" back in college, I knew that in my simplicity, I merely wanted to live a life of faith as a real Christian--following and obeying. Over the past 24 years, I have called others to that same road---it is the hard and narrow road. I've been accused many times of demanding too much, expecting people to go deeper than they naturally will---I simply see no other option. This IS the call of the gospel. So, I feel compelled to tell you, remind you, exhort you, urge you, admonish you, beg you to really live out a real life of faith and here (simplicity, sharing) is one place of discipleship.

As we head into Christmas, I just simply want you to experience that deep walk with God in real areas of faith. . .and I believe you are, all of you. But we can go deeper and how we go deeper is exactly what Paul said--beat our bodies into submission so we continue to live by faith, not trusting in the flesh, not trusting in wealth, not trusting in anything but God. And I know you want to go there. . .though you may be afraid of what it could entail. Of course, I could tell you more about how I think we won't have an option (either go deeper or be forced to recant), but I'll leave that for later.

I hope you will pray with me and take these steps. Let's see just how powerful a body of believers who hold tightly to real faith is.

December 24, 2008

Tomorrow can be so busy and fun, I thought I might not get the computer on to tell you how much I love you.

It is very hard to believe that 10 years has flown by since Kim and I bravely stepped into the "next step" of God's plan for our personal journey. Little did we know that it would, 10 years later, involve all of you. The path has not been what I imagined, but as I testify about Kim, my beautiful and precious godly wife, it (and she) is more (and better) than I could have imagined. I always think about Paul's prayer in Ephesians when he prays "God is able to accomplish infinitely more than we could ever dare to ask or hope, more than we could even imagine." (read the whole prayer at Eph 3:14-21)

I don't know all the reasons He felt like moving the idea of Numinous this direction, but we submit as happy slaves to our loving Master, knowing He always has our best in mind in keeping with His larger plans in life. But I do know that it is a tremendous honor to lead you, to pray with you, to cry with you, to watch and empathize through your disappointments, to rejoice with you through the excitement of success. I tell people all the time that this, Numinous—this quest of community of the "called out ones" in the manner of the first church—is the hardest thing I have ever done. And it is. It often tears out my soul, much like Paul said to the "called out ones" in Corinth when he wrote, "I carry the daily burden of how the churches are getting along. I mean, who is weak among you without my feeling that weakness? Who is led astray, and I do not burn with anger!?"

Yet, though it is so hard, it is also a joy. As Paul wrote many times, when I think of you, I fall to my knees in prayer and rejoice over you. You are my crown and the evidence of the power of our God. Next time we get together—look around. Look deeply at the faces. Here are former murderers, addicts, worshippers of Satan, adulterers, liars, gossips, those who cursed God, some who believed there was no God, some who practiced witchcraft, many who hated their parents or whose parents hated them, broken, torn, weak and bitter people. And yet, look at the faces—each gladly lifting their faces to worship the God of all creation. These faces are evidence that something has changed! Some nay-sayers may accuse us of being weak minded to follow a myth. Others might accuse me of being a pied-piper or even a magician, a worker of evil, leading you poor confused people astray. They, these who dismiss your testimony, miss the power of the Holy Spirit and all that He has accomplished in your lives.

So, tomorrow (well today too), REJOICE. Again I say to you REJOICE. Yes, some of us stumble in the pain of confusion; our path seems dark. Others are weak in our bodies, torn with illness and medical issues. Some are in poverty, seriously wondering if a call for a job, any job, will come. Some of us are in jobs not of our choosing, and though we minister in faith in the place God has put us, emotionally it is hard many days to get up and go again. But through these, we are not beaten down, but rather more dependent upon the Father. He, who loved us so much to give His own Son for our good, has not forgotten you. He is the "God who Sees" and as Immanuel, God is INDEED WITH US!

Please take 5 minutes tomorrow, early in the day, perhaps with

262

your family, certainly with your children (yes, even with the weeks old child for now is the time to lay the foundation), and pray thanksgiving and joy for the birth of His Son who is STILL with us (and that indeed is GOOD NEWS)! I love you all!

January 23, 2009

Hi gang—I know that typically you don't know what I know about what God is presenting to us, showing us. I wonder if I need to do a better job of including you in those thoughts. There's never an idea of "I shouldn't share," but usually just not even thinking about it.

This has come up, though, this week as I have been pondering Sunday. For the past 6-8 months, I've been in prayer and wrestling with God about what He wants for us, where He wants to take us, what He wants us to hear and think about. For the past 3 Sundays, we have embarked on that.

This Sunday will be a wonderful celebration, a kick-off in some senses, of where God is taking us, of what God is reminding us of. I wanted you to know so that you were as eager as I to be there, fully engaged and hungry for this connection with God and each other. Boy, I REALLY want to see each of you there. I wish I could fly Andrea and Gretchen down here, I wish I could drive up to G-ville and get Trish and Rusty down here. It's like planning a special party and you want all of your friends there, eager, excited and engaged!

I plan on spelling out in greater detail what I have meant by this "30 reaching 30" thing, which from here on out I will indicate by writing "3r3." There are plans for various graphics and designs, perhaps even a T-shirt (though that may come across as cheesy, so let me know what you think about that). We are going to have some eats, Chris is going to lead us in a few simple songs, we are going to read the Word and we are going to pray with each other. All of the children are going to be with us, so its going to be a fun atmosphere.

Please prioritize our time together. I really believe that God is pressing the 3r3 concept for us! I know stuff comes up; we are all in prayer for the Porters as they travel today and are in mourning for their loss. Yet, typically, not as much comes up like that and our time together is our only chance to really see one another each week. Our 4 bliss groups stand on the foundation of our larger unity which is supported mainly through our coming together here, online, and there, at fluid. I know you know this, and that in general terms, you care. But, if you are like me, it helps to be reminded. One of my Christian students, not in Numinous, reminded me that the passion of our gathering is ONLY built out of the passion for the relationship with Jesus, the reason for the gathering in the first place. In other words, "I" come (and I come eager and ready to participate with zest, not slumbering through or bored-ly watching) because of my relationship with Jesus, to enjoy this date with Jesus and to hear all that He has to say to me, say to me THROUGH the gathering of the community.

Well, I know you love Jesus and wish for that same experience each week as I do. Everyone who volunteers their time to help prepare, move chairs, sing, bring pillows and the like all do that because they want each of us to have a blast, really experience the joy of our gathering.

I look so forward to seeing you this weekend. Remember to do all in your power to protect our community and our gathering together. Get enough sleep Saturday night so as to be fully engaged. Build your calendar around being there. Trust God in things like your education so that you don't ever neglect the date He has planned for you at fluid on the thought of "I need to study"--make sure you plan your life well to get that kind of stuff, or any other kind of task, handled during the rest of the hours of your life.

We are going to have yet another super time together—snacks, songs, laughter, love, teaching, testimony, care and community. I will see you Sunday night!

February 21, 2009

It is clear that we remain under attack. I cannot separate what is going on to Vernon, Kelly C, Jen A, Gwenda, the Porters and perhaps others that I am momentarily forgetting.

These are not isolated events.

Perhaps God is only questioning each one of us as to just how serious we are about the community thing. Perhaps we are facing our finest hour when we will dig deeper than before. Perhaps this is nothing more than an early taste to what lies before us in the years to come when if we hope to make it through, it will only happen as we turn to a deeper trust with each other.

We will not have the financial strength to merely "muscle through." We can only hope to come through on our weakness--so that when we are weak, He is strong. We MUST turn to Him and plead for His protection. You must seek His face while it may be found and remind God of his promise to us.

PLEASE--I am begging you. Do not neglect the body in this time, and by that, I mean seriously turn before the Lord. Please, tomorrow, or if you don't read this till Monday or Tuesday, then immediately when you read this--take serious time. This is not a "pray while you are in the shower" or "pray while you are getting dressed" type thing. I am begging you to kneel or sit before the Lord--perhaps you may feel led to lay prostrate before Him.

--Pray for his healing for Kelly and Jen.
--Pray for him to protect us.
--Pray for those who need work such as Matthew and Gwenda.

--Pray specifically for Vernon to have a place to stay.
--Pray for God to deliver.
--Pray for wisdom so that we can know what God wants us to do.

Yes, we may be facing times when merely needing space for a teen or a baby isn't a good enough reason and we find ourselves with many people sleeping on floors together. Yet, for now, I have to believe that in some of our couples, or singles, there is a spot for Vernon.

So, again, if you have ever loved me enough to follow me, I am begging you now to stand together for the body and pray for this and the other things I have listed above.

March 10, 2009

We talked Sunday night about what it means to be a Christ-follower. We didn't get into the details, or perhaps better stated, I merely covered the many details we've talked about over the past 10 years together. Bottom line, we are each called to follow—he is the Shepherd, he leads the sheep, we merely follow him to safe pasture and food. He protects us.

So, all of that to say that again and again, we are stressing our message we tell others (3r3) is the message of hope and good news—that God is with us. Of course, that then really means that He is WITH us and wants to speak with us, lead us, protect us and show us the way. Yes, I realize that for many of us we still are not good at hearing Him, or we think that we have been following Him but things haven't turned out great so thus (we think) God isn't really in the business of speaking to us (or protecting us or caring for us). Of course, we know (or should know) those are lies of the enemy who is the best liar in the world and loves to screw with us. We remember (or should remember) that we are in a war and our enemy is stronger than us (us in our own strength). Today, Meryn read Psalm 21 in our family Bible time that reminded us that the victory is in the Lord and His strength. So, our challenge is to be strong in the Lord, wearing His armor in the daily battle, and seeking to make sure that we are indeed listening well.

We'll be covering this more in the weeks to come—a lot of what I just wrote has been my own personal struggle over the past 1.5 years which has led us to this place where we are more intentionally engaging in 3r3.

May 4, 2009

I suppose as we continue to enter this stage of the coming crisis, I have a grim satisfaction that I have been telling people for years about this. I'm not sure others have listened, but I maintain a hope that you, at least, have listened and are on some solid financial footing. I do realize how tough this is for all of us; as I have loudly testified, I can shop and spend with the best of them. All the research shows that it is the men who will crash and burn more quickly with very large purchases and thus ruin budgets. Yet, by maintaining a constant focus on this Spiritual Discipline, we build in a habit of tuning out the consumerist siren call to spend, spend, spend.

Perhaps these articles will, then, be a healthy reminder of all we have said on this topic. And, for some newer people, perhaps these articles will be a good starting point to take a long, hard look again at your budget. Kim and I did our annual financial summit over our budget, made some decisions, restructured some money, saw where we had grown lax and lazy, chastised one another for wasteful spending, and reprioritized our commitment NOT TO mere frugality or self-denial BUT RATHER TO A DEEPER FOCUS on God and His ways. Remember, simplicity not allows for me to be financially stable, but also allows God to have more of HIS OWN RESOURCES to use---I live on only 60% or 70% of what I make allows for Him to use the other 40% for His needs—feeding the poor, giving to the body, helping my neighbors, etc.....

This is why we live this way; as I said last night, we live in the world "very differently" than those around me. They notice. Trust me; as you embrace simplicity—others will notice. So, when I get a raise, it is not a license to spend more, but rather a chance to give more to God. When I pay off my debt, it is not freedom to start spending that money elsewhere, but a chance to give more to God. When I pay off my house, I don't just turn around and invest all of that money to my own retirement or other things "I want," but rather a chance to give more to God. Sure, in all these instances, I am commanded to be a sharp, wise, Godly Resource Manager, watching over his trust that includes my family, my house, these possessions. I should not default on my house debt while I pay money to the poor, thus assuming God will rescue me. But I also should not be wasting money each month on things like cable, cell phones, eating out, random purchases, multiple cars, new clothes and then wonder why God is not making the house payment.

June 14, 2009

Wow—what an incredible weekend. You know, every time we come back I can't believe it was as good as it was, yet God continues to blow us away.

So many thoughts right now, but one big thing to say openly so that everyone sees it.

Our over-arching theme was the notion of "into the next decade." Where does God want to take us? Well, as I try to wrap-up each retreat, I usually ask a certain question. This year I laid it out on Thursday night and now am asking it again to all---

Are you with me? I hope and pray that you are.

As I said today, challenging days are ahead of us. This has little to do with any specific world situations or world leaders---as you know, I've been saying this for over 15 years now. It seems clear that things I thought about back in the 90s, things I said to Chris Kutcher, D, and Matthew as young men are now happening. Things Stephanie Hill heard me say at UCF, speaking to her BSU group, are the things that Stephanie Porter now sees happening around her. So, the other question also remains, "are you ready?"

Perhaps we aren't, just as you can't totally be ready for a hurricane, but we can do a few things—we can make sure that spiritually we are on the same page as God, and we can make sure that we are deep into the community!

At the retreat, I laid out one major (perhaps shocking) change that God has directed for us to undertake this year. It is something He has been leading me to for about 6 months or more. It's so big, that I didn't trust myself, so I laid it before the elders 2 months ago and confessed that my spirit or heart might be wrong on this. They prayed. They agreed that God was leading us this way.

We are not going to hold *fluid* for a month!

When I first told the elders, Stephanie said she almost immediately knew it must be God because she couldn't imagine me even joking about that. I love worship so much. I love how we hear from God at this time. However, I think He is determined to teach us a few things in this. There is a lot to say and I will share more in person at our last *fluid*, June 21 (which also happens to be Father's Day). For now, realize that perhaps one of the biggest points is for us to realize how serious God is about worship and about His glory.

Do you love worship as Jesus did?

There are other things God wants us to take from the retreat as it relates to fluid and we'll see those over the next weeks. I am eager, though a bit nervous, to see what all God does do!

I know this may be sad for some, or nerve-wracking for others. At least 4 different people on the retreat expressed their clear concern and unhappiness with me on this. Not anger at me, but sadness at losing fluid, losing the month of worship. That is, to a very large degree, what I hope to hear from the other 36 people on retreat and the 10 or so of you who weren't on the retreat. A sadness, a longing, a deep desire to see one another and worship deeply.

Let me leave you with this thought—as I drove home with Kim and the girls, I remarked that what makes the retreat worship so special is that everyone really gives themselves to the Holy Spirit and to the worship! After 48+ hours of being together, there is a sense of unity, of having "been through it together" and that manifests itself in retreat.

Fluid is supposed to be that way EACH WEEK. It should be, in your mind, like a mini-retreat—a moment when we, those who are going "through it together," get to come together, and be before our God. A time when the frustrations of the week can be set aside, when I can turn to these around me who truly love me, perhaps to cry, or to dance, or to simply lay my head on their shoulder and have them pray for me. . .just like we saw today in worship.

So, what happens to you? I think you forget. You forget how it feels. You forget to celebrate. You forget to invest during the week, so unlike retreat, you come to the House of God somewhat a stranger, having had little to no contact with each other. You forget to allow the Holy Spirit to move. You forget you are an owner!

My prayer, and what I think God is trying to say during this "Fast from Fluid," is that you don't forget. When its November or early

February, when life has come at you hard, when you are tired or perhaps ill, when temptations have come up (maybe temptations presented by your own family members) that try to lure you away on a given Sunday—DO NOT FORGET!

Come to the "Weekly Mini-Retreat" that we call *fluid* with a heart as eager to be with God as we felt today at *fluid* on retreat!

God is good and God is great! He will sustain us during this month-long fast. We will emerge stronger.

Welcome to the Revolution!

July 22, 2009

For the past 4 weeks, we have been fasting from fluid, looking for multiple things to happen and they have. I know that much of what God has been doing or showing may be "beneath the surface," perhaps subconscious at this point, things that He will bring out in the days to come. I hope that you will continue to pray deeply for what God is saying to you, and noticing the critical connection of worship, community, God, AND YOU!

Just today, I was having a conversation and making the point that EACH person's connection at fluid and Bliss is critical! I think this is why I get so sad, and frustrated, when people miss. As we've said many times before, sure—some people are missing for very valid reasons like vacations or illnesses; but so many other times, people miss just because, well, I don't know, they miss for vague reasons. So, in my conversation today I was pointing out that whenever ANY PERSON of our group is missing, then the group fails, the group is weaker, the group is NOT the same. If it were the same, if it "didn't matter" whether a person was there or not, then we become nothing more than a consumer-styled business. Yes, I have said that fluid is our "vertical time, focused on God" and that we'd go on without a given person. And we do, but nonetheless, "you" not being there is death for the group. Just remind yourself that "without me, Numinous will never be the same."

July 25, 2009

Sunday, in many ways, is the kickoff of our journey into the next decade. I hope you are excited, but moreover I hope you are more aware of God than ever before.

Numinous has always been an idea, a concept, a hope and a dream. Although early I had to do the functional stuff of officially registering us as an organization, then 2 years later, we more officially saw a part of what Numinous, Inc did as becoming "a Church," the core of what Numinous means is an idea.

It is an idea that there are people in the US who are hungry for something more. It is a concept that there is a "spiritual presence" around and within this supposedly lost, jaded, angry or bitter generation—the notion of "spiritual presence" being the core of what the word "numinous" means. It is a hope that these people will be willing to admit that how they've been living simply isn't working and that they might consider (or more likely, re-consider) the Christian God. It is a dream these people will then "go the distance" through the tough slog of life, willing to live life "God's way," letting Him mold and shape them into something radically different than the world around them.

So, ultimately, Numinous is only people. But therein lies the rub for if you've been alive at all for more than a decade or so, you know people are weird, infuriating, exasperating, thrilling, loveable, crazy, prideful, surprising and a whole bunch of other adjectives that attempt poorly to define the challenge of being around other people. It is community and, as I have said many times before, community is the hardest thing in the world to ever do.

The hardest part may be simply the "mundane-ness" to life in the body—it never ends. There isn't a completion. And, as humans, we are easily bored or distracted. So, in many other areas, I could get excited about doing a new thing, and then a year or so later, could get bored and just move on. No harm, no foul. I can change jobs if I wish. I can stop liking a musical artist or find a new TV show (leaving another show that I used to watch). However, in the faith, that is NOT what God wants NOR what community means.

God's call to the faith is predicated on a devotion to Him and to one another. It means that I will submit all other things UNDER the call to Him. Nothing gets between me and Him or His ways.

You see the problem here, don't you? In our natural state, we don't want to be that devoted long term (not to mention that we chafe at anything or anyone who tries to "tell us what to do"--of course, that ability to tell us what to do is part of what it means TO BE GOD—either He can tell us what to do or He is not God).

I tell you this (and yes, there is more I want to tell you, but. . .) to urge you to re-kindle your first love for the things of God. Don't let things like vacations, moving, children, jobs, no work, too much work, dating relationships, activities or any of the rest of life come between you and God. Instead, have Him infuse ALL of those things. That's right—God wants us to enjoy life, so we do all of those things, BUT we do them on God's terms. For instance, we know that God can't betray himself, so it is impossible for me to infuse God into my movie going life when I am watching movies that perhaps devalue life, are overly sexual or perhaps glorify the occult or evil. Or, I can't be having God infuse my life in the area of, say, taking care of my house and yet spend all my money on things like mulch for the yard, thus having none to share with others, to give to the poor or give to the Church.

As we move into this first Sunday of the next decade, I beg you to think deeply and meditate on what it truly means to be called by Him, to be His slave, owned, lead, molded and shaped by Him—all for your good. Let your actions and thoughts match what that means and re-focus your devotion on His ways!

I love you guys and Know that you can do this! You have all made such strides, huge strides, in your spiritual growth. Now, LET'S GO!! LET'S GO DEEPER! Let your light shine before all people, saving and rescuing the many who are dying simply by living your life in His ways—they see you and see the truth! They see our idea, concept, hope and dream. I believe you! Now, give evidence to what I believe to be true about you—prioritize the community, prioritize your prayer life, dig deeply into God's word, be devoted to the worship in the body (that means BE at fluid with the same passion as we had at retreat, or as we saw in that wedding video), be in love with one another in Bliss.

January 4, 2010

Why does it even matter? Why go through the bother of gathering?

Well, to start with, we are told to and as we know, choosing to be a Christian is to be someone who chooses to obey what God commands (John 15:10). Secondly, we know that the current Christian church is pretty broken when we look at the evidence of the product those churches produce. The state of Christianity in the USA is pitiful. When we started in 1998, I did research then on the state of the church and our findings, based on experts like Josh McDowell and George Barna, were troubling. Recent research from the last 2 years shows that things have gotten worse. SO, to buck this trend, we have attempted to turn back to the first church to just copy them. So, we see that gathering was a core activity, and they did it all the time.

Thirdly, we know that the human was created with an innate need to "know and be known." That need can be met in many ways and in earlier times, many had the need met through friendships, family and organizations through their local community. However, since the 1950s, we have lost all of that. Yes, the last decade has introduced us to the joys of electronic connection and various things have helped rebuild new electronic communities. Still, sociologists, psychologists and cultural experts now are putting evidence to the common sense observation that we need to be "known" with a human touch; that no electronic community can adequately replace being with real people in real connections. Thus, to remain psychologically happy and healthy, we need to gather.

Lastly, in a time of crisis, you need others to turn to. Around us we still have several who are in financial distress. We may soon need to share our food or our cars or our homes. Many of you have played "end of the world" games with zombies or war or fast cars, and you already know that in those settings, you basically have no one (or few) people you can trust. While we are not in a "end of the world" setting (though on Monday, with new classes beginning, I might see some zombies coming), as things stay basically hard, perhaps bad,--do you plan on trying to build authentic relationships of trust and devotion AT THAT TIME? Or, will you need those relationships NOW, in order to prove the trust and devotion are real? I think you know the answer.

January 24, 2010

Sometimes I think many of you don't really remember why we do what we do. Others criticize us for not being spiritual enough. I've had people ask "how can you skip a night of worship for playing games?" The answer not only lies in our history, but lies in what the Bible teaches is core to the point of our existence as a group.

Simple version—the Bible says that there were 4 core points of unity to which the church was devoted. They are listed in a simple list and there is no apparent idea of one of the 4 being more important based on where it was stated. At no point is there any concept that only a few of the 4 things matter; that we can ignore the others. Thus, we can understand the simple notion that focusing on all 4 things is central to what it means to be church. Fellowship, a deep sense of connection together, is one of those 4 things. In my experience, for many churches, fellowship is an afterthought, the little extra time spent after a service or maybe the occasional "Sunday School Class gathering." While those things are fine, they are not really giving "fellowship" the same time and effort that the 3 other things listed (worship, Bible teaching, prayer) are given.

So, when we have "4th Sunday" (of either type, but particularly a "Fourth Sunday where we do something"), that is a direct monthly attempt on our part to focus on what God says to focus on. Maybe for some of our critics, those who have left us or have derisively never joined "our weird cult thing," they will find us deeper in sin for not taking this time to do some religious activity or sing just one more song. For me, I felt the presence of the Lord sitting around a table chatting with members of His body, knowing that at that moment, being friends with these people for whom, without Christ I would never know, I was as deep in worship of my God as I ever could have been.

February 17, 2010

Was reading John today in chapter 11, the story about Jesus raising Lazarus. Take a moment to read 11:16, please.

This verse blows me away, though today I blew past it. I was so excited to get to the part where Jesus does his stuff. As I was reading more though, I was taken back to this verse. What got me there were the disciples' fears about death. Back in verse 7, Jesus announces that they are going back to Judea, basically back to Jerusalem.

Now, by this point, the disciples have seen more than you or I can really imagine. I mean, just think—dude walks on water, sins demons into pigs, feeds 5000, stops a storm, makes a lame guy walk, feeds 4000 more people—these guys have seen a ton, but honestly, they don't really believe. Jesus admits as much in verse 15. Whenever I read things like that, I wonder what Jesus thinks of my own faith. Anyway, so in verse 8, the disciples try to warn him off—they say in some shock that Jesus would be crazy for going back there because the last time they tried to stone him (10:22-33, the previous December).

Jesus answers with a predictably obscure point (which I could explain in more depth but won't for now); they don't get it, so Jesus just says it plainly in v14-15. Then comes Thomas.

You know Thomas—he's the one forever going through history as "Doubting Thomas." I wonder if 100s of years from now, one of us will have done something in our lives to be remembered for that one act. Think about it—one act and the dude is forever "doubting." Others have fared like that—Benedict Arnold is a traitor, John the Good, Charles the Great (Charlemagne). Anyway, poor Thomas was probably only saying what we'd all say. But that's after the crucifixion and this is back in chapter 11. Here, there's not a lot of doubt.

"Let's go too---and die with Jesus."

So, as I was reading, God was reminding me of my proclamations of faith and my wrestling with doubt, the times of my great triumphs in his name and the times when its sort of hard to see that I'm a Christian. And, so I was left with Thomas' words and was thinking, "is that my proclamation?" Am I ready to go with Jesus and to go knowing that I'll die. And, for most of us, we aren't really talking about physically dying, but we are talking about other kinds of death. Death to having possessions. Death to having all the time in the world for myself. Death to others' opinions. Death to getting be cool when I need to protect someone less fortunate or needy. Death to getting to have my own opinion and go wherever I wish.

Good and hard question, huh?

April 26, 2010

What God wants is fairly clearly laid out. There are a host of things, commands, that He has expressed about my connection to Him and connection to others. Some classic verses remind us to "do what is right, to love mercy, and to walk humbly with your God." (Micah 6:8). Hosea reminds us to "show love" and David tells us that God wants a "broken spirit and a contrite heart" (Ps. 51) from us (rather than pride, arrogance, or a haughty spirit). I could go on but you know the rest—He wants us to spend time with Him in the Word, talk with Him, have a spirit like Jesus and so forth. Each of these things is something that happens with me and me alone, yet depends solely upon my volition of my will. I have to choose to do these things, or, in effect, I am choosing to NOT do them. There is no "oh, I just forgot but I wanted to" concept. I either chose to do them or I chose to not do them.

At the same time, God draws us together for the entire purpose of finding strength and companionship in order to make the journey successfully. To accomplish the above paragraph, I need others on the journey with me. And not just random others, but people who invest in me deeply and in whom I invest. Again, this comes back to the volition of my will. The Bliss leaders have been working this month to remind us of the need to find harmony together, the act of living in the "pleasing combination of sounds" or the "pleasantness of arrangement."

How do we do that? Well, the same way the first Christians did it--
by choosing intentionally to interact and invest in one another.
We are told that they ate meals together, they spent time
together (both in organized religious/spiritual moments [worship,
prayer, Bliss, fluid] and in the unorganized moments of life
[shopping, playing games, movies, road trips, helping move, making
meals], and generally lived life in a deep connection.

We are close because we say we are close, and then we look for
ways to make that statement of our will tangible. We call them.
We share special days together. If we live close, then we see them,
share meals together.

But note the critical thing—it starts in the will, in the mind---"this
person is my family, my friend, and I am close to them—I care for
them." That volitional choice of my will dictates how I will treat
them. I will happily invest my time or my money into their lives. I
will pray for them easily. I will call them. How they are doing
matters to me.

This idea is, then, the entire point of why God calls his followers the
"family of God." He calls us His "friends." And in the early church,
this was the point. We are told by ancient sources that outsiders
knew this group of freaks had something unique because it was
seen that "how they love each other" was unlike anything these
outsiders had ever seen in their religious experience. This concept
is PRECISELY what God wants Numinous to be. . .and what we ARE!
:) As I look back over our 10 years, this concept is what we have
accomplished—not perfectly of course, but this is who we are.
This, also, is why so many others can't seem to "get us."

We are determined to do as God commands. And that takes you to
choose with your will to stay connected. Today, right now if you
can, call someone in our group. Reach out to someone in our
family to simply and quickly express that you love them, are

invested in them, are choosing them. Call someone who you haven't spoken to in a while and someone that you know you won't see at Bliss tonight (or if you are reading this on Tuesday, then someone you didn't see at Bliss on Monday).

Let's stay determined to use our will to choose to be in harmony together, and then, as we are doing all of the specific things He has asked of us (including sharing our Good News with those around us), the outsiders will notice "my, how those people really love one another."

April 27, 2010

Once again, as a body, we find ourselves experiencing loss. Have you looked around lately? Do you see who isn't here? Who is missing? Have you reached out to them?

Bobby and I talked last night on the way home from Bliss (while I miss riding with Kim and the girls, I have really enjoyed my time carpooling with Bobby as we share many ideas and thoughts). We noted that for whatever reason, another member of the body had passed beyond our reach, at least for now. In that conversation, facing a sadness of realization, I repeated to Bobby the idea that has been a core one from day one in Numinous—investment is a two way street.

If someone is missing for more than 2 weeks and you don't notice, don't reach out, how can we claim to be invested in one another? If you heard that your best friend or family member was struggling, was missing, was in pain for whatever reason, would you not reach out? Remember what I wrote you yesterday; this is why God calls his disciples the "Family of God." We are a family and the idea of church MUST BE SEEN in this light! But, it also cuts both ways---if a person claims to be one of us, in our family, they can't simply vanish without a trace. How does that work? What kind of action

280

is that? It is the action of someone who has cut off investment in one another.

I got an email from Gretchen yesterday and she wrote " I pray that the body can realize what a rare thing our community is there, and that they treasure the closeness they have and not take it for granted." Spoken, of course, by someone who has not had the depth of spiritual community since leaving here.

The great challenge of Christians, I am convinced, is not the fight with the enemy. In that case, when a Christian figures out they are in the battle, they get fired up, geared up and turn to the power source for help. No, the great challenge is boredom, the mundaneness of life. We get wrapped up in the NBA playoffs or mowing the grass or worrying about our job (or lack of job) or going to the grocery store and God becomes a great afterthought. If we really hope to see the Holy Spirit explode in Numinous (and OH GOD do we NEED this NOW in our body!!!!), we must be so focused on Him through the activities of our lives!

Yesterday I wrote this: "And that takes you to choose with your will to stay connected. Today, right now if you can, call someone in our group. Reach out to someone in our family to simply and quickly express that you love them, are invested in them, are choosing them. Call someone who you haven't spoken to in a while and someone that you know you won't see at Bliss tonight (or if you are reading this on Tuesday, then someone you didn't see at Bliss on Monday)." Did you do it? Please do it today.

June 1, 2010

We've been talking a lot at fluid & Bliss about how the battle relative to spiritual wellness is one in which we cannot win through effort alone. The verse that the Bliss leaders focused on last month told us the spiritual health comes IN COMMUNITY (confess to one another) and WITH PRAYER (pray...that you may be healed). We saw three weeks ago at fluid that the battle of spiritual wellness will not be won without prayer. And last Sunday, we saw that if we choose to not believe, not act in the ways God has said, that the enemy of this world can and will blind us. And, as the story in Mark demonstrated, even Jesus himself cannot just snap his fingers and eliminate spiritual blindness, particularly that caused by the yeast of the Pharisees (spiritual pride) or the yeast of Herod (pride in power, money, fame).

So, with that backdrop, and remembering what was shared last night in the house blessing, consider what Oswald Chambers wrote today:

> Can a sinner be turned into a saint? Can a twisted life be made right? There is only one appropriate answer— "O Lord God, You know" (Ezekiel37:3-- *He said to me, 'Son of man, can these bones live?'*). Never forge ahead with your religious common sense and say, "Oh, yes, with just a little more Bible reading, devotional time, and prayer, I see how it can be done."

> It is much easier to *do* **something than to trust in God;** we see the activity and mistake panic for inspiration. That is why we see so few fellow workers *with* God, yet so many people working *for* God. We would much rather work for God than believe in Him. Do I really believe that God will do in me what I cannot do? The degree of hopelessness I have for others comes from never realizing that God has done anything for me. Is my own personal experience such a wonderful realization of God's power and might that I can never have a sense of hopelessness for anyone else I see? Has any spiritual work been accomplished in me at all? **The degree of panic activity in my life is equal to the degree of my lack of personal spiritual experience.**

"Behold, O My people, I will open your graves . . ." (Ezekiel 37:12). When God wants to show you what human nature is like separated from Himself, He shows it to you in yourself. If the Spirit of God has ever given you a vision of what you are apart from the grace of God (and He will only do this when His Spirit is at work in you), **then you know that in reality there is no criminal half as bad as you yourself could be without His grace.** My "grave" has been opened by God and "I know that in me (that is, in my flesh) nothing good dwells" (Romans 7:18). God's Spirit continually reveals to His children what human nature is like apart from His grace. [emphasis added]

Of course, as you should hopefully remember from Sunday, this is precisely what Paul wrote about in I Corinthians 2:7-10. We aren't right with God or have spiritual wellness because we are special in ourselves, as if we have done something individually. Rather, we are spiritually well because of God's grace, his Holy Spirit revealing to us; in other words, God removing the blindness.

Now, before you misread Chambers, he is NOT saying "quit doing the Spiritual disciplines." But they are done NOT to somehow placate God or to earn heaven; they are done in response to understanding that only God himself produces spiritual wellness. Only God himself can make dry, dusty bones like Carl Creasman live again. As I find myself in newness of life, I then choose to embark upon the narrow road to real life, allowing God to re-make me and re-mold me. I allow Him to do that by surrender, by obeying his commands, by being in community and by growing spiritually strong through the spiritual disciplines.

I pray that this day, you will again kneel before your maker and surrender to him again—making it clear that you realize what He has done.

August 16, 2010

I just finished mowing the yard. As most of you know, we have a small walkway that leads to our front door. Over the years, I have noticed something amazing.

Weeds and grass can carry dirt.

I never knew. I mean, they have no hands, no wheelbarrows, no obvious way of pulling off this feat, but they do it.

How do I know?

Because, given enough time, my walkway shrinks in size as my grass (and some weeds) move onto the stones. If I give it enough time, say a month, before I use the edger, the grass, dirt and weeds can move as much as 2-3 inches on either side.

Sin is like that. Few of us are trying to look for ways to screw up our lives or purposefully walk away from God. Instead, we are merely going about our normal lives, trying to balance all the demands on us like paying the bills, caring for the kids, getting along at work and so forth. In the process, we don't really force ourselves to take the time to "edge back" the creeping change in our life. And, we aren't really talking about "major" sins either.

When I see a big ol' weed popping out of the walkway, I will deal with that almost immediately. Doesn't really matter what I am walking out to do, even to go on a date with Kim or head to fluid, I'll reach down and remove that offense. But the creep of the grass and weeds into an area that they shouldn't go. . .well, I might notice it, but I certainly don't go and get the edger.

Remember what Jesus told us in his last words before the cross— my followers are those who obey my commands. Obeying his commands is a lot more than just NOT doing some bad things. It is loving the unlovable. It is being merciful when you have every right to demand justice from another. It is being a peacemaker. It is reading God's word. It is being in fellowship and communion with God's people. And a lot of other things.

Those are, I think, the kinds of things that we begin to avoid under the crush of so much "other stuff."

We just got back, as you know, from a little vacation in the mountains of Virginia. There wasn't anything to do. The cabin had no Internet access and we had declared the TV off-limits. We did watch a few DVDs, something our family enjoys, but on the whole---we rocked on the porch, we put together puzzles, we read and just hung out. There wasn't any "other stuff." In that kind of quiet, it is much easier to realize that some "edging" needs to take place.

I don't know how to really bring that quiet experience back home. Its not a "city vs. country" thing---my folks live in the country and they are just as overwhelmed with "other stuff" as any of us here in Orlando. Kim and I are praying about the right kind of things to try---maybe a "electronics-free" night, or maybe a "no Internet" night once a month, or once a week.

In any case, take some time to try and sit quietly before the Lord. Ask our Friend, the Holy Spirit, to gently point out the places where you need to do some edging, places where you've let bad habits or sheer busyness creep into your life. Then, start the process of making some changes. As Paul urged, we decide to "beat our bodies into submission." I don't know exactly what you need to push back, where you need to return to the Lord or make room for Him to move in your life. I just know that if we don't determine to actually edge back the junk, before long, there isn't any space for our Christian life at all. Before long, what was a clear path of your life to following God becomes a grass, dirt and weed filled mess with no clear direction.

Well, time to hit the shower. Finished cleaning up the outside of my house; now time to do some more work on the inside of my life.

August 19, 2010

What is this thing that we do on 4th Sunday? Why do we not gather on this day? Are we somehow bored with God? Do we view fluid as a mere religious activity that we are so glad to avoid, hopeful that maybe we can get other Sunday "off" too?

No!

4th Sunday of "doing nothing intentionally" was born in the very earliest of days of Numinous, BEFORE we had fluid, BEFORE we had Bliss even. While Kim and I were in England, we met with several church leaders. One was a wonderful, though interesting (and intense) man named Baz and his lovely wife Linda, who lived in the middle part of the island, in Sheffield. While there, they told us that each summer, they "shut down" for the summer. I was stunned and perplexed by this.

If you know anything about churches, you know that at heart, they are a business. As a business, they need a revenue stream no differently than Kelly's Pizza Hut. Having been raised on "the inside" of church work, I detested this fact, believing it to be a large part of what I deemed "the problem" with the modern church, a problem that had vexed me, and consumed me, since the middle-80s when God first called me out. However, I was also aware that as someone who assumed God would provide my main income from Numinous (though not seeing it as a church), the idea of losing a week, or a summer, of "income stream" seemed amazing, perhaps foolish. Moreover, I thought, people are creatures of habit. Part of any successful group, club, activity that involves people is making it become a regular part of their routine. I saw this as a coach. I knew it from other hobbies. How could Baz just let his people wander off for 3 full months?

Well, at the time, I didn't really worry about it because I didn't think God was going to put us into a church type setting. :)

I was wrong, of course, just as I was wrong about where God would provide the main portion of my income. For 3 years, none of that stuff really mattered until our physical situation changed and our partners, Cornerstone, needed the building on the 4th Sunday of every month. As a church we pondered what to do, and from that, one enduring idea emerged---we should mimic what Baz did, at least part of those 4th Sundays.

But why? And especially "why now" that there is no real need to miss that Sunday? I mean, heck, Cornerstone doesn't even exist any more.

Baz gave some great insights when we talked back in 1999 that I've never really forgotten, and as I thought about it then (and now), I realized that what he said matched what I was believing on the inside.

--We don't worry about one of you breaking routine with us. If missing one Sunday is all it took for you to all of a sudden not want to be with us, then you weren't really with us in the first place. You should go on your merry way. We'll be sad and we'll miss you, but we reject the concept of trying to keep you here merely by trapping you with some religious activity that you feel guilted into being at.

--We don't worry about the money, because we say with King David that God is the ruler of the world and that riches and honor come from God alone; it is at his hand that sustains us as a group (remember, we do have bills to pay, as well as missionaries to support AS WELL AS supporting one another when there is a financial need).

--We realize that the worship of God FAR EXTENDS past any one meeting that happens. Remember, Paul taught in Romans that we should not necessarily highlight any one day as more spiritual or holy than any other day.

--We affirm that God calls us to rest, yet many religious organizations turn their "day of rest" into a day of activity, often soul-crushing and mind-numbing meetings, "have-tos" and other times when it clearly is implied that "you'd better be there."

--We believe that each person who claims to be a Christian is a minister, can approach God alone (without the need of any "religious leader"), and is equal "owner" of "this thing we do," THUS EACH INDIVIDUAL can and should be looking for ways, each day, **to be in communion with one another, to worship God openly, and to share their Good News with others.**

There may be other reasons for the way we do 4th Sunday, but those things get at the heart of it.

Bobby and I have been having yet another wonderful, deep and thoughtful conversation that fits into the realm of this email. We've been talking about how, exactly, do we accomplish what Acts 2 suggests a church should be (if you've forgotten, then take the time now to read it). In that, I once again came back to the fact that we count on each person to truly, and honestly, BE a Christian, and as such, to take up the leadership in their own life for these actions. So, when we talk about the idea of the church being together every day, as Acts 2 suggests should happen, we put that into action through things like various gatherings (yesterday, I spent time with Matthew, John, Chris Lewis, D, Crystal and Justin), various phone calls (spoke with Kelly K), emails (chatted with Greg, Kim Coleman, Bobby and even Brett Shouse), and probably some other ways like IM and facebook.

Fourth Sunday, then, to answer my initial questions, is a time and place to focus on the deep act of communion---with God, with the Body, with outsiders. You are freed from any supposed "have to" meeting for this one Sunday. But you are not FREED from the commands and call of your Lord. You should still worship Him on that day, just as you should this day. You should still commune with the others in the body somehow and in some way, on that day, just as you should on this day. You should be open to any move of the Holy Spirit to share your good news with an outsider, just as you should on this day.

We aren't bored with God.
We aren't bored with worship, nor glad to avoid it.
We aren't wishing for other "Days off" from fluid.

On the contrary, we see this coming Sunday as being with God, being in worship, in other words, still DOING fluid---just doing it in unique way.

I hope that you will make this 4th Sunday of "doing nothing intentionally" your best fluid experience yet!

September 17, 2010

I'd like to share something with you that I told the elders on Sunday morning.

One of our founding themes, many of which you can read on my office wall, was the sentiment of "let it be what it becomes." The "it" is Numinous. As you know our history, being a "church" was NEVER my plan. In fact, I had little of "a plan" and when people would ask me what I was doing, I stammered a bit trying to help them see what I was doing. In the end, I started reciting my little mantra of "let it be what it becomes."

For some, that is hard to comprehend. For others, they wonder if

I'm just lazy or perhaps devoid of any ideas. Some get upset with me and have left our group because I didn't have more planned. We don't have enough activities in the things they want to see or expect to see in a church.

Well, I was reading one of my favorite theologians the other day and saw the following:

> . . . *bringing every thought into captivity to the obedience of Christ . . .* —*2 Corinthians 10:5*

> Determinedly Discipline Other Things. This is another difficult aspect of the strenuous nature of sainthood. Paul said, according to the Moffatt translation of this verse, ". . . I take every project prisoner to make it obey Christ . . . ." **So much Christian work today has never been disciplined, but has simply come into being by impulse!** In our Lord's life every project was disciplined to the will of His Father. There was never the slightest tendency to follow the impulse of His own will as distinct from His Father's will— "the Son can do nothing of Himself . . . " (John 5:19). Then compare this with what we do— we take "every thought" or project that comes to us by impulse and jump into action immediately, instead of imprisoning and disciplining ourselves to obey Christ.

> **Practical work for Christians is greatly overemphasized today,** and the saints who are "bringing every thought [and project] into captivity" are criticized and told that they are not determined, and that they lack zeal for God or zeal for the souls of others. **But true determination and zeal are found in obeying God, not in the inclination to serve Him that arises from our own undisciplined human nature.** It is inconceivable, but true nevertheless, that saints are not "bringing every thought [and project] into captivity," **but are simply doing work for God that has been instigated by**

their own human nature, and has not been made spiritual through determined discipline.

We have a tendency to forget that a person is not only committed to Jesus Christ for salvation, but is also committed, responsible, and accountable to Jesus Christ's view of God, the world, and of sin and the devil. This means that each person must recognize the responsibility to "be transformed by the renewing of [his] mind. . . ." (Romans 12:2)

If you couldn't tell, that was Oswald Chambers writing in the early 1900s. Did you catch the point? Note, the bolded parts are my own, but those are the core sentiments related to what I've tried to live out. The easiest thing for a person to do is just start doing stuff for God. Now, note, the impulse to serve the Lord is RIGHT and GOOD. And, most people that I know who have done this, particularly ministers, church leaders, are not necessarily trying to be egomaniacs. Their desire to start doing stuff, create activities, comes from a good place (usually).

However, what we end up with are things that are merely started by "their own human nature." And, in the end, you end up with groups scurrying around like mice in a maze, some getting left behind while others end up bruised and hurt. Guilt gets thrown around, people get bitter and division seeps into the mix. As you know from what I've taught you, unity is the core responsibility of the church, so you can see how our enemy uses us against ourselves, particularly leaders. I think that comes to it really, for me.

My greatest fear for my own life, irrespective of anything to do with Numinous, is that I start trying to "do stuff" for God and secretly being trying to climb up on some pedestal. A moment when I get to say "hey everyone—look at me at this thing I've started—aren't I just the greatest Christian ever?" As a leader, people WANT you on the pedestal. We see this all the time and God told us about this in the Old Testament; we see there story after story of the people of God--after having God himself clearly communicate with them, save them, lead them—the people put something or someone on a pedestal to worship them rather than God. Sadly, Christian churches and Christian leaders of all kinds have allowed themselves to be put in that position, just like Aaron did in the Wilderness (Exodus 32).

So, I am determined to avoid that and to avoid in general attempts to just "do stuff" for the Lord. Not only do I not trust myself to avoid the pedestal issue, I believe that when God wants something, He will make it clear. Now how he does that is a different conversation. We've chatted about it before, and yet it does remain challenging to know when "I've heard from the Lord."

For now, in closing, just realize that Oswald was correct that in warning us to be careful in this regard. To fight as Paul said to renew the mind and capture all thoughts (note, not just the "bad" thoughts) and take them to the Lord. See, we are easily confused and our enemy is an expert in disguise, so even those thoughts that you are confident are from God should be taken captive. Take them to the Lord and ask Him about it.   In my experience, I would say that many of the things that I believed were "from God," particularly if they involved another person, GOD TOLD ME THEN to keep my mouth shut, do nothing, back off and LET HIM DO. It's a tough thing to do, and people will criticize just as Oswald wrote ("criticized and told that they are not determined, and that they lack zeal for God or zeal for the souls of others"). Still, I know that has been best for me and it allows God to stay on task, not have to mess around fixing my mess-ups.

Let it be what it becomes---that doesn't mean I am not taking my responsibility as the lead leader, the founder of this ministry, seriously. It doesn't mean the elders are not active. It means that we, Numinous, are determined to follow God and work where He is at work, even if it means we remain a small church, or even disband in order for God's glory to be manifest greater in some other way. We want what God wants, for His greater glory!

December 14, 2010

George Barna is a Christian researcher who you have heard about from me before. He is skilled at what he does, finding the point behind the data. Today as I was reading a recent blog post of his, I was inspired by the following. Take a read:

> Shared experiences – and the special moments that flow from them – are a cornerstone of marriage. They are also crucial in the formation of healthy business partnerships, vital congregations, effective parachurch ministries, influential movements, and significant community groups. When people share a passion for something, many of the typical relational barriers are minimized or eliminated. Genuine bonding happens.
>
> Most churches in America are struggling today – if not numerically, then transformationally. The lack of accountability in people's lives is just a symptom of the real problem. That problem is the absence of dynamic, frequently-shared experiences – and not necessarily the kinds of experiences we orchestrate in the "big show" environment.
>
> Should we continue to believe that the 30-second stand and greet module built into the Sunday service is a genuine or meaningful relational time? Does having 100 people gathered in a church building simultaneously singing predetermined songs at the back of someone else's head really constitute a shared worship experience? Is church membership synonymous with belonging? Do we struggle to

raise money for ministry because people are selfishly "cheating God" or because they do not feel ownership of the ministry due to having had so few times of genuine connection with God and people in that ministry? Is it wise to believe that because people attend a small group they have developed relationships that facilitate accountability? (Note: our survey decisively says "no.")

Does that make you smile? Did you immediately think about visiting Savannah Court? Did you think about enjoying the Weaver's wedding? Did you think about sometime this year when you helped someone move? I did.

I thought about how many times you've heard me say that fluid is not the main thing---an important thing, yes, but not the main thing. Nor, is "fluid=church." Church, as we have said, is a state of being—it is, in the Greek, to be among the called out ones---it is a position that I claim, and then live out the proof by my actions. It is NEVER a thing I go to, nor a thing I belong to.

We are not a church that is struggling today, or not one struggling in the issues that Barna talks about. We have Bliss, and fun moments like last night, for the express purpose of NOT limiting ourselves to some lame 30-second handshake thing and then calling that real fellowship. We wrestle with what worship really is—currently we are still deeply wrestling with this and I am in deep prayer and conversation trying to determine our way forward---yet, we know that it can't be some thing just related to everyone standing, or clapping or just singing. We know its silence, its the dance, its tears, its laughter, it IS song, it IS standing, but its a lot of things---and we KNOW it must start INDIVIDUALLY in ISOLATION— my personal worship of the Father. We are NOT struggling to raise money because you already give deeply (at least most of you) and not because I badger you about it, but because you are determined to walk faithfully with God in His ways, and you know that includes being a Godly Resource Manager—a trustee that does well with His money. So, you give. And, from day 1, we have determined to build in a clear sense of ownership—the very thing George finds lacking in his research (I could have told him that 14 years ago had he asked).

So, first rejoice that God has led you to a place like Numinous.

Then, hit your knees praying for us in Numinous—praying that we remain AWARE of what God is doing in us and around us. . .and how fragile the whole thing is. It only takes a bit for humans to get complacent, to take their "eye off the ball," to grow coarse with each other. . .and then lose the very special thing that we have. The stuff Barna writes about could become us, as it has become 100s of other churches around.

January 24, 2011

Well, by now I know you've heard about the addition of times for us to minister to others this year. If you were at fluid any time in the last few weeks, you've heard me share how God has been leading me towards His pushing us out even further into deep water.

Eleven years ago when He first said, "Push out into Deep water," part of the clear implication was that His vision for us was going to put us into uncomfortable situations. And, that is precisely what He has done, again and again. From the very start, when we had to raise $1500 to help one of the body pay for a hospital bill, so we all collectively sold possessions to raise the money or when we had to learn to be nice to one another when most of us were strangers, He has pushed us to be good representatives of His love and grace. He has put us into uncomfortable situations, usually to minister to others.

Yet, over the past couple of years, we've all gotten pretty comfortable in our surroundings. On the one hand, that is a mark of our great success in the eyes of God. He has us in deep water, with the waves pitching and the ship bobbing, and we are cool with it. We are rocking along. We are doing the same thing in the same way and its good. But, on the other hand, that comfortableness has also made us a bit distant from our passion. We've heard the same stories, looked at all the one another verses, sang many of the same songs—its all very familiar.

The moment your spiritual walk becomes too comfortable, you cease to really feel the need for God. With the loss of the need for God goes the loss of passion for God and His ways. There is a reason why Jesus said the path was narrow and we read people like C.S. Lewis down in my sig reminding us that God isn't safe. He is GOD. The Creator of the Universe. He is beyond any of us.

So, as it relates to Bliss, I have asked the Bliss leaders to help us plan five new Mondays where we can actually minister and serve "the least of these." Do you remember how incredible it was to sit together and prepare the beanie babies? It was an awesome night. Or, do you remember the fun of sharing life briefly with older people at Savannah Court? That too was awesome.

That's what God wants from us on just 5 more nights. Five nights out of 52—not exactly asking a lot from you, is it? I bet most of you are really excited already and I told the Bliss leaders that I bet we end up with a lot more than 5 new ideas. I can't wait to start hearing from the different groups about their idea. The Braun/Delaney/Porter group is first up on the 28th of February.

Realize we are testing this new deep water. We certainly haven't been here before. We are going to do all in our power to make sure these 5 new nights will each happen on Monday. Perhaps all we will do on one of those nights is meet together to prepare meals that later will be given out to a homeless shelter. However, I need you---I am pleading with you—to be graceful and willing to sacrifice if one or two of those 5 times of service may need to fall on some other time.

We honestly don't know if that will happen. We aren't going to try and make it happen. Each bliss group is praying and thinking now about what to do, and as they find options, I'm sure they'll talk about it, hoping to find something solid for us to do on a Monday night. Just keep in mind that many places that like getting "service help" often can't really use 30+ people (and us being together IS a BIG part of the point), OR they don't need us on a Monday night.

In any case, just know the initial stages are being worked out. I will communicate with you as clearly and as early as I can. Just keep this verse in mind—its one that I've up around the house for the girls to see and meditate on--"When you do things, don't let selfishness or pride be your guide. Instead, be humble and give more honor to others than to yourselves. Do not be interested in your own life only, but be interested in the lives of others." [Phil 2:3-4]

I hope you will follow me out into deeper water still. The waves are higher there. The cost is higher there. The path is unknown there. I hope you will come with joy on those 5 new Monday's of us sharing life with others, even if it costs you in some way. I know its easier to just go once again to one of our homes and eat a meal together. We still value that and will do that in this year, month after month. But, we need to get out there and touch the lives of the least of these.

I can't wait to see what God does for us in this year through this small, simple action. I hope you are excited too. Don't hold back on your ideas. Don't look around waiting for someone else to figure this out. Step up. Think creatively (can we somehow minister in a hospital—Ted, don't you work there?). Think simple (can we help people with their groceries, maybe coordinating with an extended living facility)? Wash cars in an extended living facility? Prepare meals for the homeless? So, get your ideas to your Bliss group and let's get going.

God is already at work. Let's continue to join in.

May 23, 2011

Why Bliss? Why this small group thing?

Simply put, God calls us into relationship with others. You can simplify the entire Christian message into "Love God, Love others." But, the "love others" part is where the challenge lies. Sure, loving God is hard too, but that's easy to lie about, telling myself I love God and just going on in my deception. But "loving others" cannot be hidden! Of course, John tells us this in his letter called 1 John (go read it sometime).

Now, loving others is EASY when those people are just like me. Every group does that. When there is a common affinity that connects us, say around a hobby, it is easy to be in a group relationship with those people. It's especially true when I am with people who are like me, people that I naturally connect with. Now realize, those kinds of relationships are not bad—they are normal.

God calls us to be ABNORMAL! What He wants for his believers is to create one body of disparate parts. He calls us all to his side, from all types of personalities, from all different backgrounds. He throws us into the same mix and then wants us to experience real life together. This is where Bliss comes in.

Left to my own devices, I will either pull into isolation or I will spend time only with those people who are a lot like me. Heaven will NOT be that way, and the church is to demonstrate what heaven will be like. You get that in all of the commands: love one another, be patient with one another, be kind to one another, be devoted to one another, and so forth. Think about it—you are typically NOT those things to people that you don't know or know but don't really like. Even if you don't hate or dislike them, if they are not someone whom you connect with, you simply are not going to go out of your way to exhort them or be devoted to them, or even express real kindness or patience to them. None of us will.

August 17, 2011

Was reading Oswald again today and where I read Romans 6:13; then I backed up to v. 12 to get a running start

"Therefore, never let sin rule your physical body so that you obey its desires. Never offer any part of your body to sin's power. No part of your body should ever be used to do any ungodly thing. Instead, offer yourselves to God as people who have come back from death and are now alive. Offer all the parts of your body to God. Use them to do everything that God approves of." (God's Word version)

Earlier today, I was chatting with a few of the Numinous guys and something around this same point came up, so when I read this later, I was paying attention. I wonder how often I fail to offer all the parts of my body to God, especially when I sin in pride assuming I have already done such (offered Him my body). In thinking that way, I grow lax and lazy.

This verse also made me jump to later in the same letter. Paul obviously had a point to make with the church in Rome, because 6 chapters later, as you hopefully remember from the last series at fluid, we read this in chapter 12:1-3--And so, dear brothers and sisters, in view of God's mercy, I plead with you to give your bodies to God--a living and holy sacrifice -- the kind he will accept. This is your reasonable act of service, act of worship. Don't copy the behavior and customs of this world, but let God transform you into a new person by changing the way you think. Then you will know what God wants you to do, and you will know how good and pleasing and perfect his will really is. As God's messenger, I give each of you this warning: Be honest in your estimate of yourselves, measuring your value by how much faith God has given you.

Paul is obviously hammering this point home about how our lives are meant to be lived as ones who have been called out of darkness, out of death, into the wonderful experience of real life. But many think they can have this apart from God and his ways.

Back to Oswald, he wrote *"If I construct my faith on my own experience, I produce the most unscriptural kind of life— an isolated life, with my eyes focused solely on my own holiness. Beware of that human holiness that is not based on the atonement of the Lord. It has no value for anything except a life of isolation— it is useless to God and a nuisance to man.*

The atonement of Jesus must be exhibited in practical, unassuming ways in my life. Every time I obey, the absolute deity of God is on my side, so that the grace of God and my natural obedience are in perfect agreement. Obedience means that I have completely placed my trust in the atonement, and my obedience is immediately met by the delight of the supernatural grace of God."

Good stuff there—caught my attention for my own heart and thought it would be useful to you. Give your body to Him. Stay alert at all times about your how you are using your body and where you obedience lies to the things He has commanded.

September 2, 2011

Sunday is going to be the start of an exciting next journey for us as we head into the fall. There is, perhaps a feeling that I have, that this Sunday could be the start of a culmination of prayer from the past two or even three years.

In 2008, we spent the first half of that year investigating the Nature of God---at the time, I didn't necessarily think anything of it, but now as I look back, I believe God was laying some foundation for us as we started to approach some trials and rocky times, both in Numinous as well as in our country. I think He was determined to make sure that we had some common language and ideas based on the Bible's declaration as to who he is!

In 2009, we started the year pressing again to remind ourselves of our great desire for the "other person" in our lives when I introduced the 3r3 concept (see my little logo below, wonderfully created by Greg). We closed that year and started 2010 by reviewing solid basics of being a Christian: we talked about how to pray (Oct 2009), how to worship (Nov 2009), hearing from God (Dec 09, Jan 10), basics of the Bible (Feb 2010).

The rest of 2010 had us looking deeply at the life of Jesus through the book of Mark, more about reaching others and then Godly Resource Management (reinforcing both 3r3 and handling my money in increasingly trying times).

Now, in 2011, we have just completed the study of growing and fostering spiritual maturity.

Behind all of this has been, I think, questions and concerns, especially when looking at the world, but also when looking at Numinous. At the core of that has perhaps been the wondering "what exactly are we doing or becoming." IF you have noticed in the past month, I have been trying to slowly remind us of who we are and what we are. Don't miss this Sunday as we continue this journey.

And that brings me to Monday.

Perhaps I wasn't very clear in my previous email, so let me say a few things first before I tell you what we are doing.

Why do we gather on Mondays? (can you tell this relates to the above paragraphs about our journey?--LOL). :) But seriously, why do we do that? Is it mere religion? Just some "Numinous created" holy day that then others beat down upon you? God forbid. No, Bliss connects directly to our attempt to be that group that values the first-century documents and directions, but reflects our 21st century world.

So, what are our values here? We first value every chance to glorify God, both individually and collectively. How does that happen in this setting (Monday nights)? He has commanded a devotion to koinania. Our leadership has put our first effort to devoting ourselves to koinania at Bliss. That is not the only time---as I have told people again and again--there is both the organized and the unorganized moments of this koinania—we NEED BOTH!

I simply know of no evidence that any group of believers who are supposedly, intentionally together, can or have existed only through unorganized koinania moments. Sure, a clique can—a tight group of friends who all think the same with all the same values probably can exist through only unorganized random moments, but the not everyone else. And, if you stop to think about it—those kinds of groups (say a bowling group, a group of coffee lovers or maybe even an inner-city gang)—they actually DO HAVE ORGANIZED moments! We have long proclaimed, "Bliss is the crutch of a lame generation." What do I mean? Well, just like I shared in that email last night, people today know best how to do the weak connection, something through social media, but we do not understand what the depth of commitment is, the kind of commitment God has called every Believer to. I said this a few weeks ago; you'll probably hear it again---did God not call us a body? Both the larger, universal (often called "invisible") Church and the smaller, local (often called "visible") church? If I know my body needs a shower, my feet don't get to say "well, not me big guy, so I am out of here."   When I know that I must exercise and my feet are excited, my lungs don't get to say "well, no one asked me so I am leaving." We must have the organized, intentional gathering as a body. That's what Bliss is.

What other values guide us here—we value the need for simplicity and the need to actually relax---we are a harried generation, flitting from thing to thing, and we are bombarded with noise. When can anyone in that world ever sit and hear the voice of another, let alone the voice of God?

October 28, 2011

I am so excited about Sunday. I know for many of you, you are perhaps not excited (you've told me). Some are tired of talking. Some are tired of seeking the Word for God's ways (I think you prefer when I or someone just tells you). Some are tired of hearing OTHERS talk. God, however, is not unhappy with us nor tired of us. He is working in and through us, and even though the enemy has meant some things for evil, God will use them for good.

My boss at Valencia gave me an assignment today to investigate a ministry, a group that he might want to get involved with, taking me and a few others with him to a conference or to partner in some way with these people. The group is called Lionshare, and yes, the focus of my boss is an education mindset, but being used as Christians to be salt and light within academia and culture---but as I was searching, I went to the bio page of the founder of this thing. His name is Dave Buehring---I am certain I know him or his name from something, but I can't place it---on the page, there were two random video clips. I mean, they can't be random because they have to be there intentionally, but the topic wasn't necessarily connected in any way with the bio or information about the ministry.

The topic was about "Guarding the Heart." He doesn't talk about this in the dating relationship vein that I sometimes talk about with you, but in the larger vein from where my dating comment comes, that the heart is the center of who we are.

In the first video, Dave lays out what the Bible teaches about the heart, how it is vulnerable. In particular he spends some time on Prov 4:23. In the second clip, Dave talks about five aspects of how to guard our hearts. The last few minutes is what Dave says is the most important. I agree! Privately, as I have prayed for each of you, I have felt that many of you are here, right were Dave talks.

As I leave you for now, let me be as clear as possible---I think God sent me to my meeting with my boss in order to hear about this group so that I could find these 2 videos SO I COULD HEAR GOD ABOUT ME! As I listened, just now, to this man speak for God, I knew this was for me, and then also for you. These things are not issues I am unaware of, but know that God is working with me on. You pray for me as I pray for you.

I tell you that so that you won't sit there, arms folded, mind already made up that somehow I was specifically thinking of you and only you when Dave made certain statements. I was thinking of you--- God brought you to mind--but I was thinking of me as well. REMEMBER, God sent me to this page through my boss---I didn't go searching for this in order to harm you. Hearing this is for your good, and subsequently, for achieving the God-aim, the goal of God, in your life.

Please always know that God has placed me here as your shepherd. Everyone on this list, from my wife through all the elders, down to the newest persons and youngest members (yes, Brynn, that means you too, BUT we'll give Asher, Zander, Emmalyn and Ian a break on this one) needs to listen. As the person responsible (with God's Holy Spirit as power-provider, for only HE deserves our worship) for bringing you to safety, to good pasture, and to wholeness, I urge you to take the 20 minutes or so to at least listen to the parts that I referenced.

Start it up, then put it on pause, do something else for 15 minutes, then come back once it is all loaded and skim to the parts I suggest.

You can do this. I urge you to do this. I love you tons, EACH AND EVERY ONE OF YOU!

November 19, 2011

I was reading Dietrich Bonhoeffer's *Letters and Papers from Prison.* Late in his life July 1944, Bonhoeffer wrote about the challenge of being salt and light in the world in a letter to his friend Eberhard Bethge:

> "During the last year of so I've come to know and understand more and more the profound this-worldliness of Christianity....I don't mean the shallow and banal this-worldliness of the enlightened, the busy, the comfortable, or the lascivious, but the profound this-worldliness characterized by discipline and the constant knowledge of death and resurrection....I discovered later, and I'm still discovering right up to this moment, that it is only by living completely in this world that one learns to have faith. One must completely abandon any attempt to make something of oneself, whether it be a saint or a converted sinner, or a churchman, a righteous man or an unrighteous man, a sick man or a healthy on. By this-worldliness, I mean living unreservedly in life's duties, problems, successes and failures, experiences and perplexities. In so doing we throw ourselves completely in the arms of God, taking seriously, no our own sufferings, but those of God in the world— watching with Christ in Gethsemane. That, I think, is faith."

One month later, he created an outline for a book that obviously never was written (he was executed 8 months later) about Bonhoeffer's view of Christianity, of the church. In it, he continues the theme he had come to in his letter of July. He is calling out to a German church that, in his mind, has hid its eyes from the excess evil of the government itself. But, in his charge to his fellow Germans, the pastor has spoken powerfully to all Christians.

"The church is the church only when it exists for others. To make a start, it should give away all its property to those in need. The clergy must live solely on free-will offerings of their congregations, or possibly engage in some secular calling. The church must share in the secular problems of ordinary human life, not dominating, but helping and serving. It must tell men of every calling what it means to live in Christ, to exist for others. In particular, our own church will have to take the field against the vices of hubris, power-worship, envy, and humbug, as the roots of all evil. It will have to speak of moderation, purity, trust, loyalty, constancy, patience, discipline, humility, contentment, and modesty....it is not abstract argument, but [human] example that gives [the Church's] word emphasis and power."

Yet, Bonhoeffer also saw the need, the critical understanding, for the committed, intentional community of faith. His view of the church was not merely of the Universal, Invisible Church to which all Christians belong. Living at that time when many Germans spied on another, he understood the call for a people to be devoted to one another in a way that demanded trust. Writing in 1943, Bonhoeffer reflected back on the previous 10 years since Hitler had been elected to lead the nation.

"There is hardly one of us who has not known what it is to be betrayed. The figure of Judas, which we used to find so difficult to understand, is now fairly familiar to us. The air that we breathe is so polluted by mistrust that it almost chokes us. But where we have broken through the layer of mistrust, we have been able to discover a confidence hitherto undreamed of. Where we trust, we have learnt to put our very lives into the hands of others; in the face of all the different interpretations that have been put on our lives and actions, we have learnt to trust unreservedly. We now know that only such confidence, which is always a venture, though a glad and positive venture, enables us really to live and work. We know that it is most reprehensible to sow and encourage mistrust, and that our duty is rather to foster and strengthen confidence wherever we can. Trust will always be one of the greatest, rarest, and happiest blessings of our life in community, though it can emerge only on the dark background of a necessary mistrust. We have learnt to never trust a scoundrel an inch, but to give ourselves to the trustworthy without reserve."

Immediately after reading in his book, I read Paul's words in 1 Thessalonians. The connection between Bonhoeffer's call for devotion and trust, and then Paul's words about how the local community of faith must live, should be easy to see. Paul was writing to a small church in one of the largest Greek cities, Thessalonica. That church had also been facing major persecution and stress; some had even left the church through the stress while some members had stopped working in their jobs, assuming the church would just take care of them. Paul was concerned that the entire group might be collapsing, so he sent Timothy to check on them. Upon getting a report that they were still a church, but having some issues and concerns, he wrote to them. I have quoted Eugene Peterson's paraphrase from *The Message* because I love some of his phrasings (highlighted below). Take a moment and drink in the Word of God written to a specific church in a specific place. I've removed all verse numbers so you can simply soak in the Word—so much of what Paul wrote reflect my thoughts, and those of Kim, for you, especially the first paragraph.

*What would be an adequate thanksgiving to offer God for all the joy we experience before him because of you? We do what we can, praying away, night and day, asking for the bonus of seeing your faces again and doing what we can to help when your faith falters. May God our Father himself and our Master Jesus clear the road to you! And may the Master **pour on the love so it fills your lives and splashes over on everyone around you,** just as it does from us to you. May you be infused with strength and purity, filled with* *confidence in the presence of God our Father when our Master Jesus arrives with all his followers.*

*One final word, friends. We ask you - urge is more like it - that you keep on doing what we told you to do to please God, **not in a dogged religious plod, but in a living, spirited dance.***

You know the guidelines we laid out for you from the Master Jesus:
- *God wants you to live a pure life. Keep yourselves from sexual promiscuity.*
- *Learn to appreciate and give dignity to your body, not abusing it, as is so common among those who know nothing of God.*
- *Don't run roughshod over the concerns of your brothers and sisters. Their concerns are God's concerns, and he will take care of them.*
- *Just love one another! You're already good at it...keep it up; get better and better at it.*
- *Stay calm; mind your own business; do your own job.*
- *We want you living in a way that will command the respect of outsiders, not lying around sponging off your friends.*

*You're sons of Light, daughters of Day. We live under wide open skies and know where we stand. So **let's not sleepwalk through life** like those others. Let's keep our eyes open and be smart. People sleep at night and get drunk at night. But not us! Since we're creatures of Day, let's act like it. Walk out into the daylight sober, dressed up in faith, love, and the hope of salvation.*

So speak encouraging words to one another. Build up hope so you'll all be together in this, no one left out, no one left behind. I know you're already doing this; just keep on doing it.

And now, friends, we ask you to honor those leaders who work so hard for you, who have been given the responsibility of urging and guiding you along in your obedience. **Overwhelm them with appreciation and love!**

- *Our counsel is that you warn the freeloaders to get a move on.*
- *Gently encourage the stragglers, and* **reach out for the exhausted, pulling them to their feet.**
- *Be patient with each person, attentive to individual needs.*
- *And be careful that when you get on each other's nerves you don't snap at each other.*
- *Look for the best in each other, and always do your best to bring it out.*
- *Be cheerful no matter what;*
- *Pray all the time;*
- *Thank God no matter what happens. This is the way God wants you who belong to Christ Jesus to live.*
- *Don't suppress the Spirit,*
- *Don't stifle those who have a word from the Master.*
- *On the other hand,* **don't be gullible.** *Check out everything, and keep only what's good. Throw out anything tainted with evil.*

Do you see both ideas? Bonhoeffer reminds us that we have been saved, we have been changed through the love of God, so that we can offer a cup of cold water to anyone in need. We are God's representatives to the world.

And, to accomplish that, we push deeper as Paul urged, to a unity that isn't drudgery, but rather a "living, spirited dance." That dance, that love, works itself out into a place where we experience a trust that most people never know.

"Oh Father, even so bring both ideas more firmly into focus in my eyes, that I live my life in a way that others can see You, and builds up the body of Christ in Numinous."

January 14, 2012

Yes, yes, yes! Thank you John for sharing with the body. I think it is on point. I did want to make one tiny correction and then share one more corroborating evidence with everyone that God is saying the same thing to me.

We have actually grown over the years. As John said, when we started, we were about a dozen. Well, actually, we started with 2, then 5, then at Bliss about 12-15. Our first fluids in spring 2000 had lots of visitors who were personal friends, so we skip that to summer to say that we had about 20 faithful people with 11 going on the retreat. Today, we have about 30 (including teens, but not little children---we've never really counted them). Over the years, we have lost about 20-30 people. So, overall, we could say that we've had growth of about 50 people, but have kept about 20 out of that 50. Those are rough numbers, but fair. I wish we had about 40 of the 50, thus we'd have about 50 total----40 plus the original 11 at retreat.

Now to the corroborating evidence with John---John said, "No one can drum up excitement." AMEN, and AMEN. Years ago, God told me directly the same thing, way back in 1996. I wrote the following in my journal then:

> *As I drove home from a Bible Study the next day, God began to speak to me. As I found my lonely place at home, He continued to speak. Here's the gist of the thinking.*
>
> **No program, no event, no teaching, no thing that you (Carl) do will be the thing, in and of itself, that will spark a passion in these people for Me. It is My will, My Spirit that**

draws and calls and nothing you (Carl) do can change that.

Two weeks ago, during the Ember Days reflection, God and I were talking. I said, "Well, here's what I want:
- people to find God
- for those people to learn how to live for You
- for those people to live well for You
- for those people to excitedly tell other about finding You.

I then asked Him, "Is there a 'how' for that?   Is there something that will help people become excited for God?"

His reply was simple: "Only the Holy Spirit; Only Me---No program or type of worship or event or teaching or anything else will produce sustained excitement for Me."

Shows how loving God is (and probably how slow or dense I can be) that He has to tell me the same thing 16 years apart.

In that same time period of January 2012, then, God gave me a verse for my year, to guide my steps, from Galatians. Galatians is somewhat like II Corinthians in that Paul is defending his ministry. Others have left his church; many have attacked his style, his leadership and the fruit of his effort. In both letters, he somewhat lashes out strongly, but continues to point to God. Finally, at the end of the letter, in something of a deep sigh after his frustration (you can almost see Paul sitting back, praying, listening, maybe slouched over leaning back in his chair, before somewhat wearily but with confidence and a deep conviction about His God and his own course of action), Paul wrote this (6:14): **"As for me, may I never boast about anything except the cross of our Lord Jesus Christ. Because of that cross, my interest in the world has been crucified, and the world's interest in me has also died."**

Let's boast in the cross. As John said, let's relinquish the critical spirit returning to being "more forgiving of a lot of the faults." Let grace abound. Let's hit our knees together as friends, eager to see God's Spirit move in each of us, and through each of us. Let's beg Him to use us however He wishes and for His Spirit to touch the lives of those around us.

God is good. God is very good!

In Closing....

I wrote the following in 2003 while working on my first book, my first effort to describe our theology of community. My daughters were then very young: Logan was just 8, Meryn was turning 6, and Brynn was 3. This is the last chapter, last "letter" that would have closed that book [Section 1 in this compilation]. As I reflected on what I wrote, I felt that it still needed to be the closing comment. What I have done has largely been done for future generations, for my girls and their families to come. So, read on with my closing thoughts as to why I do what I do. I have changed nothing from that document:

Dear Logan, Meryn, and Brynn,

I wanted this last letter in Daddy's book to be written to you. In the end, I suppose I am being as selfish about this as I am being jealous for God. I stand convinced that America is in peril and that peril has arisen as our country has walked away from God.

Not that it's their fault, per se. Instead, the fault must lie with ordinary Christians like myself who forgot to really look in God's book for direction. The fault must also lie with churches and church leaders who lost their way, who forgot the main commands, and turned a family of God into a consumer institution. Well, I for one, plan on trying to convince the world (or at least those around me) that we must return to that basis for life.

I honestly do believe that there is a real world beyond the one we can see, a spiritual world. That world continues to be in struggle and as spirits in that world, we are not allowed to be neutral. Thus, I (like my forefathers before me, at least four generations back) have chosen to stand with God in this struggle. As such, I am attempting to live with credibility, both individually and collectively.

I am doing that for selfish reasons in that I want your grandchildren to live in an America that remembers God. Of course He is NOT an American God, but nonetheless, our history is not casually founded on or by Him. No, our history contains a very clear guiding hand, just as our first President George Washington stated. So, in these days around 2003, I think that our country slips further and further away from our foundation.

Since I feel that the onus of fixing this lies with ordinary people like me, I have attempted to do exactly that with this book. Of course I know one book can't fix everything, but with God's help it can perhaps be a key ingredient in helping.

Thus, I am writing you now in the hopes that years from now when you read this as adults, you'll look around at a church that has returned to its Biblical mission. I pray that you will be strong women of faith whose families will demand to participate in gatherings of believers supported by principles like the ones I've laid out in these pages.

Never forget that you have a mission as individual women. You are God's representative and that is a critical mission. How He has you carry that out is only a guess from my end, so I won't try. Just remember that you are more than you seem and that you really aren't from here, but your real home is with God.

While you are carrying forth your individual mission, never forget to draw close to others like yourselves. God's plan from the start is for community. Jesus explained in his last words to his inner group of followers that they must stay united, loving as He loved them. As they were about to embark on sharing the truth (in essence, as they started doing the mission each Christian has), Jesus knew that they must not be alone.

You girls and your families must cling tightly together in community with others. Love deeply. Accept others quickly. Be devoted to one another in your group. Stand behind and beside whoever are currently the leaders, if you are not said leader. Never forget that you are members of one another in your gathering.

So, while my writings are selfish in one sense that I want your descendents to live in an America that knows God, my writings are also jealous for God's glory. In the end, your lives must shine brightly for God like stars in the sky.

If you do that, then I'll know my work here was not in vain. I love you deeply and pray the best for you. Even if I have passed on to the other spiritual world, I believe in you and will see you again. Cling tightly to the truths contained in God's word and never let go of what I have taught you. Go for this! You can do it! Accept nothing less than the best, even if that means you have to start anew in a new city that does not have a church like the one I have described here and led. If so, then you start one!

are you ready?

Love,

Daddy

Appendix

One Another Verses

The "Love" section

- Rom. 13:8 Let no debt remain outstanding, except the continuing debt to <u>love one another</u>, for he who loves his fellowman has fulfilled the law.
- Gal. 5:13 You, my brothers, were called to be free. But do not use your freedom to indulge the sinful nature ; rather, <u>serve one another in love</u>.
- Rom. 12:10 Be <u>devoted to one another in brotherly love</u>.
- Hebr. 10:24 And let us consider how we may <u>spur one another on toward love</u> and good deeds.
- John 13:34 "A new command I give you: <u>Love one another</u>. As I have loved you, so you must love one another.
- John 13:35 By this all men will know that you are my disciples, if <u>you love one another</u>."
- 1 John 3:11 This is the message you heard from the beginning: <u>We should love one another.</u>
- 1 John 3:23 And this is his command: to believe in the name of his Son, Jesus Christ, and <u>to love one another as he commanded us</u>.
- 1 John 4:7 Dear friends, <u>let us love one another</u>, for love comes from God. Everyone who loves has been born of God and knows God.
- 1 John 4:11 Dear friends, since God so loved us, <u>we also ought to love one another</u>.
- 1 John 4:12 No one has ever seen God; but <u>if we love one another</u>, God lives in us and his love is made complete in us.
- 2 John 5 And now, dear lady, I am not writing you a new command but one we have had from the beginning. I ask that <u>we love one another</u>.

- 1 Pet. 1:22 Now that you have purified yourselves by obeying the truth so that you have sincere love for your brothers, <u>love one another deeply, from the heart</u>.
- 1 Pet. 3:8 Finally, all of you, live in harmony with one another; be sympathetic, <u>love as brothers, be compassionate</u> and humble.

The "Do not" section

- Lev. 19:11 'Do not steal.' 'Do not lie.' '<u>Do not deceive one another.</u>'
- Rom. 14:13 Therefore let us <u>stop passing judgment on one another</u>. Instead, make up your mind [do] not to put any stumbling block or obstacle in your brother's way.
- Mal. 2:10 Have we not all one Father ? Did not one God create us? Why do we profane the covenant of our fathers by <u>breaking faith with one another</u>?
- Hebr. 10:25 <u>Let us not give up meeting together</u>, as some are in the habit of doing, but <u>let us encourage one another</u> —and all the more as you see the Day approaching.
- James 4:11 Brothers, <u>do not slander one another</u>. Anyone who speaks against his brother or judges him speaks against the law and judges it. When you judge the law, you are not keeping it, but sitting in judgment on it.
- 1 Peter 3:9 <u>Don't repay evil for evil.</u> Don't retaliate when people say unkind things about you. Instead, pay them back with a blessing. That is what God wants you to do, and he will bless you for it. [One Another implied!!]

The "acceptance, unity" section

- Rom. 15:7 <u>Accept one another</u>, then, just as Christ accepted you, in order to bring praise to God.
- 1 Cor. 1:10 I appeal to you, brothers, in the name of our Lord Jesus Christ, that all of you <u>agree with one another</u> so that there

may be no divisions among you and that you may be perfectly united in mind and thought.

- Rom. 12:16   Live in harmony with one another. Do not be proud, but be willing to associate with people of low position. Do not be conceited.
- Rom 15:5   May God, who gives this patience and encouragement, help you live in complete harmony with each other – each with the attitude of Christ Jesus toward the other.
- 1 Pet. 3:8   Finally, all of you, live in harmony with one another;

The "encouragement" section

- 1 Thess. 5:11   Therefore encourage one another and build each other up, just as in fact you are doing.
- Hebr. 3:13   But encourage one another daily, as long as it is called Today, so that none of you may be hardened by sin's deceitfulness.
- Eph. 5:19   Speak to one another with psalms, hymns and spiritual songs. Sing and make music in your heart to the Lord,
- Col. 3:16   Let the word of Christ dwell in you richly as you teach and admonish one another with all wisdom, and as you sing psalms, hymns and spiritual songs with gratitude in your hearts to God.
- Hebr. 10:24   And let us consider how we may spur one another on toward love and good deeds.
- Hebr. 10:25   Let us not give up meeting together, as some are in the habit of doing, but let us encourage one another —and all the more as you see the Day approaching.

The "Miscellaneous" Section

- Gal. 5:13   You, my brothers, were called to be free. But do not use your freedom to indulge the sinful nature ; rather, serve one another in love.
- Rom. 12:10   Be devoted to one another in brotherly love. Honor one another above yourselves.

- Prov. 27:17   As iron sharpens iron, <u>so one man sharpens another</u>.
- Eph. 4:32   <u>Be kind and compassionate to one another</u>, <u>forgiving each other</u>, just as in Christ God forgave you.
- Eph. 5:21   <u>Submit to one another</u> out of reverence for Christ.
- 1 Pet. 5:5   Young men, in the same way be submissive to those who are older. All of you, <u>clothe yourselves with humility toward one another</u>, because, "God opposes the proud but gives grace to the humble."
- Eph. 4:2   Be completely humble and gentle; be patient, <u>bearing with one another</u> in love.
- Col. 3:13   <u>Bear with each other</u> and forgive whatever grievances you may have against one another. Forgive as the Lord forgave you.
- Galatians 6:2   <u>Share one another's troubles/burdens and problems</u> and in this way obey the law of Christ.
- James 5:16   Therefore <u>confess your sins to each other</u> and <u>pray for each other</u> so that you may be healed. The prayer of a righteous man is powerful and effective.
- 1 Pet. 3:8   Finally, all of you<u>, live in harmony with one another</u>; be <u>sympathetic</u>, love as brothers, be <u>compassionate</u> and <u>humble</u>.
- 1 Pet. 4:9   <u>Offer hospitality to one another</u> without grumbling.

The "holy kiss" section

- Rom. 16:16   <u>Greet one another with a holy kiss</u>. All the churches of Christ send greetings.
- 1 Pet. 5:14   <u>Greet one another with a kiss of love</u>. Peace to all of you who are in Christ.
- 1 Cor. 16:20   All the brothers here send you greetings. <u>Greet one another with a holy kiss</u>.
- 2 Cor. 13:12   <u>Greet one another with a holy kiss</u>.

Church Study from 1997

These notes are my personal musings and have never been published before. The thoughts and ideas were written to myself.

OK, here is the premise or question. In the totality of the commands of God regarding his followers, is there a difference between the directives for the individual and those for the church as a body? I know that I may be splitting hairs here, but the question about the mission of the church cannot be answered without an understanding of this matter.

Is the church responsible for missions? Is the individual Christian responsible for the care of widows? Does the directive of the individual disciple fall under the umbrella of the church? What is the mission of the church, anyway?

Before we go any further, let me lay down this presupposition: the "church" is nothing more than the collection of individual disciples, believers. "Well, if that is true," you ask, "why all the bother?" Okay, the church is the believers collectively, but if there are direct commands for the church as an entity above and beyond the individual, would it not seem proper that those commands are the chief thought for the mission?

So, before I wax anymore philosophic, lets look at God's word. I looked up every occurrence of ecclesia (eck-lay-see-ah); there are 114 occurrences in the New Testament. Many of these are merely in conjunction with the title of a town or in mention of a person's house church. Other passages were examined, as I knew of their relationship with the idea of church. There are probably other passages that are useful for this study, but these are the ones that I observed.

Jesus builds the church - Mt 16:18, Ac 9:31, Rev 3:18
Christ in head of the church - Col 1:28, Eph 1:22, Eph 5:22
The church is on the move, attacking - Mt 16:18, Rev 3:8
Gates of hell cannot prevail (hold out) the kingdom of God - Mt 16:18

Disputes between believers handled within framework of church - Mt 18:15-17,

I Co 5:9-13, I Co. 6:1-8, Acts 15:1-23, Acts 5:11

Evil people to be cast out of church - Rv 2:2, I Co 5:9-13, Rv 2:14-15, Rv 2:20-23

Church has a fear (reverence, awe) for the Lord - Acts 5:11, Acts 9:31

Church met together to be taught by apostles - Acts 2:42

Church met together to fellowship - Acts 2:42

Church met together to "break bread" - Acts 2:42

Church met in public place, participated in public life of city - Acts 2:46, I Co 5:10

Church shared all things - Acts 2:44, 45

Church used resources to care for each other - Acts 2:45, Acts 6:1-5

Church met together to pray - Acts 2:42, Acts 4:23-31, Acts 12:1-5

Church comforted by Holy Spirit - Acts 9:31

Leadership

- Apostles (teach, lead) - Acts 2:42, Acts 6:2, I Co 12:28, Eph 4:11
- Deacons (serve widows, needs)- Acts 6:1-5, I Tim 3:8-16
- Overseer (leadership) - I Tim 3:1-7
- Prophet (edification) - I Co 12:28, Eph 4:11, Acts 13:1, I Co 14
- Teacher   - I Co 12:28, Eph 4:11, Acts 13:1
- Shepherd   - Eph 4:11
- Elders (teach, rule, shepherd, pray for sick, preach)
            - Ac 20:17-38, I Ti 5:17, James 5:14,

Leadership chosen out of church - Acts 6:1-5, Acts 15:1-23ff, Ro 16:1ff

Elders commanded by Paul to: Acts 20:17-28

--watch themselves first

--Holy Spirit declares them overseers

--also called shepherd

Church will be attacked from without - Acts 20:29, Rev 2:10

Church will be attacked from within - Acts 20:30

Paul served Ephesus on his own resources - Acts 20: 31-38

Paul was served by Philippi while he served Thessalonica - Phil 4:15-16

Deacons can be women - Ro 16:1

Leaders can be women - Ro 16:3-5, I Co 16:19, Acts 18:2, 18, 26 (this only suggests that a woman was a leader of at least a house church, does not suggest that she was the elder or shepherd or held any other office nor that she did or did not do the teaching; the key fact is that Priscilla is mentioned with Aquila and that seems to imply that she had an important ministry in Paul's eyes)

Church not to judge those outside of church - I Co. 5:12

Church is a body - I Co 12:12ff; Eph 5:22ff, Col 1:24

Church to care for a needy person only if an individual can not do it - I Tim 5:16

Church to work hard - Rev 2:2

Church to persevere - Rev 2: 2, 2:3, 2:13, 2:19, 3:10

Church not to forsake "first love?" - Rev 2:4

Church to have faith - Rev 2:19

Church to have love - Rev 2:19

Church to have service - Rev 2:19

Church to "hold on to what you have?" till Jesus comes - Rev 2:25 (this might only be referring to holding on to proper doctrine in face of heresy)

Church to be awake - Rev 3: 2-3

Church to complete its deeds - Rev 3:2

Church to keep the word of Christ - Rev 3:8

Church not to deny name of Christ - Rev 3:8

Church to be hot, not lukewarm - Rev 3:15-16

Church service to have order - I Co 14

When all come together, all to have (at least one): a hymn, word of instruction, revelation, a tongue, an interpretation (of a tongue is suggested)

Coming together is to be done to strengthen the church - I Co 14

About the Author

Carl Creasman has been speaking professionally for over 25 years to a wide variety of audiences here in the United States and abroad in such diverse places as Haiti and England. A gifted communicator, one College President stated, "Carl has a gift for making complex ideas easily understood," reaching audiences "with a style and message that transcends the cultural challenges of postmodernism." A speaker for numerous colleges, churches and professional organizations, he urges his listeners to achieve excellence in their personal, educational, and professional lives.

Carl began speaking during college at Auburn University, and continued to do so while earning two Master's Degrees, one a Master's of History and the other a Master's of Divinity. Throughout his adult life, Carl has combined his ability as a communicator with his love of working with people. He has worked in diverse arenas such as coaching an Olympic training swim team, working construction for a custom homebuilder and ministering as the Student Pastor of First Baptist Church-Winter Park, FL.

Currently both the Senior Pastor at an innovative young church, Numinous Inc, and a Professor of History at Valencia College in Orlando, FL, he is known for his inspiring presentations and his concern for his students. At Valencia, his student reviews tell a consistent story of value as reflected by a common statement—"you are one of the best teachers I have ever had; thank you for changing my life."

Carl is married to Kim, recently celebrating 23 years of bliss together. They have three lovely daughters, Logan, Meryn and Brynn. Since 1993, they have lived in Winter Park, FL, moving from Wake Forest, NC where Carl completed his seminary degree.

As a Professor, Minister and Speaker, Carl mixes history and spiritual depth with motivational, value-laden stories to drive home a passionate message that will leave your participants "inspired, encouraged and ready to charge forward into life." Or, as one recent participant stated, "Your words have inspired me to take a deep leap of faith and change my young life for the better."

"You need to bring Carl Creasman to your campus ministry group! He will bring a word and story to students that will ring with authenticity . . .and plant seeds of transformation in their thinking.
Ken Dillard, University of Cincinnati, Campus Pastor, Collegiate Ministry

"Carl Creasman is an innovative speaker. Students relate well to the ideas, presentation, and realization of all that Carl offers."
Amy Boyer, College of Holy Cross

"Carl has a unique way to speak the truth in a way that communicates to a 21st century audience.
E. Bailey Marks, Campus Crusade for Christ, Leader-Led Movements

"Your presentation on 'Extreme Living Extreme Valor' drove home a message that was critical to the times we are living in.
Michael Cowles, SkillsUSA Ohio Director

"Your words were inspirational, humorous and timely."
Dr. James T. King, Vice Chancellor Tennessee Board of Regents

"You have a special talent to inspire, motivate and excite others toward being the very best they can be."
Dr. Kermit Carter, Dean for Student Affairs, Calhoun Community College, Decatur, AL

"Carl has real insight and an ability to convey truth to the most practical of minds, both across cultural and generational divides. At this time, perhaps more than any other, we need God's straight talking messengers to shake us from the foundations up."
Garry "Gaz" Kishere, Pastor, Love146 European Operations Director

"Carl's ability to relate to students and professionals alike makes his work extremely relevant to both audiences."
Victor Felts, South-Eastern IFC Executive Director

To invite Carl Creasman to speak at your school, conference, or church, contact:

Carl E. Creasman, Jr.
P.O. Box 2031
Winter Park, FL 32790-2031
407.949.4171 or creasman@mac.com

www.carlcreasman.com